Sustainable
Networking

FOR SCIENTISTS AND ENGINEERS

Sustainable Networking

FOR SCIENTISTS AND ENGINEERS

Christina C. C. Willis

SPIE PRESS
Bellingham, Washington USA

Library of Congress Cataloging-in-Publication Data

Names: Willis, Christina C. C., author.
Title: Sustainable networking for scientists and engineers / Christina C.C.
  Willis.
Description: Bellingham, Washington : SPIE Press, [2020] | Includes
  bibliographical references and index.
Identifiers: LCCN 2019017034 (print) | LCCN 2019020370 (ebook) | ISBN
  9781510629844 (pdf) | ISBN 9781510629851 (epub) | ISBN 9781510629868
  (mobi) | ISBN 9781510629837 (softcover)
Subjects: LCSH: Communication in science--Problems, exercises, etc. |
  Communication in engineering--Problems, exercises, etc.
Classification: LCC Q223 (ebook) | LCC Q223 .W55 2019 (print) | DDC
  650.1/30245--dc23
LC record available at https://lccn.loc.gov/2019017034

Published by
SPIE
P.O. Box 10
Bellingham, Washington 98227-0010 USA
Phone: +1 360.676.3290
Fax: +1 360.647.1445
Email: books@spie.org
Web: http://spie.org

The content of this book reflects the work and thought of the author. Every effort
has been made to publish reliable and accurate information herein, but the
publisher is not responsible for the validity of the information or for any
outcomes resulting from reliance thereon.

Printed in the United States of America.
First Printing.
For updates to this book, visit http://spie.org and type "PM309" in the search field.

For the late Dr. Katharine Gebbie

Contents

Foreword

To many of us in the STEM fields, engaging in networking is like starting to exercise or eating more healthily or backing up the files on our computers. We keep reading here and there that we should, that it's important in the long run, that there will be consequences if we don't. We may even be aware that others around us do it—regularly and, it would seem, effortlessly. And yet, we fail to. Why? As usual, there might be many reasons. Let me mention three.

First, we may doubt the benefit of networking. Isn't it overrated? Something for salespeople, yes, but not for scientists and engineers? Admittedly, we may not see any immediate, tangible outcome of our networking efforts. Networking is about uncovering hidden opportunities. If they are hidden, we do not realize what we are missing out on.

Second, we may feel that we are not up to the job. It must be easy to network for so-called "people persons" with plenty of time on their hands, but what if we are introverted individuals with a busy enough schedule as it is? Fortunately, networking is just another learned skill, and scientists and engineers are usually good at learning.

Third, and this is where this book comes in handy, we may not have a clear picture of what networking is all about. True, we might be anxious at the prospect of delivering a research talk, but at least we have some idea of how to go about it, such as build a story, create slides, and practice; we might learn public speaking by imitating others. In contrast, we might not know how to go about networking; in fact, we might not even recognize when or how others around us are engaging in it.

If any of the above excuses sounds familiar to you, rest assured you're not alone. Myself, I may have a Ph.D. in optics from Stanford University, I may have been invited to address researchers at some 200 universities in over 30 countries, I may even be a "wild card" in the seating chart of my friends' weddings because I will gracefully make conversation with anyone on any topic in any of four languages, yet I'm still a shy individual who would rather hide in his hotel room than face a conference reception. Over the last several decades, I came to terms with this personality trait by recognizing how it has been instrumental in my success as a professional speaker and by learning to mitigate its less positive consequences. All the same, I never thought of myself as a networker.

Paradoxically, it was my network—the one I was not aware I had—that convinced me otherwise. Friends and contacts told me: "Oh, come on. You started a career off the beaten path, from scratch, no one was there to show you the way, and now you receive more requests for speaking engagements than you can accept? Of course you have been networking. It would not have happened otherwise." In other words, and as is often the case, it was a matter of perspective. To me, the word *networking* had always evoked noisy rooms full of people approaching one another with greedy eyes and mere pretenses at politeness. I had never realized it might also mean authentic volunteer work mainly for the satisfaction of helping out or perhaps for the possibility of sharpening one's skills, and only incidentally for bringing about further professional opportunities. (In this respect, my accepting to write this foreword qualifies as networking.)

In other words, it took me a while to come to grips with networking, and I hope that others around me will be faster learners than I have been. Learning can use guidance, though, and if someone can provide such guidance on networking, it is Dr. Christina C. C. Willis. With her Ph.D. in optics from the University of Central Florida, Christina is of course "one of us" to start with, but she is obviously so much more, such as a world traveler, a dedicated volunteer, and a great conversationalist.

It's been 10 years since I first met Christina at the closing reception of a student conference, but I remember this first encounter as if it were yesterday. There I was, in a corner of a large, open space, feeling awkward, when Christina noticed me and went out of her way (literally, in this case) to strike up a conversation with me. (I had delivered a plenary address the day before, so she did know who I was—a memorable talk can afford you so much visibility.) I remember how we talked about travels and her year in Japan—and how she had had to use expressive gestures to make a Japanese pharmacist understand she wanted aspirin. I remember how she then introduced me to other students and made me feel so at ease that we ended up taking silly group pictures (and, no, I had not consumed any alcohol).

In this book, Christina shares her view of networking in the broadest possible sense—from motivation to social graces, all the way to specific media such as poster sessions or LinkedIn. All along, she shares personal anecdotes from someone who has been through her own discovery process and has learned from it every step of the way. The result is a text rich in recommendations yet respectful of everyone's identity, serious about the topic yet not without humor, digestible as a whole for the thorough reader yet made of reasonably stand-alone chapters for the more selective one.

Before I let you enter Christina's story, let me end on a story of my own. Over a quarter century ago, launching my own business consumed me beyond what I had imagined, as I spent not just days but also nights, weekends, and holidays at the office. No regrets: I was making a dream come true and enjoying the intensity of the challenge. Still, three years of this spartan regimen brought my social life to its lowest point ever: I was not seeing any friends or family, let alone dating anyone. As a remedial strategy, and not unlike Jim Carrey in *Yes Man*, I decided I would (for a while) accept any social invitation I received, whether I felt like going or not. Soon enough, I met new people, through whom I met yet other new people, and so on. Some of the social events I thus attended were delightful; others were dreadful. One such event was a friend's birthday party, which I definitely did not feel like attending. Although I liked this friend (and still do), I did not care for the crowd she was hanging out with at the time: shallow, self-conceited show-offs looking down on nerds like me. As expected, I had a miserable evening. Still, I did notice on that occasion a young woman who was different. She and I eventually got married, had two kids, and launched a successful company together. I shiver at the thought I might have missed out on that opportunity had I turned down my friend's invitation.

If you want to create opportunities, I similarly encourage you to step out of your comfort zone. As Christina concludes (spoiler alert), it's OK to start small, so I'll make it easy for you: next time you attend a conference or similar gathering, make sure to be there every time there is free food. After a while, you might just realize you come a little less for the food and a little more for the people.

Jean-luc Doumont
December 2019

Preface
Who Wrote This Book? And Why?

"A bit of advice. Always… No. No. *Never* forget to check your references."

~ Dr. Meredith (played by Severn Darden),
Real Genius (1984)

The goal of this book is to help you understand what networking is and how to do it sustainably with a method and strategy that is right for you. It is intended to help you raise your self-awareness and communication skills, address relevant anxieties that you may have, and give you the tools and strategies to apply networking in your life and career, for your own success and the success of your network. It is part philosophy, part strategy, and part application.

But why should you listen to anything I have to say? What makes me an authority on the subject of networking? And what prompted me to write this book?

I've done a lot of successful networking, a lot of research on the subject, and I've got a message that I think is worth sharing. As a scientist, I believe in a data-based approach, and so while my personal experiences have greatly shaped the content of this book, as much as possible I offer you, my reader, the supporting research and references to back up the statements made herein. This preface is also the only portion of this book written in first person; any personal anecdotes elsewhere are separated from the main text.

What follows here is my story and how this book came to be. It is a story heavily influenced by networking, and it illustrates some of the principles that are discussed in this book. It will give you some useful context about me and the perspective with which I have written this book. However, if you are not one for anecdote (and as a scientist, I would hardly fault you for it), then I suggest looking at the list of lessons learned at the end of this section before moving to Chapter 1.

My personal story and the origins of this book begin when I was a junior studying physics at Wellesley College in the fall of 2004. One of my professors advised me to apply for a summer internship at the National Institute of Standards and Technology (NIST) in Gaithersburg, MD. I took his advice and applied, and was accepted into the Summer Undergraduate Research Fellowship (SURF).[1] This was one of my first major networking lessons: When a teacher or trusted advisor suggests you apply for something, be it an internship, a grant, or an award—*do* it.

As a SURFer, I spent the summer of 2005 living and working in Gaithersburg. While I was there, Dr. Katharine Gebbie,[2] who was then the director of the Physical Measurement Laboratory, gave a presentation welcoming the summer students, and she encouraged us to make an appointment to meet with her. While I didn't know much about networking at the time, I did know that (a) an important person was offering to make time for me and that I should probably take advantage of the opportunity, and (b) I needed to come prepared to the appointment with something to say. I knew that I shouldn't just show up to say, "Hi! You said to come say 'hi'." So I set up an appointment, and I prepared a question.

My question related to my plans after graduation. I knew that I wanted to go to graduate school but also that I wanted to do something else first. Something like traveling. When the time came to meet with Dr. Gebbie, I asked her what I should do if I wanted to travel and eventually go to graduate school. She gave me a great piece of advice: she told me that I should work abroad, because traveling without working would make it too hard for me to return to school.

Then she asked me if I knew anything about Japan. I admitted that I didn't really know anything, except that sushi was my favorite food and I knew how to use chopsticks. But I said that I would love to learn more.

From there, Dr. Gebbie referred me to another NIST scientist who had connections with the Japanese standards institute, the National Metrological Institute of Japan,[3] part of the Advanced Institute for Standards and Technology. I met with him, and he passed my resume along to his contact in Japan, which lead to an interview later that fall and, ultimately, to me spending a year living and working in Japan after graduating from Wellesley. That was my next big networking lesson: when someone important, established, or advanced in their career offers you some of their time, accept the offer. I never could have envisioned the outcome, but I never would have achieved it without making the appointment.

Accepting that job offer was one of the more terrifying things I have ever done, but it was one of the best decisions I ever made. I got to learn a lot about physics, optics, and electronics. I made friends with my Japanese colleagues, as well as other researchers living in my apartment building. And I learned a lot about Japan—way more than just how to use chopsticks! This was another important networking lesson: some opportunities that offer a lot of growth and learning can also be very scary, and I would have missed a lot of life-changing experiences if I had let fear stop me.

If I hadn't taken my professor's advice and applied for the internship, I wouldn't have had the chance to meet Dr. Gebbie. And without accepting her offer and setting up a meeting, I never could have asked her my question, and she never would have introduced me to her contact. None of the subsequent networking that led to an interview and a job offer would have happened either. And by accepting that job offer, I did something that pushed me far outside of my comfort zone and fundamentally changed me as a person and a scientist, in ways that have been very valuable to me. This is part of why networking is so powerful; it will give you access to career and life opportunities that you may not have known existed.

While I was in Japan, I applied for graduate school, and when my year was over, I matriculated at the Center for Research and Education in Optics and Lasers (CREOL), the College of Optics and Photonics, at the University of Central Florida.[4] While at CREOL, I got involved in several student organizations, including student chapters for professional societies such as OSA and SPIE. I became the treasurer of the SPIE student chapter, and organized optics outreach and professional development events.

Then I made a mistake. Really, it was the entire Executive Board of the chapter that made a collective mistake. We were all senior graduate students, busy with research and dissertation work. After a year of solid chapter programming, we failed to hold an election for a new Executive Board. Then we ceased activities all together. I felt awful about it, and avoidant, and for almost a whole year I procrastinated. But as the time for a new election rolled around, I decided that something had to be done.

I took action and got in touch with the SPIE staff person in charge of Student Chapter relations at the time, Dirk Fabian. Fearing admonishment, I sent him an email, explaining, apologizing, and asking how to fix things. But instead of chastising me, Dirk was very understanding and helped me make the arrangements necessary to get our chapter back in good standing and hold the election (which we did, happily passing the torch to new leadership).

Dirk and I stayed in touch, and later when I needed additional support for conference travel, he helped me find volunteering opportunities. This was another important networking lesson: by staying in touch with a new connection and establishing a mutual understanding of needs (I needed funding to attend a conference; Dirk needed volunteers for the conference), we created a mutually beneficial networking relationship. This is the heart of sustainable networking.

It was also how I discovered that I loved volunteering and organizing, and so I kept looking for more opportunities. I found that the more I volunteered, the more volunteering opportunities became available to me. I call this phenomenon *Opportunity Momentum*: the more you participate in an activity, the more skills you build and the more people will associate you with that activity, which results in more opportunities to do that activity. As I gained Opportunity Momentum by volunteering with SPIE, my roles expanded to include conference media coverage, panel moderation, and facilitating at the Student Chapter Leadership Workshop, which then led to sitting on panels, judging the Optics Outreach Games, and serving on several SPIE governing committees. Then something amazing happened: I was put on the ballot and elected to the SPIE Board of Directors! As I write this book, my term as a Director is coming to a close. It has been an *immense* honor to serve SPIE in this manner, and I have learned so much.

Which brings us to the book.

I won't say "never," because I am a physicist, but I will say that the probability of me deciding, on my own, to write this book was negligible. Which rounds down very easily to "never." So I was surprised when I received a message from an SPIE staff member, asking if I would be interested in writing a networking book for scientists and engineers. This person knew that I enjoy writing, and about my volunteer work with SPIE, and thought that I might be interested. In considering that idea, I saw that I would not have gotten to where I was without a lot of networking and that I (probably) would never have received that message. This was another valuable lesson: if I hadn't shared my passion for writing with this person, they probably wouldn't have thought of it either. Sharing about my work and interests had brought me a wonderful opportunity without even asking for it.

I also know how hard-earned some of my basic networking skills are, such as social interaction and conversation. They are a huge part of networking, and I used to be terrible at them. Really terrible. It resulted in a lot of social rejection during my childhood, and I still regularly battle social anxiety relating to the acceptance or rejection of my peers. Learning how to cope with that anxiety has been a big part of my networking strategy, especially at conferences, where the socializing can reach a frenetic pace. But over the years I have learned a valuable networking lesson: I am not alone when it comes to social anxiety. Many people have it, and there are many strategies that I can use to mitigate its effects.

Growing up, I remained a socially awkward, nerdy kid, but I gradually got better at socializing and making friends. As my self-awareness developed, I began to realize something else: I was pretty terrible at making conversation. I saw that I was missing out on getting to know other people, because I spent so much time talking that I never got to listen to what they had to say.

So what does a nerdy, twenty-one-year-old physicist do when she realizes that something needs to be fixed? Study it. Do research. Experiment. I got on the internet and looked up how to be a good conversationalist. I found articles and forums, and took notes. I read books, such as *Emotional Intelligence*[5] and *The Art of Civilized Conversation*,[6] making highlights and writing in the margins. It opened up a new world to me. I practiced the principles I learned and slowly got better at being a good conversational partner, asking questions, and sharing the spotlight. This was another valuable networking lesson for me: social skills are trainable, like any other skill, and I can change myself through practice and concerted effort.

I've told you this story about myself to give you some context about who I am and why I wrote this book. It illustrates some important lessons about networking:

- When a trusted advisor or mentor suggests you apply for a fellowship or award, do it (see Section 7.4 on mentoring relationships and Section 7.5 on applying for awards and scholarships).

- If someone talented or important offers to give you some of their time, take the opportunity and ask questions (see Section 7.12 on following up and Section 8.2 on networking in your workplace).

- Opportunities that offer a lot of growth and learning can also be very scary, but don't let fear stop you from taking advantage of them (see Section 3.2).

- Staying in touch and establishing a mutual understanding of needs is key to effective and sustainable networking (see Chapter 1).

- Volunteering is one of the best things you can do for your network and your career, and it is a path to leadership (see Section 7.2).

- The more you do of something, such as volunteering or working on a specific topic, the more of that something you will get—a phenomenon I call *Opportunity Momentum* (see Section 2.2).

- Sharing your work and interests with your network connections will bring opportunities to you without you asking (see Section 1.2).

- Social anxiety is a common problem that you can develop positive strategies to address (see Section 3.4).

- Networking, conversation, and self-awareness are learned skills, and they can be improved with study and practice (see Section 3.4 and Chapters 4 and 5 for ways to improve your self-awareness and conversational skills).

- A diverse network that includes people outside your subfield can lead to opportunities you couldn't have imagined—such as writing a book (see Chapter 6).

In addition to my own experience, I have done a lot of research to prepare this book so that you don't have to simply take my word on it. References are listed at the end of each chapter. The appendix contains suggestions for further reading.

I wish you all the best in your endeavors, and I hope you enjoy the book.

Christina C. C. Willis
August 2019

References

1. SURF Gaithersburg, www.nist.gov/summer-undergraduate-research-fellowship-surf/surf-gaithersburg.
2. Gaal, R., "Katharine Blodgett Gebbie (1932–2016)," *APS News* **25**(8), www.aps.org/publications/apsnews/201608/gebbie.cfm (2016).
3. National Metrological Institute of Japan, www.nmij.jp/english.
4. CREOL, the College of Optics and Photonics, www.creol.ucf.edu.
5. Goleman, D., *Emotional Intelligence*, Bantam Books (1995).
6. Shepherd, M., *The Art of Civilized Conversation*, Three Rivers Press (2005).

Acknowledgments

The book owes its existence to valuable contributions from a number of special people who shared their time, feedback, and ideas with me.

I am incredibly grateful to SPIE and its staff for the vital role they have played in my life, career, and the creation of this book; I cannot count the number of opportunities, colleagues, and friends that I have had or made thanks to my involvement with SPIE and its wonderful staff. Special thanks to my editor, Scott McNeill, for patiently guiding me through what has been an unconventional project and manuscript preparation process. Many thanks also to Tim Lamkins; this book would not exist without his creative thinking, initiative, and belief in my writing abilities. I am thankful to Dirk Fabian for his valuable suggestions at the start of this project, and for opening my eyes to the world of volunteering and all its possibilities; I am forever, happily, in his debt. I am also pleased to thank and acknowledge Colin McCormick and Jean-luc Doumont for their thoughtful feedback during the initial stages of the project.

I extend my sincere thanks to Daniel Ott for being a patient and attentive sounding board for many of the ideas in this book; I am fortunate to have such a life partner. A special thanks to my in-laws, Larry and Peggy Ott, for their generous hospitality; it was in their home that the first draft was composed. Finally, I would like to express my deep gratitude to my own parents, Nan and Jerry Willis, for their love and encouragement; the sacrifices they made to ensure the quality of my education enabled me to grow up and do things like build lasers and write books.

Chapter 1
Sustainable Networking, and Why You Should Do It

"You can't hack relationships."

~Scott Gerber and Ryan Paugh,
Superconnector (2018)

1.1 Sustainable Networking and Helping Others

Networking is a tool and an investment. Networking can help you solve research problems, find friends or employment, get advice and support, meet collaborators, and increase your knowledge. And if you wield this tool in the service of your network connections, you will help to create success not just for yourself but for everyone. Done well, *sustainable networking* is an investment in both your community and your career.

But investments take time to mature, whether it's money in a mutual fund or seeds planted in a garden. Just as much of science is a process of slow and diligent preparation for the collection of a few minutes' worth of crucial data, so too is network building a slow process of preparation for that critical moment when you need to call upon your network for assistance. Except there isn't just one moment, there are many, and the persistent cultivation of your network is a continuous and ongoing process that is never finished.

There will always be people who try to hack the process, whatever it is, to make it quicker. But "get rich quick" schemes applied to networking typically focus on short-term personal gains, not on generating mutual success. This kind of selfish behavior has given the term *networking* a bad reputation and caused people to question the ethics of networking.[1,2] If you think of help as a finite resource created by people, and you take more of a resource than you create, then your behavior is unsustainable: the resource will run out. If you try to get rich quickly and always ask for help and never give it, eventually no one will want to help you. So when networking is *not* done in a sustainable manner, it becomes that sleazy, transactional caricature that is used to describe those who seek unfair advantage over others.

This has led some to declare that networking is dead[3] and to attempt to migrate to other terminology such as "connecting," "relationship building," or "community building." The framing used in this book is "sustainable networking," but whatever the nomenclature you prefer, networking is an important concept to understand and to practice, and it is not going away. The landscape has changed dramatically with the proliferation of digital and online networking opportunities, but the way that relationships function has not. Developing quality relationships and networking sustainably with generosity takes time and effort. There is no way to hack your network, just your networking skill set.

Sustainable networking, as discussed here, is an exchange of information and assistance between two or more parties that allows everyone to benefit, increasing the success of the community as a whole. By helping others, you make sure that your network and your relationships are successful and fruitful for years to come. The reputation that you develop through networking will open or close doors for you, depending on how you treat others. Ideally, you want to offer real, useful help before asking someone for assistance, but sometimes you may need to call upon a new connection for help right away, and that is okay. That need may be the reason why a mutual connection introduced the two of you in the first place, but it is important to remember the principle of sustainability: think of help as a resource, and create more of it than you take.

In some discussions on networking, people use the term "return on investment," or ROI. This is an investing and business term that describes what benefits are reaped in exchange for the time, effort, or money originally invested in an enterprise. The ROI of networking is typically high; however, this framing and phraseology, due to their implied transactional nature, are avoided in this text in favor of the concept of sustainability. But if ROI is a useful framework for you, then use it. This is again a nomenclature issue and a matter of personal preference.

The above discussion relates to networking as a concept, but it is also important to understand what behaviors qualify as networking. Networking and socializing are not the same thing. If you have a positive or memorable exchange with someone, get their contact information, and follow up, that is networking. Sustainable networking means creating ongoing relationships based on mutual understanding and support, whether it is in person or online. Networking often involves socializing in a professional context, but there is more to it than that. To turn socializing into networking, you need to (a) have an exchange of information where both parties talk and listen, (b) remember each other, (c) reach out and contact each other at a later date, and (d) maintain that initial contact, even if it is infrequently.

Sustainable networking is both a philosophy and a set of actions. It is a way of looking at your interactions in the light of how you can help people and how your network gives you the opportunity to help others. As Keith Ferrazzi, author of *Never Eat Alone*, says, "*Real* networking is about finding ways to make *other* people more successful."[4] And the success of your network becomes your success.[5,6]

1.2 What Is a Network, and What Makes It Function Well?

Your network is the people you know, and the people who they know, and so on. From your relative perspective, you are at the center of your own network, but examined from a distance, you are just one node in a much larger web. It's important to think about yourself as a part of this broader community and how much you can do for that large number of people. For example, when attending an event, framing your thinking around what value or information that you can offer the other attendees will serve you and your community better than focusing only on what you want (though having your own goals is also important and will be discussed in Chapter 2). Helping others has tangible benefits for you, but it should be done with a spirit of generosity; telegraphing an expectation of return spoils the good will you created by helping.

The philosophical and mathematical principle of "six degrees of separation" is intimately related to the idea of networking and gives networking its power. The *six degrees* principle, first proposed by the Hungarian author and poet Frigyes Karinthy in his short story "Chain-Links,"[7] states that you can connect any two people in the world by five other people, or six steps of interconnection, thus creating a chain of acquaintances. This is the worldwide network of people that we all exist within, and as Karinthy wrote "the population of the Earth is closer together now than they have ever been before" because of it. And he wrote that in 1929, well before the inception of the internet and before commercial air travel became common.

It turns out that the world is even smaller than Karinthy thought, or at least it is now. A study by Facebook in 2011 found that the degrees of separation for Facebook users are on average 4.74 degrees,[8] with a degree being a social (inter)connection, i.e., there is a high probability (92%, according to Facebook) that if you are a Facebook user and you meet a stranger who is also a Facebook user, you could create a chain of only four people (five degrees) to connect the two of you. Facebook, LinkedIn, and social media in general give us valuable insight and analysis tools to see and understand the network of connections that already exists around us.

Which means that you already have a network. There are many different kinds of networks, defined not just by discipline but by geography, culture, language, school, university, interest, and religion. Your network is made of family, colleagues at work, and friends from school or childhood; they are all nodes in your network. Your network is everyone you already know, and each of those people represents potential access to an entirely new set of people. Networking, in a sense, is the maintenance and creation of these relationships. It can be thought of as the process of finding, developing, and maintaining professional connections, though of course, networking is just as important in the personal sphere as in the professional one. This book focuses on professional networking, but many of the principles that will be discussed here also have applications in the personal realm.

For your network to function well, your connections need to be built on a mutual understanding of needs. If you don't know what someone needs, you can't really help them. Assistance based on what you *think* a person needs may be a hindrance if it is not what they actually need or want, and it is a waste of your time and energy. This is where communication and empathy are important, because they allow you to understand others as well as express yourself effectively (more on these concepts in Chapter 3), so that a mutual understanding can be established.

Diversity is also important for the health of your network. Your close work colleagues have access to most of the same people and the same information as you. With so many resources and experiences in common, you are less likely to be able to answer questions that they cannot, and vice versa. Cultivating relationships with a broad swath of people from diverse backgrounds will make your network a stronger, more powerful tool, and you will be more able to solve problems. The strength of diversity, as it applies to networking and the workplace, will be discussed in Chapter 6.

1.3 Motivations and Benefits

It might be tempting to dismiss networking as an activity for businesspeople and not something that scientists, engineers, or anyone in STEM fields need to concern themselves about. But the importance of networking extends far beyond your career: STEM fields and the scientific method itself depend upon it. Sharing experimental results so that they can be replicated is at the heart of science, and it is a facet of networking. While working in solitude can be productive and is especially important for creativity,[9,10] collaboration and networking are often necessary to advance particularly large projects or intractable problems.

On an individual level, networking has a wide variety of benefits, ranging from professional to emotional. These benefits include career security, being a better employee, increasing your productivity and knowledge, living longer (yes, you read that right, references to come), and feeling happier and more satisfied with life. Networking can get you jobs, promotions, awards, committee and board positions, speaking engagements, invitations to apply for or review grants, and (book) writing opportunities.

In many places, stable life-long employment at one employer is a thing of the past, if it ever existed. In 2018, the U.S. Bureau of Labor Statistics released a report stating that the median number of years that salaried employees had been at their current job was 4.2 years, and that for workers in the age range of 24 to 35 years it was shorter: 2.8 years.[11] The fact is that your employer has many considerations beyond the quality of your work that you cannot control, and it is possible to be let go even when you have been producing good work. If you network sustainably and regularly, whether you choose or change jobs or are forced to by circumstances, you will have at your disposal a network of people who you have helped to succeed and who will be happy to help you, which will make the transition smoother. And your network will follow you over the course of your entire career. In the modern era, a good professional network *is* the new career stability.

There are also many interesting job opportunities that are not promoted through official channels and that can be accessed only through networking. It is estimated that between 40–85% of job opportunities are never advertised.[12] On the more conservative end, the 40% value is generated by looking at data published by the U.S. Bureau of Labor Statistics and noting that *more* people are hired than there are open, advertised positions. The higher end (85%) takes into account the use of advertising on social media and people who are hired through referrals or networking, even if it is an advertised position.

This is the hidden job market: jobs that you can only access through networking. Your networking activities will also give you access to unadvertised opportunities to collaborate, learn, expand your knowledge and experience, and help others to do the same. Access is one of the most significant career benefits of networking. Success and access are a virtuous cycle; the more access you have, the more resources you have at your disposal to help your connections, and the more success you can help people generate within your network, which in turn feeds your career success and improves your access. This virtuous cycle is much the same as the one associated with Opportunity Momentum: the more you engage in an activity, the more access you will have to opportunities to do that activity. (Opportunity Momentum was introduced in the Preface and is discussed in more detail in Chapter 2.)

You may think that if you are happy in your job, then you have no need to network because networking is a job-seeking activity, and it is. A 2019 LinkedIn survey revealed that 85% of the approximately 3,000 survey respondents found their current job through networking.[12] But while networking is an excellent way to find a job, as discussed above, if you treat it as *only* a way to find a job, and only at the moment when you change employment, you will fall into the unsustainable, transactional-side of networking. It becomes totally about what you want and when you want it, without consideration for the needs of others. How to sustainably network your job hunt is the topic of Chapter 12.

Beyond finding or changing employment, networking increases the breadth of your understanding. This is why volunteering is such an excellent networking activity; you help someone by giving your time and, in exchange, you learn valuable new things and meet new people. Networking with people outside of your niche of expertise is also important, as well as networking with people outside of your discipline. Often, we are too close to a problem to see a solution, but those who are further removed will ask new and surprising questions, and generate fresh and novel solutions, specifically because of their distance from the problem. This is how networking can serve you as a collaborative problem-solving tool.

Getting things done at work is also a lot easier when the people in your organization like you and want to help you. Networking within your place of work, including across disciplines and departments, gives you opportunities to help your colleagues, and generates ideas and goodwill. So thinking proactively about how you can help them is a valuable investment in your own work and in the success of your company.

The ability to network and connect with others is important in both work and personal life. People typically collaborate with and hire people whom they like, and people who have strong personal networks have a greater sense of well-being, live longer, and have greater overall happiness than those who are less well networked.[14,15] A 2012 study published in the British Medical Journal, showed with statistical significance that people over 75 who had a rich social network on average lived 2.7 years longer than those who did not.[16] A 2006 study demonstrated that people get a greater sense of well-being from making new acquaintances than from spending time with people they already know, even if they are introverts[17] (more on introversion and extraversion in Chapter 3). So networking is not just a career skill, it is a life skill.

Studies have also shown that helping others generates feelings of happiness and wellbeing,[18] which is another excellent argument for sustainable networking: it feels good. TED speaker and author Adam Grant discusses in his book *Give and Take* how helping others not only makes us feel better but also motivates us to work harder.[9] So networking in a fashion that helps your contacts can boost your own productivity. Grant's studies show that people who give a lot but maintain self-interest and keep up their own work tend to be the most successful. These people also tend to control their time by scheduling how much of it they give to their contacts, so they still have time for themselves and their own projects.

You may be wondering how all this touchy-feely, emotional stuff is relevant to a book on *professional* networking for scientists and engineers. It's a fair question. Emotion is relevant because there is a lot of crossover and blending between our personal and professional networks. Some of your strongest and most valuable professional networking connections will also be your friends and classmates from graduate school, with whom you bonded through the process of research and graduation. You will likely socialize and develop friendships with your colleagues at work. Sometimes you may have purely personal relationships develop professional facets, as friends and family have careers and jobs, too.

Human beings are emotional creatures that are capable of science and logic. Part of what makes us human, and what makes networking as much an art as it is a science, is our emotions. Humans make many decisions based on emotion, not logic; there is evidence that we *cannot* make decisions without the use of emotion.[19] Our awareness of our emotions, how we handle them, and our ability to empathize and recognize emotions in others is vital for our ability to communicate effectively and is therefore an important part of networking.

Becoming a good networker is one of the best things that you can do for your own happiness and success, as well as the success and happiness of those in your network, both personal and professional. Networking done right, i.e., sustainably, is a win–win situation that makes things better for everyone.

1.4 Communication, STEM, and Networking

We as scientists and engineers can tend to have a dim view of social skills, communication and networking included. There is a proclivity to either box ourselves in as being bad at networking and social interaction, or to downplay their importance as skills. Or perhaps we do the former because of the latter: to excuse ourselves from the need to do something that we fear doing because we feel inept.

We call social abilities "soft skills," which sounds derogatory next to the important "hard science" that we do.

Compounding the issue, networking and communication are typically not part of a formal STEM education, and as such, many scientists and engineers do not know how to do it well, nor do they consider it to be important. Actor, author, and science communication advocate Alan Alda wrote in his book *If I Understood You, Would I Have This Look on My Face?* about speaking with the presidents of higher-learning institutions and asking if they would consider educating their science students in communication.[15] The response was almost invariably no, because there is too much science to teach.

And so, in STEM, our communication education is typically left to chance. After all, if our institution of higher education did not place a premium on it, then why should we as individuals? We spend years honing our analytical and problem-solving abilities, training how to align an optic, calibrate a device, or meet a specification, and then we neglect our communication and networking skills, or make them low priorities.

But communication skills are critical for science. You may not need a lot of communication skills to do your lab work or to make derivations, generate part drawings, or model complex phenomena, but without communication, science is dead. First and most fundamentally, if scientists had not shared and published their knowledge and findings, we wouldn't live in the world that we do today, and that includes not having all those nice textbooks we used in school. Being able to communicate and convey your results is as important to science as the measurements and data themselves. If you can't share or communicate your results so that others can replicate your experiments and add them to the body of scientific knowledge, is it really science?

Beyond that, much of the money that funds scientific research, at some point up the hierarchical chain, is not awarded by a scientist or engineer. In many countries, few policymakers have a scientific or technical background. If scientists and engineers cannot communicate to funding agencies and decision makers why their work is important, and cannot get the funding to do the work, that is science that doesn't happen. As to the future of STEM and the next generation of scientists and engineers, young people will be more likely to study STEM if they can understand what it is and why it is interesting and important. And it is the scientists and engineers of today who need to explain this to them.

Being able to communicate well is also important on an individual and everyday level. You need to be able to discuss your work with your research group or coworkers, and to get help when you need it. You can be incredibly talented technically, but if you can't work well with a team, i.e., communicate effectively with others, you are less likely to be considered a good hire and to get a job. It doesn't matter how good your work is if you never get the opportunity to do it.

Communication does not happen simply when something is said. If your audience cannot understand you, nothing is being communicated, even if you are speaking and they are listening. You can speak all day in ancient Greek, but if your audience doesn't speak ancient Greek, then nothing will be communicated. As a speaker or communicator, it is your responsibility to make sure that your audience is following you; it's not the other person's job to catch up if you have lost them. This is called *adapting to your audience*, and it involves changing your content and mode of expression to make it easier for your audience to understand. If you want to communicate something, you need to check your approach, explain it differently or with different words as needed, so that your audience can follow what you are saying. In this way, communication is like a partner dance, and it requires empathy and self-awareness (more on this in Chapter 3).

Improving your networking skills is an investment in your network, your career, and in science itself. Your abilities to get a job, win funding for your research, do your job effectively, share your data and results, negotiate a salary, and meet new people depend on your communication skills. Communication is also important in your friendships, filial relationships, and intimate partnerships.

Communication skills are to networking what a saw, hammer, and nails are to carpentry: essential tools necessary to get the job done. This may all seem like a daunting task, but the good thing is that all of these networking, communication, and social skills are *teachable*. They are something you can tackle the way you would any research problem: with study, analysis, and data collection. And practice. Lots and lots of practice. Chapters 4 and 5 go into detail about conversational in-person communication skills, and Chapter 10 covers topics related to remote and written communication for networking.

1.5 The Dunning–Kruger Effect

When it comes to networking and communication, it is important to be able to make (accurate) assessments of our own abilities to find areas that need improvement. And we need to beware of feeling too confident. While a lack of confidence and social anxiety are their own obstacles, overconfidence can be worse, because it can lead us to dismiss the idea that we need to improve and subsequently result in inaction. The Dunning–Kruger effect describes how this ignorance of our own ignorance (meta-ignorance) can lead to inaccurate, and inflated, assessments of our abilities.[21] In other words, the less you know about something, the less you are able to assess your ability related to it. This is because the ability to make an accurate assessment depends on an understanding of the topic, and if one does not understand the topic, the skills for assessment are also missing. A quote often misattributed to Einstein, Aristotle, and several other historical figures is, "The more you know, the more you know you don't know." The complement to this statement would be, "The less you know, the less you know you don't know." That is the Dunning–Kruger effect.

This phenomenon is mentioned here because it is a reminder that there is always room for improvement, even (and especially) if we believe that our skills are complete. Networking and communication are often neglected or dismissed by STEM professionals, but they are activities and abilities that, if you work at and practice them, will benefit you and those around you. The Dunning–Kruger effect will also enter into the discussion on self-awareness, empathy, and communication in Chapters 3–5, as well as the exercises that appear at the end of each chapter.

Author Anecdote

As mentioned in the Preface, for a long time I had trouble being a good conversational partner. I dominated conversations, barely letting others get a word in edgewise, and I thought I was good at conversation because I talked so much. This was the Dunning–Kruger effect in action: I thought that dominating conversations made me good at conversation because I didn't understand that a conversation should flow in both directions. It took me a long time to understand what I was doing wrong. It was a slow process as my overall self-awareness developed, even after I realized that I had a problem. But as will be discussed in Chapter 3, self-awareness is important for networking and communication, and it can be consciously practiced and improved, as can conversational skills which are discussed in Chapters 4 and 5.

Exercises

(1) Spend some time thinking about and examining your existing networks. Take notes or look through your LinkedIn and/or other social media connections. Think about your connections, both personal and professional: coworkers and colleagues, family, neighbors, old classmates, teammates, and childhood friends. Having a clear picture of who you are already connected with can help you when you begin to consider your networking strategy in Chapter 2.

(2) Consider your current career and professional situation, both good and bad. Take some notes about how you could use the good parts of your situation to help others and the ways in which you might be able to improve the bad parts of your situation with the help of others.

(3) Think about your communication skills, both written and verbal. What are you already reasonably good at? What do you think needs improvement? (Hint: If you think your communication skills need no improvement, please revisit the discussion on the Dunning–Kruger effect.) Is there anything holding you back from making those improvements? This exercise will help you begin to become more self-aware, an important trait discussed in Chapter 3.

References

1. Nemko, M., "The Case Against Networking," *Psychology Today* (24 June, 2014). Retrieved from psychologytoday.com/us/blog/how-do-life/201406/the-case-against-networking. Accessed February 17, 2019.
2. Dobos, N., "Networking, Corruption, and Subversion," *J. Business Ethics,* **144**(3), 467–478 (2017) [doi:10.1007/s10551-015-2853-4].

3. Gerber, S. and R. Paugh, *Superconnector: Stop Networking and Start Building Business Relationships That Matter*, Da Capo Lifelong Books, Boston, MA (2018).

4. Ferrazzi, K. and T. Raz, *Never Eat Alone*, Crown Business, New York (2005).

5. Grant, A., *Give and Take: Why Helping Others Drives Our Success*, Penguin Books, London (2014).

6. Price, S., "Why Helping Others Is Key to Accelerating Your Career," *Huffpost* (August 17, 2017). Retrieved from huffingtonpost.com/entry/why-helping-others-is-key-to-accelerating-your-career_us_598dbe1ce4b0caa1687a5f71. Accessed on February 18, 2019.

7. Karinthy, F., "Chain-Links," *Everything Is Different*, Athenaeum, Budapest (1929).

8. Backstrom, L., "Anatomy of Facebook," *Facebook* (November 11, 2011). Retrieved from facebook.com/notes/facebook-data-team/anatomy-of-facebook/10150388519243859. Accessed February 18, 2019.

9. Cain, S., *Quiet: The Power of Introversion in a World That Can't Stop Talking*, Broadway Books, New York (2013).

10. Babauta, L., "The No. 1 Habit of Highly Creative People," *Zen Habits* (May 27, 2010). Retrieved from zenhabits.net/creative-habit. Accessed March 24, 2019.

11. "Employee Tenure in 2018," *Bureau of Labor Statistics* (2018). Retrieved from bls.gov/news.release/pdf/tenure.pdf. Accessed February 18, 2019.

12. Rothberg, S., "80% of Job Openings Are Unadvertised," *College Recruiter* (March 28, 2013). Retrieved from collegerecruiter.com/blog/2013/03/28/80-of-job-openings-are-unadvertised. Accessed February 18, 2019.

13. Adler, L., "New Survey Reveals 85% of All Jobs are Filled Via Networking," *LinkedIn* (February 29, 2016). Retrieved from linkedin.com/pulse/new-survey-reveals-85-all-jobs-filled-via-networking-lou-adler. Accessed February 18, 2019.

14. Yang, C. et al., "Social relationships and physiological determinants of longevity across the human life span," *Proc. National Academy of Sciences of the United States of America* **113**(3), 578–583 (2016).

15. Holt-Lunstad, J. et al., "Social Relationships and Mortality Risk: A Meta-analytic Review," *PLoS Medicine* **7**(7) (July 27, 2010) [doi:10.1371/journal.pmed.1000316].

16. Rizzuto, D. et al., "Lifestyle, social factors, and survival after age 75: population based study," *British Medical Journal* **345**:e5568 (30 August 2012).

17. Lawson, W., "Howdy Stranger!," *Psychology Today* (June 9, 2016). Retrieved from psychologytoday.com/us/articles/200601/howdy-stranger. Accessed February 18, 2019.

18. Thoits, P. A. et al., "Volunteer Work and Well-Being," *J. Health and Social Behavior* **42**(2), 115–131 (2001).

19. Damasio, A., *Descartes' Error: Emotion, Reason and the Human Brain*, Grosset/Putnam, New York (1994).

20. Alda, A., *If I Understood You, Would I Have This Look on My Face?*, Random House, New York (2017).

21. Kruger, J. and D. Dunning, "Unskilled and unaware of it: How difficulties in recognizing one's own incompetence lead to inflated self-assessments," *J. Personality and Social Psychol.* **77**(6) 1121–1134 (1999) [dx.doi.org/10.1037/0022-3514.77.6.1121].

Chapter 2
Networking and Strategy

"Would you tell me, please, which way I ought to go from here?"
"That depends a good deal on where you want to get to," said the Cat.
~Alice, speaking with the Cheshire Cat,
Alice's Adventures in Wonderland, by Lewis Carroll (1865)

2.1 Strategy Is Built on Goals

Sustainable networking is a multi-tool that can be used to help you and those around you to succeed. But what is a tool without a plan or project? Imagine what the final product would be if you took a hammer and began to nail boards together with no end in mind. It would probably be a waste of effort and nails! Generally, to build something useful, you need to know what you want to build (your end goal) and how you will build it (a strategy or plan to achieve your goal), and networking is no different.

Networking strategically is important, because it allows you to focus your efforts and be more efficient with your time. And fundamental to your networking strategy is your goal or goals. Knowing yourself and what you want to achieve is how you set a goal, which is the foundation upon which you develop your networking strategy. The more specific your goal or goals, the more effectively you will be able to focus your efforts. Your goals will also act as a metric by which you assess which networking opportunities to pursue and which you should forego.

You are the ultimate orchestrator and architect of your career; just as you would not do an experiment in the lab without a hypothesis or a plan for what measurements to take, neither should you haphazardly go through your career without some sort of goal. What goals you choose to pursue is a personal matter that depends on your history, current circumstances, likes and dislikes, and aspirations for the future. Goals can be long term and ambitious, such as getting or creating a dream job in a different industry, sector, or country. Goals can also be short term and straightforward, such as taking a course to get certified for a new skill. Or you might pick a goal that is focused on your colleagues and community, such as forming a journal club or organizing a happy-hour social event.

You may not have any specific goals in mind yet, and that's okay. Goals and plans can change as you change and acquire new data about yourself, your work, and your surroundings. Like the quest for better networking, communication, and social skills, you can bring your research and study skills to bear upon the problem of goal setting. Mentors can also be invaluable during this discovery process;

13

the value of being a mentor or a mentee is discussed in Chapter 7. And if you want some out-of-the-box career inspiration, consider looking through the American Physical Society News Series *Profiles in Versatility*, by Alaina G. Levine.[1]

If the idea of having a master plan seems daunting, don't worry, but do set *some* kind of goal. Start with something concrete and achievable. It could be about acquiring a particular skill or simply getting back in touch with people in your network who you haven't spoken to in a while, at a rate of one person a week. In fact, reconnecting with old friends and colleagues is a great way to maintain your network (see Section 2.5). But large or small, near or far, set a goal. The goal doesn't have to be perfect or forever. Do not be afraid to experiment and try new things that present themselves to you. There are valuable lessons to be learned from new experiences. Even if it means discovering new things that you didn't like, that is also valuable data to have.

On the other end, if you have a large or long-term goal, tackle it by breaking it into smaller goals and achievements. Identify skills, contacts, or experience you need to achieve in order to obtain your goal. Setting small, easily quantifiable goals in the direction of your ultimate goal will give you confidence and help you consistently move towards what you are trying to achieve.

While working towards your goal, don't be afraid to reassess and change directions. If your goal, or your approach to it, doesn't seem to be working, tweak a parameter and try again until you find something that does work. Negative results are still useful results. Steve Kamb's article "How to NOT Suck at Goal Setting" on the *Nerd Fitness* website addresses these issues of goal setting, specificity, and breaking down larger goals with respect to physical fitness,[2] but many of these lessons are transferable to networking goals and other areas.

An important part of goal setting is self-awareness. Self-awareness is also key to empathy and communication, as will be discussed in detail in Chapter 3. It requires being attentive to and honest with yourself, examining what you do and do not like about your current situation, and what you want from your job, your career, and your life. Being or becoming self-aware means recognizing emotions within yourself and discovering what makes you happy or fulfilled. You can think of your life experiences as data and analyze them as you would if you had collected them in a lab. What trends do you see? Do the data support your hypothesis? Do they suggest other useful experiments to perform?

Having a goal is also good for time management. Your time is precious, and while it is important to be generous and network sustainably, make sure that you do not go overboard. Do not allow too much of your time to be drawn away from your own goals and what you are trying to accomplish. If a request doesn't take long, then it is easy to decide to help, but for more time-consuming tasks, make sure that you have enough time to take care of your own work before committing your time elsewhere. In its own way, protecting your time and the quality of your work is supportive of your network, because the more successful you are at your job, the more resources you will have at your disposal to assist your network. Your goal is a metric for prioritizing tasks and requests, allowing you to decline or avoid activities that would be detrimental to your progress.

2.2 Networking Strategically

Being selective and using your time and energy for the greatest benefit and impact is very important. It means being intentional about how you network. Even if you're not looking for a new job, you should be cultivating your network, because it affects how you get your job done, and it allows you to help others succeed. Networking strategy is about being able to maintain the quality of your work output while maintaining your network, helping your connections, and accessing your network to work towards your goal.

Your networking strategy will do many things for you. It will keep your networking efforts on target so that you don't waste time and can stay focused on your main concern: doing science or engineering. Your networking strategy will help you curate and filter the inputs you receive via your network, and act as the algorithm that helps you choose how to spend your time. You cannot have a reputation as a successful scientist without doing good work, but you also cannot have a reputation as a good scientist if no one knows about your work. You need to do good work for the former, and you need to network for the latter. Your abilities will not advertise themselves; waiting to be acknowledged for your talents and abilities does *not* constitute a strategy. When there is a talent that you want to showcase, seek out opportunities to exercise it. Be proactive and let your network know what you are trying to accomplish so that they can help you.

It is especially important to network strategically if you are planning on doing something new or outside your current comfort zone. For example, if you are planning a career transition from academia to industry, industrial contacts will be invaluable in your transition. If you have cultivated a diverse network, you should already have some contacts in the relevant area, but adding further to your network when you know you want to make a change is very important. This means reaching out to your existing network and asking them to make introductions to people you would like to meet, attending the types of events where you can meet such people and gain relevant skills, and researching the subject online.

Strategic sustainable networking is a long game. Cultivating your network in a kind, sustainable fashion is like growing an orchard or building a cathedral brick by brick. Being consistent in terms of helping others and your community, meeting people, and establishing relationships is the best way to network. Think of your network as a long-term investment (not something you pay attention to only when you need a new job), and it won't be hard for you to find a new job or ask for help when you need it.

There are those who consider time spent networking to be a waste of time, but networking is to your career what exercise is for your body. If you don't occasionally take some time out of your busy schedule to exercise and care for your body, it suffers. And just as exercise can be a boring, miserable thing that you have to drag yourself through if you don't pick an exercise that suits you, networking can be too with the wrong approach. This is why it is important to find your own optimal way of networking as you design your strategy, just as it is important to find a type of exercise that you enjoy, so that neither is an onerous task. Just as you improve at fitness activities with practice, so too will you improve at networking if you make a strategy that works for you and stay consistent.

Because of this unfortunate, commonly held attitude about networking being a waste, learning to be a strategic networker gives you immediate access to some low-hanging fruit. Most people don't have a plan or strategy, so even doing a minimum of these activities will give you a significant advantage in your career. Following up after meeting or making contact with someone is one the most important networking habits to practice, but following up with consistency is hard. Even sales people, whose success is typically dependent upon networking to find new clients, often fail to follow up with prospects.[3]

Whatever activity you do gives you experience doing that activity and ultimately yields more opportunities to do more of that kind of activity. Like generates like. Idioms such as "you reap what you sow" and "the rich get richer, and the poor get poorer," and the concept of compound interest, are all related to this principle, which is referred to in this book as Opportunity Momentum. It applies to networking and professional opportunities, as well as personal hobbies and activities. The more you network, the better at it you will be and the more networking opportunities will come your way. People will associate you with that activity and present you with more opportunities to do it, and that gives you access to things you might never find otherwise.

Author Anecdote

I first experienced Opportunity Momentum when I began volunteering. I served as Treasurer of my SPIE student chapter in graduate school, and I was able to refer to that experience when asking for other volunteering opportunities. As I received more publicly visible volunteering opportunities at conferences, other people began to see me as a volunteer and think of me when they needed one. Each volunteering task I did, I gained more volunteering experience and more Opportunity Momentum for volunteering.

A good networking strategy built on your goals, preferences, and abilities will help you find the best and most effective ways to use your time and play to your strengths. For the introverted or the shy (which are not the same thing!), who may avoid networking or find it arduous or draining, having a strategy based on goals allows for a straightforward selection process (and being an introvert doesn't mean you can't be a good networker; more on that in Chapter 3). Using your strategy will allow you to be targeted in your networking and to attend or participate in specific events where you expect a high success rate in meeting either the type of people you want or a particular person. A networking strategy will also help you resolve feelings of anxiety that you may have associated with networking, because you will know why you're participating and what you want to accomplish, making you more relaxed, focused, and productive. It will also save you time by enabling you to avoid events that are unlikely to be fruitful.

For example, imagine two people attending a conference, Andy and Elif. Andy's goal is to make a career change from academia to industry, so his strategy for networking at the conference will be to attend professional development classes on the subject and meet others there. He'll also attend the career fair to see what industry jobs are available and talk with recruiters. He might visit the exhibition and talk to vendors in the sectors that interest him, asking about what their work is like and what skills he needs. Elif, on the other hand, is a tenured professor not looking to make any career changes, but she may have a new project in mind for which she will need funding and collaborators. She will probably set up meetings with people she already knows who work in the area relevant to her new project, as well as attend talks and meet speakers presenting relevant work. She might also attend a course on proposal writing to brush up on her writing skills to prepare for applying for funding. There might even be people at the conference who work at a funding agency that she will be applying to, and she might meet with them to discuss what they are looking for, if appropriate.

Even if both of these people are attending the same event, they will have very different experiences based on their respective goals and strategies. And this sort of goal setting and strategy development applies to any kind of networking activity or venue. How you network at a conference, online, or within your own company and town, can be strategized based on the goal or goals you set for yourself.

Another important part of strategic networking is knowing your network well. The more you know about what people are doing, and what their interests and expertise are, the better you will be able to help them in their endeavors, and the better you will understand what you can and cannot reasonably ask of them. Knowing what's going on with your contacts can help you to know when you should offer support, or when not to ask for assistance. If you know someone is looking for a collaborator or to change jobs, then you know to pass along someone's contact information or offer to review their resume. Or maybe they have a big project and they are incredibly busy, or they are coping with something like an illness in the family, and it would be inopportune to ask for anything.

Likewise, you want your network to know you and what you do, so that when information and opportunities arise, they think of you or know that you are the right person to ask about something.

Finally, as you network strategically, remember to keep your efforts in perspective. While you have control over your own actions, you typically have no direct power over the result. The Hindu practice of Karma Yoga emphasizes a lack of attachment to the fruits of one's actions, because it is only the action that one can control, nothing else.[4] While networking is a personal and professional practice, not a spiritual one, this is an important parallel. Do your best to create the result that you want, but recognize that there are many aspects of networking that are out of your control. If things don't turn out exactly the way you planned, don't be hard on yourself. Simply examine if there was anything you might have done to achieve a different result, if applicable, and move forward, absorbing the lesson.

2.2.1 Following up

Following up is a key aspect of sustainable networking. This means making a second contact with someone after an initial interaction. Typically, following up happens digitally after an in-person contact, but not necessarily. It is key to being able to continue and solidify new networking connections, thank people for assistance and advice, let people know you appreciate their time, express your interest after an interview, and get feedback from others. Following up is discussed in a general sense in Section 7.12, in reference to conferences in Section 9.9, and in terms of content and medium in Section 10.2, but it is a concept that appears throughout this text.

2.2.2 Personal branding

In terms of strategic networking, personal branding can be a useful way to think about yourself, the work that you produce, and the value that you can offer others. Brands are about consistency and expectation management. If you are familiar with a brand, you know what to expect from it. What comes to mind when you think of Starbucks? Or Thorlabs? Or Chanel? Each of these brands has an image and identity that give you an idea about what to consistently expect from their products. Your personal brand lets others know what they can expect from you.

Think of yourself as a business or company, and your work outputs as your products. From there, you can craft a brand statement that expresses what someone can expect from you and your work. And you won't have only one brand statement, because the value that you can offer to someone will depend on *their* needs, work, and understanding. The brand statement you would give to a scientist in your field would be necessarily different from what you would give to a CEO of a company or a new acquaintance who does not work in STEM. This is about adapting to your audience, as discussed in Section 1.4.

While personal branding is a useful conceptual framework, it is not treated extensively in this book due to scope. Many of the concepts discussed here fit well into a discussion of personal branding, and it is just as useful for people working in STEM as it is for other fields. To read more about personal branding, the book *Networking for Nerds*[5] treats it well as a networking concept for a STEM audience, and the book *Brand You*[6] is wholly dedicated to the subject as written for a general audience.

2.3 Kindness Is Imperative

As you are thinking about your goals and designing your networking strategy, it is important to remember to do so sustainably, and core to sustainable networking is kindness. It is important to be kind to everyone. Whether or not you believe that being kind to others is the right thing to do, being unkind will affect you and your career negatively, whereas being consistently kind to others will work in your favor. People will notice if you are rude, mistreat others, or are dismissive of people whose value to your career is not immediately obvious. It will reflect poorly upon you as a person, and it makes you unlikable.

Overwhelmingly, people hire, choose to work with, and help people whom they *like*. If two candidates are equal in their qualifications, the more likeable one will be hired.[7] This is human nature and psychology, and though it is irrational and frustrating, it is a reality.[8,9] It therefore behooves everyone to be kind. Beyond generally making life more pleasant, kindness makes interactions with others more enjoyable, and it makes it easier for you to find collaborators, opportunities, and new employment.

To this end, an important aspect of strategy in networking is to widen your focus beyond the people who are currently the most powerful. Your network is a long-term investment, and getting to know people before they rise to positions of power is much more effective than the other way around. Today's graduate student is tomorrow's CEO, and they will probably remember if you were unkind to them. They will remember when they were starting out, at their point of greatest need, if you didn't help because they weren't "useful." So if being kind isn't simply the right thing to do, then do it because it will help you achieve your own goals. This includes the gatekeepers and assistants for people important enough to need a filter, and anyone else not in a traditional position of power. Make sure to be kind and gracious, and acknowledge their help when they provide it.

Being a kind, sustainable networker means using your network to help others solve their problems, anticipating people's moments of need and asking how you can help, following up on introductions or leads, following through, and giving people answers to their questions. It's about recognizing that each of your contacts has their own goals that they want to achieve and finding ways to help them. It involves understanding the other person, including knowing the other person's communication preferences. These are all acts of kindness, and they have the nice side effect of benefitting you down the road. Avoid the dark, transactional side of networking, and embrace sustainability and kindness; the success of your network will support your success.

While it is easy to be kind to people who are kind to you, it can feel impossible and frustrating to be kind to people who are not. Unfortunately, sometimes you will encounter people who are either inadvertently or intentionally unkind, and you may want to pay them back in the same currency. This desire for revenge is also part of human nature.[10,11] Instead of succumbing to temptation, you can use your self-awareness to recognize what feelings are provoked when someone is unkind, and choose your response rather than instinctively react with unkindness.

2.4 Care and Maintenance of Your Network

While regularly putting effort into maintaining and caring for your network is very important, it doesn't require a large amount of time. You also don't need an enormous network to be successful at networking. What you need is to keep your network informed about what you are doing so that they know when you are the right person to seek out and so that you can ask the right questions to the right people in your existing network. The information should always flow both ways, which requires you to stay in touch with your contacts by performing routine maintenance of your network.

You can easily imagine how this might turn into a time sink or a distraction. And your existing network is probably bigger than you think it is. It's not just the people with whom you work: it's the people you went to school with, your friends from non-work activities, your neighbors, etc. Fortunately, with the flourishing array of digital networking tools available, from email and LinkedIn to things like Twitter and blogs, keeping up with your network is easier today than it has ever been (digital networking methods and platforms are discussed at length in Chapters 10 and 11). Having a strategy, and being disciplined and consistent with your network maintenance, will eventually make it a habitual and easy task to perform. And you can aim for a level of involvement that suits you and your goals; for some, that will be daily, and for others, weekly or biweekly, depending on what you want to accomplish and what works well for you.

A quote attributed to the late martial artist and actor Bruce Lee is that "Long-term consistency beats short-term intensity." This principle has been studied with respect to health and fitness,[12,13] and it applies to many other areas, including networking. Consider two hypothetical extremes: networking for three consecutive days once a year versus networking 15 minutes every workday for a year (which is a little less than three days total). What do you think would be more effective? The latter would allow you to stay current on things that are going on and respond quickly, but a three-day-marathon networking session would only give you a snapshot of your network once a year. While this is an improbable example, it is a good illustration of how short, regular exchanges are more effective than infrequent information dumps.

It is human nature to avoid change and uncertainty, to stick with routine, and to not deviate unless forced.[14,15] However, this is an ineffective strategy for success and happiness in today's working world. Often, we get wrapped up or trapped in a mode of managing crises or simply doing daily tasks. But regularly managing and expanding your contact base is an important investment in your future success and the success of those connected to you. Make a point to regularly comb through your connections and see who you haven't spoken with in a while, and check in with them to hear how they are doing or ask them if they need anything (digital networking makes this process quick and easy).

As you make it a point to be regularly in contact with your network, your goal should be to find ways to benefit your connections, which requires familiarity with their needs and interests. You can send them messages to check in and ask them how they are doing, ideally when you don't need anything. You can also check their activity on social media platforms such as LinkedIn, or follow their blogs or newsletters. This can mean sharing articles or papers that seem relevant to the person's interests, sending a handwritten note or gift, or giving them a phone call, if appropriate. Sharing other people's content with your network is another sound way to help, such as sharing their blog post, article, or paper on your own account. This helps raise your connection's visibility with the rest of your network.

In terms of meeting your contact's needs, remembering their work and personal details is important. It is up to you and how you want to do things, but many people find it helpful to take notes about their professional contacts. For example, remembering that your boss's partner's name is Umar and that they have three children together (and the children's names and ages) might be a challenge for you, but it's also something that may mean a lot to your boss. Putting forth the effort to remember shows that you care, and taking notes on these sorts of details is one way to do that if you don't have a good memory for that sort of thing.

Some people keep notes on business cards, spreadsheets, etc. It can help to categorize your contacts by characteristics such as their specialties, where they are from, where they are now, how you know them, etc. You can keep a notebook, a file, notations in your contacts, or even a spreadsheet to remember details about your contacts that can help you to help them. There is also "client relationship management" (CRM) software that can help you keep track of people, often used in business, marketing, and sales.[16] Taking notes about things that you can't find in someone's LinkedIn profile, such as where you met them, can help you keep track of your contacts and find ways to be more helpful to them. Making a few notes about someone you just met can also help you remember them and enable you to better maintain the relationship moving forward. If you choose to take these kinds of notes, make sure you do it in an organized and easily accessible fashion, so that you can find them when needed.

Author Anecdote

I only recently began keeping notes on contacts, because at some point I recognized that my network had grown to the point that I wasn't able to remember certain details. After looking into my options, I began recording details in the notes section of my Google contacts. I use Gmail and an Android phone, which means I have easy access to my contacts and notes at any given time. Because I am usually connected with people on LinkedIn, where their professional details are available, I typically only record significant personal details, about family or where they grew up, or anything else I learn that seems important.

In addition to notes, digital and online networking accounts will also play a key role in your networking strategy. Given how international science and engineering are, your network could potentially be spread all over the planet. Networking online and through social media are important ways to maintain your connections, but you should seek out face-to-face meetings whenever you can, especially at the beginning of a relationship. Whenever you travel, look into your contacts and see if anyone may be nearby, and check in with them to set up a meeting. If you attend a conference or trade show, make a point to catch up with people you don't see very often but who will likely be in attendance. Digital networking platforms are incredibly powerful and important, but it is improbable that anything will ever fully replace the experience that you get by seeing someone in person. A networking strategy that incorporates both in-person and online approaches will serve you well.

Attending social or networking events is an important way to maintain your network. When a group of people you already know gather together, showing up and engaging with them is an efficient way to perform maintenance. This is part of what makes conferences (see Chapter 9) such amazing networking events: they do the work of bringing many of your existing connections together in the same place in a way you never could alone.

You can also include your connections in activities that you are already doing. This is a matter of personal preference and style, but, for example, if you are a runner and you have a professional contact who is also a runner, then going running with them to do connection maintenance is a great idea. You were already going to run, so it doesn't take a new time commitment, but it allows you to keep up with this person. This applies to any hobby or activity that you do that is professionally appropriate, and you can even include multiple contacts in these activities, as a way to cross-pollinate your network. Networking expert and author of *Never Eat Alone*[17] Keith Ferrazzi is a strong advocate for this approach, but it is a matter of personal taste. It can be a very effective networking habit, but you need to be comfortable engaging with other people this way.

Your main focus in networking should be to help your connections in a way that is consistent with, or at least does not detract from, your career goals. You will ideally receive regular requests from your network for your time or assistance. With that in mind, you want to say yes as much as you can. For requests that are easy or require little effort or time commitment, saying yes should be obvious, but you need to be careful with your time and be more selective about high-commitment requests. The greater the commitment, the more important it is that it aligns with your goals and networking strategy. Saying yes to chairing a committee for an organization you care about is a good commitment to make if you want to find a leadership position in that committee or if leadership experience is important for you.

The reality is that sometimes you will need to decline because you are busy, under a deadline, or determine that the request is not a good fit for you. You want to network sustainably and perform network maintenance by participating, but not at the expense of the quality of your work (the basis of your reputation). If your reputation is harmed, it's not just bad for you but also for your network, because it hinders your ability to be helpful. So saying no and *not* over-committing yourself is not only good for you, it's good for your network.

When you recognize that a request is not timely, too much for you to handle, or not in line with your goals, politely decline and do so promptly. Don't make the person wait or have to guess your answer from your silence. Simply explain that due to the nature of the request and the time that it would take, you cannot help, but ask how you might be able to assist in a less-time-consuming way (if you want). And of course, referring someone else who might be interested and have the time to help is always a good idea—and a win–win if you find someone who would benefit from the opportunity.

2.5 Expanding Your Network

In addition to caring for your existing network, once you begin networking strategically, you will also want to think about expanding your network. There are a variety of methods, both active and passive, that you can use to begin adding connections to your network. As defined in this book, active methods include seeking out individuals, groups, organizations, or events that you want to become involved with, whereas passive methods mean sharing your information and ideas in places where others can find it and reach out to you.

Active methods can be exercised in person or remotely, but most passive methods are remote, through online social media profiles, activity on social media, or electronic and print publications. Presentations and talks given to a public audience, as well as recordings of them, can also be considered passive methods, because they make you more visible without seeking out a particular audience or person (except to the extent that you chose the venue or conference at which you are speaking). Passive networking is about making yourself visible so that other people can approach you, not the other way around.

2.5.1 Intentional relationship cultivation

Using your time effectively means networking in the right areas to achieve your goals. A part of this is intentionally cultivating relationships. Who you know and who will call upon you for assistance, and vice versa, have a powerful effect on your career and how well you can implement your knowledge and ideas.

The idea of strategic relationship building might make you squeamish, bringing the dark, transactional side of networking to mind. It might make you shy away from the idea. But with strategic relationship cultivation, as with all your networking efforts, if you do it sustainably with kindness and the ultimate goal of mutual benefit, then there is nothing wrong with it. If you seek to help first, ask favors second, and produce mutual success, then you are using the sustainable approach that benefits everyone.

It should go without saying that you should not spend time forming a connection with someone solely thinking about what you can get from them or how they can help *you*. This doesn't treat them like a person; it treats them like an object whose value is based solely on its leverage, which is not kind. The German philosopher Immanuel Kant described this as the "Formula of Humanity," which states that you should "Act so that you use humanity, as much in your own person as in the person of every other, always at the same time as end and never merely as means."[18] It is okay to have in mind that someone might be able to help you, and if you are looking for help, you should be transparent and honest about that. But you should first consider if there is something you can do to help them with their goals and career.

When you want to begin strategically acquiring new connections, research your new or desired contacts and work to understand what they do. This advance preparation will help you understand what they might need and how you might open the relationship in a generous way. Your research should cover the person's professional history, their research interests, and public social media accounts. Knowing this kind of information gives you the opportunity to establish a greater connection with them. You can use a variety of search engines, find them on LinkedIn or Twitter, and see what is important to them and what interests them. LinkedIn will also tell you if you already have a mutual connection, so that you can ask for an introduction instead of sending a cold email (how to write a good cold email is discussed in Chapters 10 and 12). If you can get an existing contact to introduce you, the person is more likely to respond, and respond favorably. If you already know that you went to the same university, studied the same subject, or have similar travel tastes, you can spend more time discussing those subjects.

You can work towards creating a connection with a person of interest by following them on social media, commenting on their public posts, attending events where you might encounter them, or contacting them directly with questions. During your initial meeting or in your opening message, let them know why you are interested in them, compliment their work, or congratulate them on an accomplishment, if applicable. Ask them questions about themselves, and if you have found a way that you think you can be of service, mention that as well. If you are looking for help, be honest and upfront about it. Remember to be concise and respectful of their time. If your initial contact leads to a phone call or in-person meeting, always follow up via email or other relevant medium with thanks and action items.

In a follow-up with a new contact, make a point to remind them of the things that you can do for them, not the other way around. You want to motivate them to stay in touch with you. Calendar alerts can help you stay in touch with people. After a meeting with someone, if you want to cultivate the relationship or if you discussed an action item with them, leave yourself a reminder to follow up with them in a week, month, or any amount of time you think appropriate. If it's a new connection you are trying to cement, don't let too much time pass without communication. And if someone referred you for the introduction, make sure to follow up with the original referrer and let them know what happened, especially if it went well and you can deliver good news; regardless of the outcome, thank them for their effort.

Ultimately, as you build relationships this way, you will augment your network such that when you are ready to commence a new project or make a career change, you will not be stepping out unsupported. You will be advancing with the aid of friends and colleagues.

In terms of relationship cultivation, people who are especially good to know because of their wide contact networks include journalists and recruiters. They are generally very well connected and are likely to remember you if you help them find someone to fill a position or with a story they are working on. So take the call or email from recruiters or journalists, because even if you aren't the person they need, you can try to help them find the right person and benefit everyone, including the connection that you refer.

2.5.2 Other ways to actively expand your network

There are a number of ways to expand your network beyond seeking out specific individuals. These include attending social and networking events, conferences, volunteering, and becoming involved in online groups and discussions that are relevant to your field, interests, and goals. Activities such as these can help you engage with others and make new connections. See Chapters 7–9 for more details.

Another good approach is to revisit old relationships from your past that have become neglected. This increases the number of active contacts in your network in a way that requires less effort than establishing brand-new contacts. People are more likely to respond to people they already know. Catching up with someone about what they have been doing since you fell out of touch is a great way to open a conversation and re-establish a connection. These can be thought of as dormant connections that need reactivation.

2.5.3 Passive network expansion

Methods for passively expanding your network are about making yourself available to be approached by others. You do this by increasing your visibility through social media, online communities, and publications. This includes your technical publications. Your conference presentations, proceedings, and any other public speaking engagements you make also serve this purpose, especially if your talk is recorded and posted online where it is searchable. Public speaking (discussed further in Section 7.7) and presenting are a grey area between passive and active, in that you can actively seek a particular venue or audience, but who approaches you afterwards is outside of your control. Asking questions during question-and-answer sessions after talks also serves as a sort of passive networking (see Section 9.3), because you are putting yourself in front of an audience. Like presenting, because you have actively chosen to attend that talk you have some impression of who the audience will be, but it is passive because it allows others to approach you if you asked a memorable question.

Passive networking means using things such as personal websites, publications, Twitter, and LinkedIn to publicly share your work and accomplishments, and generate useful content for others, including actively taking part in discussions. Your replies to someone's question in an online forum can prove useful to others, which develops your reputation as a helpful and knowledgeable person.

Ultimately, anything that can be found about you online should be considered a form of passive networking, one that requires maintenance, including being aware of and managing any negative information (e.g., you share a name with a prominent criminal). Generating content and managing negative information is discussed further in Section 10.8.

2.6 Planning versus Serendipity

While planning and strategy are essential to making your networking efforts effective, you should not make your plan so rigid that you do not allow for a bit of serendipity. As scientists and engineers, we should have an appreciation of the value of the serendipitous and the accidental. There is a long precedent of unexpected and important scientific discoveries, including nuclear fission,[19] x-rays,[20] and penicillin,[21] which is why no phrase in science is half so exciting as "Huh, that's strange." Studies have shown that densely populated areas afford unplanned face-to-face interactions and the development of rich networks, which increases productivity,[22,23] and has inspired designs and architecture intended to encourage serendipitous encounters.[24,25]

Accordingly, if you network in an exclusively strategic fashion, attempting to plan every move with no space for spontaneity, you will make it harder for serendipity to strike. While you should have an overall strategic plan for developing your network, make sure to leave space for accidental encounters, meeting someone at a coffee break, or on public transit. Attend the occasional networking or social event outside of your expertise or comfort zone. Some of these incidental encounters will lead to nothing, but some might become powerful collaborations or friendships.

One of the benefits of serendipity is that it is likely to result in a diverse network connection. It may be someone from a different company, field, gender, background, or country. Diversity immensely strengthens your network, making it a more powerful tool for success. The strengths and challenges presented by diversity, how to embrace diversity and reap its benefits, are discussed at length in Chapter 6. Serendipity in reference to conferences is discussed further in Subsection 9.8.6.

Exercises

(1)   Spend some time considering one or more career goals. For the purposes of this exercise, you want to generate at least one, but feel free to generate as many as you like, both large and small.

(2)   Develop a networking strategy for (one of) the goal(s) you came up with in the first exercise. Concentrating on that goal, do some thought experiments and research on general ways you could accomplish it through networking. Don't worry about the details yet; you'll be able to flesh those out as you keep reading.

(3)   Think about how you interact with others, especially people who are in service or administrative positions. Are you kind to these people? Do you treat everyone kindly, or do you have a tendency to correlate the kindness that you offer with the person's material value to you? Why? This can be a very difficult exercise that requires a lot of self-awareness and can bring up some unpleasant feelings, but try as best you can.

(4)   On what occasions have you been unkind to others? Thinking about it now, how would or could you behaved differently?

(5)   Think about some general ways that you can begin to care for and maintain your network. You could begin to reconnect with old friends, classmates, and colleagues; address overdue follow-ups; begin organizing your contacts; or start to take or organize notes on them.

(6)   Returning to the goal and strategy you created in Exercises 1 and 2, identify a relevant potential network connection and spend some time researching them. Run searches on them, find them on LinkedIn, see if they have a Twitter account or other social media presence. Try to think of ways that you could offer assistance to them or interesting questions you could ask, and find out if you have any mutual connections already. You don't need to contact them yet (unless you want to), but spend some time doing the initial preparation as practice.

(7)   Research some organizations, conferences, or events that you might attend to expand your network. Get involved or attend an event.

References

1. Levine, A. G., "Profiles in Versatility," *APS News*, American Physical Society (2007–2018).
2. Kamb, S., "How to NOT Suck at Goal Setting," *Nerd Fitness* (January 2011). Retrieved from nerdfitness.com/blog/how-to-not-suck-at-goal-setting. Accessed on February 19, 2019.
3. Brooks, M., "Following Up with Prospects: 90 Percent Never Do," *Sales Gravy*, Retrieved from salesgravy.com/sales-articles/closing-techniques/Following-Up-with-Prospects-90-Percent-Never-Do. Accessed on February 20, 2019.
4. Kumar, A. and S. Kumar, "Karma yoga: A path towards work in positive psychology," *Indian J. Psychiatry* **55**(2) (2013) [doi: 10.4103/0019-5545.105511].
5. Levine, A. G., *Networking for Nerds*, John Wiley & Sons, Hoboken, NJ (2015).
6. Purkiss, J. and D. Royston-Lee, *Brand You: Turn Your Unique Talents Into a Winning Formula*, Pearson FT Press, Harlow, UK (2012).
7. Higgins, C. A., and T. A. Judge, "The Effect of Applicant Influence Tactics on Recruiter Perceptions of Fit and Hiring Recommendations: A Field Study," *J. Appl. Psychol.* **89**(4), 622–632 (2004).
8. Dvorsky, G., "The 12 cognitive biases that prevent you from being rational," *io9 Gizmodo* (January 29, 2013). Retrieved from io9.gizmodo.com/the-12-cognitive-biases-that-prevent-you-from-being-rat-5974468. Accessed February 20, 2019.

9. Soll, J. B. et al., "Outsmart Your Own Biases," *Harvard Business Review* (May 2015). Retrieved from hbr.org/2015/05/outsmart-your-own-biases. Accessed February 20, 2019.

10. Harmon, K., "Does Revenge Serve an Evolutionary Purpose?" *Scientific American* (May 4, 2011). Retrieved from scientificamerican.com/article/revenge-evolution. Accessed on March 25, 2019.

11. Fehr, E. and S. Gächter, "Fairness and Retaliation: The Economics of Reciprocity," *J. Economic Perspectives* **14(3)** 159–181 (2000) [doi:10.1257/jep.14.3.159].

12. Kim, S. H. et al., "The Relationship of Exercise Frequency to Body Composition and Physical Fitness in Dormitory-Dwelling University Students," *J. Men's Health* **14**(1) (2018) [doi:10.22374/1875-6859.14.1.6].

13. Laskowski, E. R., "Which is better — 30 minutes of aerobic exercise every day or one hour of aerobic exercise three times a week?," *Mayo Clinic Expert Answers* (December 14, 2018). Retrieved from mayoclinic.org/healthy-lifestyle/fitness/expert-answers/aerobic-exercise/faq-20058561. Accessed March 25, 2019.

14. Eidelman, S. et al., "Longer is better," *J. Experimental Social Psychol.* **46**(6), 993–998 (2010) [doi:10.1016/j.jesp.2010.07.008].

15. Ryback, R., "Why we resist change," *Psychology Today* (January 25, 2017). Retrieved from psychologytoday.com/us/blog/the-truisms-wellness/201701/why-we-resist-change. Accessed March 25, 2019.

16. "What is CRM? A Marketer's Guide," *Mailchimp*. Retrieved from mailchimp.com/crm/what-is-crm. Accessed on March 25, 2019.

17. Ferrazzi, K., *Never Eat Alone*, Crown Business, New York (2005).

18. Kant, I. and M. J. Gregor, *Groundwork of the Metaphysics of Morals*, 4:429, Cambridge University Press, Cambridge, UK (1998).

19. Tretkoff, E., "December 1938: Discovery of Nuclear Fission" *APS News,* **16**(11) (2007). Retrieved from aps.org/publications/apsnews/200712/physicshistory.cfm. Accessed March 26, 2019.

20. "November 8, 1895: Roentgen's Discovery of X-Rays," *APS News* **10**(10) (2001). Retrieved from aps.org/publications/apsnews/200111/history.cfm. Accessed March 26, 2019.

21. "Discovery and Development of Penicillin," *American Chemical Society International Historic Chemical Landmarks*. Retrieved from acs.org/content/acs/en/education/whatischemistry/landmarks/flemingpenicillin.html. Accessed on March 26, 2019.

22. Pan, W. et al., "Urban characteristics attributable to density-driven tie formation," *Nature Comm.* **4** (2013). [doi: 10.1038/ncomms2961].

23. Waber, B., *Understanding the Link Between Changes in Social Support and Changes in Outcomes with the Sociometric Badge*, Ph.D. dissertation, Massachusetts Institute of Technology (2011). Retrieved from dspace.mit.edu/bitstream/handle/1721.1/67762/766797397-MIT.pdf. Accessed March 26, 2019.

24. Kettelhut, K., "Chasing Productivity And Innovation: Can The Workplace Get Us There?," *Work Design Magazine* (July 11, 2018). Retrieved from workdesign.com/2018/07/chasing-productivity-and-innovation-can-the-workplace-get-us-there. Accessed on March 26, 2019.

25. Wagner, J. and D. Watch, "Innovation Spaces: The New Design of Work," Anne T. and Robert M. Bass Initiative on Innovation and Placemaking (April 2017). Retrieved from brookings.edu/wp-content/uploads/2017/04/cs_20170404_innovation_spaces_pdf.pdf. Accessed on March 26, 2019.

Chapter 3
Self-Awareness, Social Anxiety, and Communication

"Know thyself."

~Delphic maxim,
Temple of Apollo at Delphi, 7th century BCE

3.1 Knowing the Terrain

Communication is an essential part of networking and science, and how we communicate is shaped by our own internal landscapes. In this landscape, you will find personal characteristics, such as whether you are more introverted or extraverted, your levels of self-awareness and empathy, and the way you interpret information that you receive from others. You may also encounter fears and social anxieties, which can make interacting with other people challenging or even unpleasant. Knowing this terrain, and being able to navigate it effectively, allows you to improve your communication skills and develop an effective, sustainable networking strategy that suits your personality and your goals.

Being able to understand and navigate this internal landscape is about self-awareness, which is the ability to recognize our emotions and understand who we are. It is an essential skill for being able to empathize with others. Empathy is an important skill, because it allows you to adapt to your audience and communicate effectively.[1] There is a positive correlation between empathy and self-awareness,[2,3] because the ability to recognize emotions in others is dependent upon our ability to recognize our own emotions.

Self-awareness also allows us to approach and mitigate common issues such as social anxiety. One study estimated that globally 275 million people suffer from anxiety *disorders*, representing 2.5–6.5% of a country's population.[4] Another study found that 13.7% of the population in Ireland experiences a social anxiety disorder at some point in their lives,[5] and the number is 12.1% in the United States.[6]

When we are self-aware, we are also better able to optimize our communication and networking strategy based on the knowledge of who we are. The best strategy for an introvert is necessarily going to be different than for an extravert. Extraversion may be a trait that is often praised in many Western societies,[7,8] but it is important not to pathologize its counterpart, introversion.

31

In fact, research shows that groups with a mix of introverts and extraverts on teams and in leadership perform better than a homogenous group of one type or the other (more on diversity of all kinds in Chapter 6).[9,10] Both introverts and extraverts can be excellent networkers, but their respective approaches to communication and networking require different strategies, so knowing yourself in this area is important.

But the subject of communication (and its component skills) is typically not included in STEM education programs.[11] As scientists and engineers, we are expected to pick those things up as we go (by osmosis, perhaps), leaving many lost or frustrated as to how to improve. Many of us end up neglecting or avoiding the topic of communication all together, or the Dunning–Kruger effect convinces us that we don't need any improvement. But poor communication can hinder our relationships, careers, and even the science that we do.

Fortunately, communication and self-awareness are trainable abilities, and you can take matters into your own hands. This chapter will give you an overview of these subjects, including anxiety, introversion and extraversion, empathy, and how they relate to your communication style and networking strategy. The goal is to help you to find a way to express yourself more effectively, to have a better understanding of yourself and by extension others, and to find ways to address your social fears or adapt your approach according to your personality and preferences.

3.2 Fear, Rejection, and Anxiety

Meeting new people and attempting to engage strangers in conversation is an exercise in vulnerability, because you are opening yourself up for rejection, but it's also something you will need to do in networking. Rejection is unpleasant; studies have shown that the same part of the brain is activated for both physical pain and verbal rejection.[12,13] Pain and fear of rejection are useful feedback mechanisms that have kept human beings alive in dangerous situations,[14] but they can backfire in certain modern circumstances, such as in-person networking events, making us want to run for our lives and find somewhere to hide when no life-threatening circumstance exists.

There is also the fear of saying or doing something wrong, looking stupid, and exposing ourselves to ridicule. This is a different type of fear of rejection, with a more dramatic outcome than being told no. Human beings are highly social animals, and prehistorically it was our ability to collaborate that allowed us to protect ourselves from large predators.[15] The fear of rejection is so powerful, because for our ancestors, it could mean death if they were ostracized.[16] This is why a party or reception with strangers, meeting new people, and public speaking can be so intimidating. When you attend a networking or conference event and see people chatting naturally with others, it is probably not as easy as it looks and there are many others in the room who feel the same. In fact, to use the American population as an example, research shows that anywhere between 40% and 60% are shy, and that the number is increasing over time.[17,18]

Hopefully, knowing that you are not alone in your fear of rejection (and why) gives you solace, but there are additional things that you can do to ease your social anxieties. Recognize your fear, but do not chastise yourself for experiencing it. While you may never completely eliminate your fear, you can learn to mitigate it by improving your social skills and getting practice at meeting and speaking with others. Like any skill, networking, communication, and meeting new people take study and practice. And social anxiety is something that can be reduced through training.[19,20]

One of the ways you can begin training yourself is through observation. As a scientist or engineer you already have a powerful set of observation and analysis skills that you can bring to bear. First, you can begin to observe people who are successful in ways that you wish to be, and then imitate them or seek their aid. You can also observe the reactions of people you are interacting with and make changes to your behavior. Keeping a lab notebook is probably already a habit that you possess, and you can begin recording your observations to help you remember and make plans to practice new techniques. Journaling, including gratitude and visual journaling, is also a well-known technique for processing and relieving anxiety.[21–23]

What if, even after acknowledging that others share your fears and finding people to observe and imitate, you still struggle with anxiety? You can pursue things like formalized public speaking practice, such as through Toastmasters International,[24] get involved in a professional organization or volunteering opportunities where you are required to interact with others, or see a therapist. Studies show a high rate of success for counseling and psychotherapy to alleviate anxiety that can inhibit socializing.[25,26] Acting and improvisation classes can be very helpful in overcoming the sort of social anxiety that makes it difficult to start conversations and attend social events. The American idiom "fake it 'til you make it" is about acting the way you wish you were and, with practice and repetition, ultimately learning to embrace and become the desired image that you are presenting.

One of the most anxiety-inducing networking experiences most people face is a large room of people, mostly strangers, with whom you are expected to mingle. First, it is important to acknowledge that this is just one of many types of networking events, and that you do not have to attend such events in order to network or to be a good networker. However, when chosen strategically, these types of events can offer a lot of great opportunities, and so it's not a bad idea to have a plan for how to handle your anxiety and find a way to participate without excessive stress.

One such strategy for dealing with the "scary room full of strangers" scenario is to show up close to the start of the event, when there won't be many people there yet. When you arrive, walk into the room and don't hang out in the doorway. You want to appear approachable and easy to talk to; hesitating in the entrance works against that. So even if you feel like running away and *are* hesitant to enter, just walk straight in. Then make a point to introduce yourself to the organizer, see if there's anything you can do to help, and familiarize yourself with the space.

That way, by the time most others arrive, you are already comfortable and more prepared to interact. It can be tempting and easy to stay within the circle of people we know, but this does not expand or build a diverse network. Staying with people we already know is comfortable because we avoid rejection, but in this way, the fear of rejection can stop us from putting ourselves out there. More on strategies for formal networking events will be discussed in Chapter 9.

Another anxiety you may face if you are an early career professional (ECP) is the fear that more senior people may not be interested in talking to you. However, many senior-level scientists and executives recognize that the ECPs of today are the leaders of tomorrow, and they will be interested in fostering and interacting with you. They may even be interested in mentoring you. There are some people who fall prey to snobbery and will not give you their time because you are junior, but do not take this short-sighted behavior personally; it is their failing, not yours.

When dealing with people who are senior, it is important to remember that, by merit of their advanced positions, they tend to be very busy with full agendas. A polite person, who is not on their way to an appointment or late getting somewhere, will make a few minutes of time for you. But it is important for you to remain cognizant of treating their time with respect. Do introduce yourself to senior scientists and executives, but do not monopolize their time or be offended if, after a few minutes, they excuse themselves. This applies to anyone, but doubly so to executives and their equivalents. If you have a positive interaction with someone, even if it is brief, make sure to get their contact information and follow up with them to cement their memory of you. High-level individuals meet a lot of people, so you need to make an extra effort to ensure that they remember you by following up promptly.

Ultimately, feeling comfortable with the idea of rejection will help you with social anxiety, both personal and professional. This is a valuable skill that will aid you in most facets of life. This is not to say that you should stop caring entirely what people think or that you should not care if you are rejected. What it means is becoming comfortable enough with the idea of rejection that you do not avoid the possibility of rejection purely out of fear. Much of science is a process of repeated failure until something goes right, and in both science and your career, negative results can provide useful information about how to refine your approach going forward.

To become more comfortable with rejection, you can practice something called "rejection therapy." This a concept created by entrepreneur Jason Comely and subsequently purchased by TED speaker Jia Jiang.[27] It is a formalized methodology (game) for becoming comfortable with rejection. The goal of rejection therapy is to intentionally seek out small, inconsequential rejections, such as making a request to a stranger that is non-offensive but likely to be rejected, e.g., asking if they have gum or a lighter, or if they could give you a ride to the store. One seeks these opportunities to deliberately acquire a rejection, and by making rejection a desirable result, it makes rejection a more manageable and a less frightening thing to receive.

Whatever strategies you elect to deal with your social anxieties, something you need to make sure to do is to *practice*. Practice is one of the best ways to get better at interacting, calming your anxiety, and reducing your fear of rejection. If the problem seems insurmountable and you experience significant physical symptoms of panic, you may want to consult a counselor or physician. Blushing, sweating, trembling, avoidance of socializing due to fear, and dwelling on perceived mistakes are known symptoms of Social Anxiety Disorder (SAD),[28] and if that seems familiar, doing more research and seeking outside assistance may help.

Self-care after social interaction can also be very important, especially when you have social anxiety. A component of social anxiety is ruminating on actual or perceived social mistakes after they have taken place. The Mayo Clinic describes this behavior as "spending time after a social situation analyzing your performance and identifying flaws in your interactions."[28] If you do this, finding ways to calm yourself by performing activities you find soothing, such as journaling, meditation, exercise, or drinking tea, can help relieve your post-social anxieties. More on the topic of self-care is discussed in Chapter 9.

3.3 Introversion and Extraversion

Something that affects your style of networking, and the types of events and social engagements that you prefer, is whether you are an introvert or an extravert. Know that one is not better than the other; introversion and extraversion are merely terms that describe sets of personality traits that tend to be clustered. Introverts are generally considered to be quieter and more solitary, whereas extraverts are considered to be outgoing and gregarious.[29] Another way of differentiating introversion and extraversion is to look at how the act of socializing impacts an individual.[30] Under this definition, if an individual finds that social interaction uses up a lot of energy and they require downtime afterwards to recover, they are considered an introvert. Conversely, gaining energy from social interaction is considered to be a sign of extraversion.

There is even a new term, ambiversion, which describes a person who does not shy away from social interaction, nor do they find it especially taxing, but who still needs private time to recover and relax from large social events.[31] An ambivert lies somewhere between an extravert and an introvert. Ultimately, the need to define the concept of ambiversion is an indicator that extraversion and introversion are not binary states, but that they exist in a continuum, with most people lying somewhere between the two extremes. You will likely find that you possess some characteristics that are considered extraverted and some that are considered introverted.

While the dynamic and charismatic personality has become popular and desired in many Western cultures,[7] it is important not to devalue the qualities of introversion. Introversion is often also characterized by attention to detail and strong observation skills, characteristics that are highly valued in STEM fields and elsewhere. Many Eastern cultures do not have the same fascination with, nor do they prize, extraversion in the same way as some Western cultures.[8] Neither extraversion or introversion is better than the other, and it is a mistake to pathologize or consider introversion a deficiency.[32] However, due to the highly social nature of many in-person networking events, introverts face some obstacles that extraverts do not, and therefore they especially benefit from having a goal-driven networking strategy.

Author Anecdote

By most measures, I am an extravert. I am outgoing and talkative, and rooms full of strangers don't bother me. But I find social interaction exhausting, and I am prone to post-social bouts of anxiety and rumination over my perceived mistakes. In other words, I strongly exhibit characteristics of both extraversion and introversion, with a side of social anxiety. I don't identify strongly with ambiversion, though I perhaps fit the definition. Many people, like me, will not fit tidily into a single box, and it is also not necessary to do so. These definitions are simply helpful nomenclature to help us understand these concepts and ourselves.

Regardless how you identify—extravert, introvert, or ambivert—you can be a talented networker without attempting to change your personality. Because introverts tend to avoid busy social situations, there is a misconception that they do not make good networkers. Many excellent networkers are introverts, possibly due to the more strategic approach that introverts tend to take to networking. Finding opportunities that are high impact, in order to get the greatest effect from their efforts, or focusing on one-on-one interaction are things that will come more easily to an introvert, who naturally has a more limited bandwidth for dealing with people and social situations. Introversion is not mutually exclusive with networking; it just requires a different strategy than extraversion.[33]

If you are an introvert, conferences and public speaking may be things that you shy away from instinctively. Recognize that you don't have to participate in those kinds of activities to network, though a strategy can make it easier to participate. When approaching large, "room of strangers" social situations or anything that can be generally over stimulating, a good strategy for introverts is to have a specific goal for that exact event. Do advance preparation and, if possible, decide who you want to meet, or simply give yourself a set number of people with whom you would like to connect. Setting a goal or goals of this kind is useful for non-introverts as well. Then when you have achieved your goal, you can allow yourself to leave if you find the situation taxing. These kinds of opportunities can be high impact for networking efforts, and they tend to be of short, fixed duration, so even though they may be daunting, you know when you can go home to recharge, having made a lot of new contacts.

If you are an introvert, it may also be a challenge to speak up and ask for what you want in your work environment, but this is something that you should make a point to do, both for the quality of your work and for your local networking strategy (more on this in Chapter 8). This means finding the best circumstance to do this. If you can't bring yourself to speak up in meetings, make sure you get face time with your boss. Part of networking, either at your company or a conference, is about sharing your work, the goals you have, and the obstacles you face. Introverts may be tempted to listen rather than speak or share, but remember that networking is about an *equitable* exchange of information. So if you cannot bring yourself to speak in a meeting, find a way to talk with your boss or coworkers in a setting where you feel comfortable so that you can share your accomplishments.

Extraverts may have the opposite issue in networking, where they may easily meet people and share information but not ask enough questions to receive information in return. This is an issue especially if an extravert is interacting with an introvert; the natural tendency of both will be for one to talk and the other to listen (more on this in Section 4.3). If you are an extravert, make a point to listen and ask questions as well as speak. Pay special attention to the balance of the conversation (whether it is in person or electronic), and if you notice that you are doing most of the information giving, throttle back and ask more questions so that the conversation is more equitable. Doing so takes self-awareness, which will be discussed in Section 3.4. Ultimately, your goal is to ensure that your networking is a two-way flow of information.

3.3.1 Sensitivity

Something that can also come into play in social interaction and anxiety is sensitivity. Some people are qualified as "highly sensitive" because they possess "sensory processing sensitivity" (SPS), which means that they have elevated levels of empathy, are very aware of their surroundings, and can be easily overwhelmed and overstimulated by large numbers of people, bright lights, and loud noises.[34,35] While the majority of highly sensitive people also qualify as introverts, there are also highly sensitive extraverts, who are invigorated by stimulating social situations but simultaneously experience sensory overload.[36]

Just like introversion, high sensitivity has valuable aspects but can also pose an obstacle to certain in-person networking events. That doesn't mean that highly sensitive people cannot be excellent networkers; in fact, their elevated levels of empathy can make them excel at communication. But as with introversion, it may require more strategy and advance planning to deal with overstimulating situations.

3.4 Empathy, Self-Awareness, and Communication

Empathy is defined as the ability to recognize emotions in others,[37] and self-awareness is defined as the ability to recognize emotions within ourselves.[38] These concepts are important to understand for effective networking, because communication, a necessity for networking, depends upon both empathy and self-awareness.[1] We have to pay attention to our audience, see if our message is being received, and adapt as necessary. We can speak at length on a topic, but if we fail to do so in a way that our audience understands, we have communicated nothing. The emotions of the person or audience listening to us are important feedback on how well we are communicating, and our ability to receive that information, or the sensor we use for collecting this kind of data, is empathy. And the ability to recognize the emotional states of others is highly dependent on our ability to recognize those emotions within ourselves, or self-awareness.[10,11]

The good news is that both empathy and self-awareness are skills that you can improve through practice.[39]

Aside from getting better at communication and networking, self-awareness allows you to assess your own abilities and have a good understanding of your strengths and weaknesses. Self-awareness and competence are positively correlated,[40] which combats the Dunning–Kruger effect. The information acquired through self-awareness and self-examination can be used to find ways to improve areas in which you are weak, such as becoming more empathetic and enhancing your conversation and communication skills, and it can help you pick career goals that will make you feel fulfilled.

Through self-awareness, you can also find ways to mitigate your weaknesses by playing to your strengths. If you have trouble networking in large groups, recognizing this and finding ways to network in smaller, more intimate settings, is an example of how you can play to your strengths. Self-awareness also allows you to form a picture of how you are perceived by others, and to behave in such a way that the perception is as true to you and your goals as possible. And when people have an accurate picture of what you do and what you are capable of, it allows them to connect you with relevant opportunities or approach you with questions.

As a scientist or engineer, you may be familiar with keeping a laboratory notebook, and noting the details of your experiments, as well as recording the data you collect. It is possible and useful to do this with yourself. Performing and recording self-assessments will help you improve your self-awareness, and making notes to yourself can help to clarify your thoughts, as well as being a useful reference later to see how you are changing and improving. You can do experiments, such as writing down your responses to certain social situations, or after attempting rejection therapy. If you want, there are also formalized models for self-assessment, such as the Johari Window,[41,42] that you can perform. Creating concrete, easily quantifiable goals (such as saying "Hello" to one new person a day), recording them, and then the results as you work towards them, can clarify your path forward and make a difficult problem feel more approachable.

Sometimes self-awareness means recognizing that you need to take a different approach than everyone else, or that a solution that works well for other people is not the best solution for you. This can be small-scale and day-to-day, or this can be large scale in terms of what kind of work you want to do or what your life goals are. When you are self-aware, you are better equipped to find the situations that suit you best and make you the happiest. It allows you to find the networking methods and strategy that works best for you, and to pass over things that don't work as well, making your efforts more focused and efficient.

An important example of the utility of self-awareness in a networking setting is how to recognize and handle negative emotions. Realizing that you had a bad day or are in a bad mood is the first step, and this may not come easily to you at first. If you have trouble recognizing when you are in a bad mood, begin by learning to recognize the physical indications. If your shoulders are tight and high, your heart rate is elevated, and your breathing is fast and/or shallow, these are physiological indicators of negative emotions.[43] To calibrate, you will also need to note your physical state when you are feeling good and neutral, as this gives you benchmarks with which to make a comparative assessment.[44] Remember that negative emotions are not "bad" but an indicator of your circumstances, and they give you valuable information about changes you might need to make.[45]

Then when you recognize that you are in a bad mood, and you know that attending a social event is going to be hard for you, you can consider skipping it and performing self-care instead. No one benefits if you arrive sour-faced and grouchy. While it is important to be forgiving and patient with others, it is also hard to dispel a bad first impression. So if you recognize that it will be a struggle to be friendly and engaging, then give yourself the option to do something else.

Alternatively, if you are aware of a negative emotional state, there are certain actions that you can take to address it. For example, posture and emotion are connected: emotions can cause you to change your posture, and changing your posture can influence your emotions.[46] Standing up straight also gives you the benefit of being able to inhale fully into your lungs. If you stand with a slouch, this compresses your lungs, forcing you to take shallow breaths, which are associated with anxiety and stimulate the sympathetic nervous system (fight or flight response);[47] standing up straight and breathing deeply can help calm you and make you feel more confident. Because of this relationship between mind and body (this two-way flow of information is called "embodied cognition"),[48] awareness of your emotions and your body is valuable. This also ties back to the idea of "fake it 'til you make it," as emulating emotions can engender them.[49]

Recognizing your negative emotions, deciding not to attend an event if you cannot support it, or shifting your negative mood all require self-awareness. You have to know yourself and whether going to an event and pretending to be happy will actually succeed, and if attending will improve or worsen your mood. You many need to stay home, rest and relax, or get some exercise, instead of forcing yourself to participate in something that you won't enjoy or be able to pretend to enjoy. For some people, doing something social and making themselves stand up straight and smile will make them feel better, and for others that's a nightmare to be avoided for everyone's benefit. Further still, your answer may be different from one day to the next, and it's in your best interest to know yourself so that you can make the right decision.

Author Anecdote

One important aspect of self-awareness is recognizing "self-talk" and whether it is negative or positive. When I am preparing for a presentation, if I realize that I am repeating to myself, "I'm so nervous, I'm so nervous" (negative self-talk), it makes me *more* nervous. Identifying negative self-talk and changing it to "I'm going to do great, I'm going to do great" reduces the sensation of nervousness and calms me. It sounds cheesy, but it lowers my heart rate.

Being self-aware also makes it easier to read and understand the emotions of others.[3] Conversely, being unable to understand one's own emotions makes it much harder to understand the emotions of others. This is why self-awareness is foundational to empathy. Being empathetic allows you to adapt to your audience by observing the signals they are sending, not just with their words but with their body language and voice. A good communicator meets their audience where they are by changing their words or method of expression so that the audience can absorb the message as best as possible. Having a conversation and trying to share an idea requires adapting to your audience of one person, just as giving a presentation requires adapting to an audience of many.

There are many studies that demonstrate the value of empathy, but a particularly dramatic one examined how the empathy of physicians affected patient outcomes.[50] Meta-analysis of 127 studies about how patients react to their doctors found that if doctors expressed empathy and concern, provided information about an illness and its treatments, and encouraged their patients to participate in decision making, then those patients were more likely to follow their physician's recommendations on things like medication, diet and exercise, than those patients with whom communication was poor with their physician. This demonstrated that a physician's ability to communicate has a direct impact on their patient's health and recovery.

Empathy is also important for leadership.[51] One study analyzing data from 38 countries looked at assessments of managers by both their superiors and subordinates.[52] Managers who were rated as empathetic (exhibiting behaviors that indicate empathy) by their subordinates also tended to be rated as the best performers by their superiors. This implies that people are who are empathetic are able to get better performances from their subordinates and therefore have better performance themselves, as observed by their superiors.

Fortunately, empathy is a social skill that can be trained and improved. Consciously trying to name the emotion that another person is experiencing improves our empathy.[53] Improvisation training helps with empathy as well[54,55] and is discussed in more detail below. You can take online assessments of empathy, including one by Lab in the Wild,[56] which is a revision of a test called "Reading the Mind in the Eyes," developed by Simon Baron-Cohen.[57] Meditation is another way to become more empathetic, though the effect is on the small side, 4.6%.[58] Reading literary fiction, where the author delves into the emotional lives of the characters, has been shown to increase empathy and improve one's ability to understand what is going on in other peoples' heads.[59] Likewise, creative writing requires one to imagine the emotional responses of characters, which also increases empathy.

Two concepts that are intimately related to empathy and self-awareness are *social awareness* and *emotional intelligence*. Social awareness is the ability to be aware of someone else's feelings, grasp their state of mind, and understand them. This term was coined by Edward Thorndike in 1920[60] and is the foundation for Daniel Goleman's book *Emotional Intelligence*.[61] Emotional Intelligence is a concept first described by Peter Salovey and John D. Mayer in 1990, which is "a set of skills hypothesized to contribute to the accurate appraisal and expression of emotion in oneself and in others, the effective regulation of emotion in self and others, and the use of feelings to motivate, plan, and achieve in one's life."[62] Emotional intelligence requires both self-awareness and empathy. [Goleman's book, published in 1995, has sold over half a million copies and remained on the New York Times Best Sellers list for a year and a half.[63]]

3.4.1 Improvisation

Improvisation (also called improv) is a particular kind of theater training that teaches an actor to respond quickly to another person, allowing them to engage in a rapid dance of ideas and feelings. It is often performed as comedy but not necessarily; the key is that the scene is unplanned, with only a premise or starting point defined. The rest is extemporaneous. Improvisation is something that Alan Alda, who founded the Center for Scientific Communication at Stony Brook, teaches to scientists to help them increase their empathy and improve their communication skills.

The goal of improvisation is to learn how to make eye contact, to quickly respond to another person's emotions and statements, and to resonate (empathize) with those emotions. The goals of small talk and conversation are much the same.

A core principle of improvisation is "yes and," meaning that you hear and acknowledge what they say and then build upon it, moving the scene forward. "Yes, and" does not reject or deny the other person's statements, and it is an excellent approach to use in other forms of communication, because it encourages instead of discourages. Learning and practicing improv can teach you useful skills that apply to work and personal issues, because ultimately, improv is just real life codified into a game. Life is unpredictable, and we are always reacting to unexpected or changing stimuli.

These principles apply to written as well as verbal communication. When you write, you need to imagine your audience, what they need to know, and the order in which they need to know it, so empathy plays a role in writing as well. Readers have basic expectations that need to be met or else they will become confused and frustrated. They expect to hear what a sentence is about at the beginning of the sentence, not the middle or the end: "Readers expect [a sentence] to be a story about whoever shows up first."[64] According to Alda, performing improvisation games before writing workshops improves the quality of writing because it gets participants focused on their audience and how they can be helped to understand.

There are many improvisation games, and all you need to practice improv is two people, though you can practice with large groups as well. The book *Theater Games*, by Viola Spolin, outlines a number of games.[65] A few examples of improv games are described below, but you can find more both in Spolin's book and on the internet by searching for "improv games" or "theater games." To see comedic improv performed as entertainment, the show *Whose Line Is It Anyway?* has some good examples.

Scientists are often called upon to explain their work to non-scientists, and there is a particularly useful improv game for practicing this skill. It requires only two people, but it can be performed in front of an audience. One person plays the role of explainer, and this person silently assigns the other person the role of a specific known person, e.g., their advisor, partner, young niece, or a celebrity. The explainer does not tell the other person their role; they simply explain their work or research to the other person as if they were the imagined person. This requires them to carefully tailor their explanation, and the goal of the game is for the other person to guess their assigned role. If playing in front of an audience, the audience can guess as well. Playing the role of the explainer will make you better at adapting to different audiences and describing your research in a variety of ways.

Another game that clearly illustrates the principle of "yes, and" is "Yes, Bob." This only requires two people but can also be done as a performance for a larger audience. The two performers are both named Bob and deliver a fake newscast together. The first Bob opens with a statement about something that has happened (which can be supplied by the audience), and the second Bob then has to reply with "Yes, Bob" and follow with an additional statement building on the first statement. The first Bob must then reply "Yes, Bob," and again build on the last statement, forming a story as statements are exchanged.

For example,

Bob 1:	"Bob, this just in. It appears the zombie apocalypse has begun."
Bob 2:	"Yes, Bob, and it's wreaking havoc on the stock market."
Bob 1:	"Yes, Bob, I've lost all of my retirement savings."
Bob 2:	"Yes, Bob, fortunately, we aren't likely to survive until retirement!"
Bob 1:	"Yes, Bob, I admire your optimism!"

etc.

Practicing improv with a friend or a group can improve your empathy and communication skills, but it may feel difficult to know where to start if you've never done something like it before. Reading about and especially watching videos of improv is a great place to start to get a feel for how it works. There are also many places where you can take improv classes if you want a more formal setting, including community centers, theaters, comedy clubs, and Meetup groups (Meetup is discussed more in Section 8.13). Just begin by searching "improv classes" and your city. If you enjoy it, there are improv troupes in many places that you can join. Whether you practice it with a friend, a group, or a troupe, improv will help you learn to respond more quickly in extemporaneous settings and increase your empathy and ability to adapt to your audience.

3.5 The Golden and Platinum Rules

You may already be familiar with the concept of the Golden Rule, which is about treating others the way you would want to be treated. The more formal name for this rule is the "Ethic of Reciprocity." The true origin of this rule is unknown, with possibly the earliest documentation coming from the ancient Egyptian story "The Eloquent Peasant" circa 2000 BCE.[66] The Golden Rule is a good starting point for interaction, but it has a significant flaw: it assumes that other people are just like you and that they want the exact same things you want. Clearly, this is not true. People are diverse within their own cities and cultures, and cross-cultural differences further add to the complexity. Starting from the Golden Rule is good, because it shows concern for the well-being of others, but there is more that can be done.

Everyone has a different set of life experiences and personal preferences, so when you first meet someone, ascertaining how they want to be treated is challenging. It's easier to know how someone wants to be treated when you've known them for a while. But a new acquaintance might have an entirely different background and be from a different place than you. Even if they are from your hometown, there is still a huge amount of individual difference. This is where you will need to rely heavily on your skills of empathy and observation to gauge people's responses to your behavior, and then change your approach accordingly.

So when you first meet someone, start with the Golden Rule and treat them the way you would want to be treated. But recognize that it is only a rough estimate and that you will need to perform a calibration to determine the differences between your initial approach and what will actually make them comfortable. You perform this calibration by interacting with them and observing their response (empathizing); you can then use that information to alter your approach, which will make them more comfortable and you more fondly memorable. This variation of the Golden Rule is referred to as the Platinum Rule, which states that you should *treat others the way that they want to be treated*, and by doing so, acknowledge that everyone has different preferences. This is also about *adapting to your audience*, as discussed in Section 1.4.

In all of your interactions, professional and personal, your goal should be to keep your audience and conversational partners comfortable; this is the source and the goal of etiquette. Just as improvisation is the codification of life into a game, etiquette is a codification of behaviors designed to minimize discomfort during social interaction. However, strict adherence to the etiquette from your place of origin falls into the same trap as the Golden Rule: it fails to account for variation. This is why you should observe the Platinum Rule as much as possible (see Chapter 4 for further discussion on etiquette).

3.6 Authenticity

A core and important part of sustainable networking is honesty. Being honest as a networker means representing yourself accurately in your interactions with other people, so that they get to know the real you. But offering an appropriate, authentic version of ourselves in a professional networking setting can be a challenge. Some of us may not naturally speak about ourselves, and we may fail to offer enough information to paint a complete picture. Or we may be the kind of people who have trouble filtering our thoughts and how we express them to others, and uncertain what aspects of ourselves should be discussed. The importance of adapting to your audience has been discussed previously in Chapter 1, and it applies to how we authentically express ourselves as well.

Adaptation in this context is about presenting ourselves and our thoughts in a way that is comfortable and understandable for our conversational partner. This may mean learning a new way of expressing ourselves, but it is important that the content of our messages (who we are and what we do) is the truth. You are a complex and multifaceted being, and so you should select the relevant facets of yourself to share with others as you network. This is not inauthentic; it is filtration and curation to convey a positive message that is consistent with your goals and networking strategy (which are an authentic reflection of you). What facets you present depend on the context and the audience.

Honesty and authenticity are especially important, because the opportunities that your network will provide you reflect how you represent yourself to your network. You want that representation to be as accurate as possible, so that the people and opportunities that you attract align with your interests and abilities. Some network connections will also become friends if you let them, and that is more likely to happen if you are honest.

Further, by being authentic and sharing about yourself and what you care about, you are opening up a space for your conversational partner to share in kind. This is called the "norm of reciprocity," where people tend to respond in kind to your behavior.[67,68] It means that people will tend to share with you the kinds of things that you share with them and that you should share the kinds of things about yourself that you would like to know about others. If you share nothing about yourself, then it is unlikely that you will make strong connections or be memorable, and remembering each other is key to integrating a person into your network. So share authentically about yourself and what you find interesting, and listen carefully to the response you get.

Authenticity is a special challenge, because it requires you to know who you are and what you want to accomplish. Self-awareness is important not only because it is foundational to our ability to empathize and communicate with others but also because it is key to knowing what you want from your career and setting the appropriate goals and networking strategy. Knowing yourself through self-awareness, and others through empathy, will help you to be authentic, communicate, and make meaningful connections with others.

Exercises

(1)   It can be instructive to do a self-assessment to practice the skill of self-awareness and identify areas that need improvement. Spend some time taking notes and writing down answers to the following questions:

  (a) What do you perceive as your strengths and weaknesses in terms of social interaction?

  (b) What kinds of networking environments make you feel the most comfortable?

  (c) What makes you nervous?

  (d) What makes you happy?

  (e) What skills do you want to acquire?

  (f) What kinds of interactions with others are challenging?

  (g) How are you at entering conversations? Leaving them?

  (h) Do you talk or listen more?

  (i) Are you able to comfortably maintain a conversation?

  (j) Are you better one-on-one or in a group? Digitally? In a large room of people? At a dinner party?

(2)   Think about where you identify on the continuum between introversion and extraversion. You will likely have features of both, but identifying them will help you find optimal networking opportunities for your traits and preferences, as well as strategies optimized for your strengths.

(3)   Reviewing the suggestions in Section 3.4, pick a strategy to practice empathy and self-awareness, and then try it out. For example, try to imagine and label the feelings of people that you see; watch and try some improv; or read some literary fiction. Do this regularly, and record your efforts and any improvements.

(4)   Think about topics of conversation that interest you and allow you to share facets of yourself with people that you meet. These topics should be personal but appropriate for professional networking situations, such as your interest in reading science fiction or the type of fitness you enjoy practicing. Keep it clean, but make sure it's authentic, which will allow you to have an interesting conversation with someone. While you will primarily discuss professional matters at networking events, preparing peripheral conversational material in advance will help you connect with others in a positive and memorable way.

References

1. Gompertz, K. "The Relation of Empathy to Effective Communication," *Journalism Quarterly* **37**(4) (1960) [doi:10.1177/107769906003700405].

2. Haley, B. et al., "Relationships among active listening, self-awareness, empathy, and patient-centered care in associate and baccalaureate degree nursing students," *NursingPlus Open* **3**, 11–16 (2017) [doi:10.1016/j.npls.2017.05.001].

3. Böckler, H. A. et al., "Know Thy Selves: Learning to Understand Oneself Increases the Ability to Understand Others," *J. Cognitive Enhancement* **1**(2) (2017) [doi:10.1007/s41465-017-0023-6].

4. Ritchie, H. and M. Roser, "Mental Health," *World in Our Data* (April 2018). Retrieved from ourworldindata.org/mental-health. Accessed on March 26, 2019.

5. "Social anxiety," *Social Anxiety Ireland.* Retrieved from ocialanxietyireland.com/social-anxiety/how-common-is-social-anxiety. Accessed on March 26, 2019.

6. "Social Anxiety Disorder," *National Institute of Mental Health* (November 2017). Retrieved from nimh.nih.gov/health/statistics/social-anxiety-disorder.shtml. Accessed on March 26, 2019.

7. Cain, S., *Quiet: The Power of Introversion in a World that Can't Stop Talking*, Broadway Books, New York (2013).

8. Allik, J. and R. McCrae, "Toward a Geography of Personality Traits: Patterns of Profiles across 36 Cultures," *J. Cross-Cultural Psychology* **35**(1) (January 2004) [doi:10.1177/0022022103260382].

9. Kristof-Brown, A. et al., "When opposites attract: a multi-sample demonstration of complementary person-team fit on extraversion," *J. Personality* **73**(4) (May 4, 2005) [doi: 10.1111/j.1467-6494.2005.00334.x].

10. Grant, A. et al., "Reversing the Extraverted Leadership Advantage: The Role of Employee Proactivity," *Academy of Management Journal* **54**(3) (June, 1 2011) [doi:10.5465/amj.2011.61968043].

11. Brownell, S. E. et al., "Science Communication to the General Public: Why We Need to Teach Undergraduate and Graduate Students this Skill as Part of Their Formal Scientific Training," *J. Undergraduate Neuroscience Education* **12**(1) (October 15, 2013).

12. Winch, G., "10 Surprising Facts About Rejection," *Psychology Today* (July 3, 2013). Retrieved from psychologytoday.com/us/blog/the-squeaky-wheel/201307/10-surprising-facts-about-rejection. Accessed March 26, 2019.

13. Kross, E. et al., "Social rejection shares somatosensory representations with physical pain," *Proc. National Academy of Science* **108**(15) (April 2011) [doi:10.1073/pnas.1102693108].

14. Leary, M. R., "Emotional responses to interpersonal rejection" *Dialogues in Clinical Neuroscience* **17**(4) (December 2015).

15. Tomasello, M., "The ultra-social animal," *European J. Social Psychol.* **44**(3) (2014).

16. Croston, G., "The Thing We Fear More Than Death," *Psychology Today* (November 29, 2012). Retrieved from psychologytoday.com/us/blog/the-real-story-risk/201211/the-thing-we-fear-more-death. Accessed on March 30, 2019.

17. Bressert, S., "Facts About Shyness," *PscyhCentral* (October 8, 2019). Retrieved from psychcentral.com/lib/facts-about-shyness. Accessed on March 30, 2019.

18. Carducci, B. and P. G. Zimbardo, "Facts About Shyness," *PscyhCentral* (First published November 1, 1995, last reviewed on September 20, 2018). Retrieved from psychologytoday.com/us/articles/199511/the-cost-shyness. Accessed on March 30, 2019.

19. Konefal, J. and R. C. Duncan, "Social anxiety and training in neurolinguistic programming," *Psychological Reports* **83**(3) (1998).

20. Scott, S., "The medicalisation of shyness: from social misfits to social fitness," *Sociology of Health & Illness* **28**(2) (2006).

21. Flinchbaugh, C. L. et al., "Student well-being interventions: The effects of stress management techniques and gratitude journaling in the management education classroom," *J. Management Education* **36**(2) (2012).

22. Mercer, A. et al., "Visual journaling: An intervention to influence stress, anxiety and affect levels in medical students," *The Arts in Psychotherapy* **37**(2) (2010).

23. Weiss, A., "7 Journal Prompts That Will Help Tackle Anxiety," *Bustle* (April 16, 2016). Retrieved from bustle.com/articles/156986-7-journal-prompts-that-will-help-tackle-anxiety. Accessed on March 30, 2019.

24. *Toastmasters International*, toastmasters.org.

25. Sauer-Zavala, S. et al., "Beyond Worry: How Psychologists Help With Anxiety Disorders," *American Psychological Association* (October 2016). Retrieved from apa.org/helpcenter/anxiety. Accessed on March 30, 2019.

26. Ali, B. S. et al. "The effectiveness of counseling on anxiety and depression by minimally trained counselors: a randomized controlled trial," *American J. Psychotherapy* **57**(3) (2003).

27. *Rejection Therapy*, rejectiontherapy.com/game.

28. "Social anxiety disorder (social phobia)," *Mayo Clinic*. Retrieved from mayoclinic.org/diseases-conditions/social-anxiety-disorder/symptoms-causes/syc-20353561. Accessed on March 26, 2019.

29. "Extraversion or Introversion," *The Myers & Briggs Foundation.* Retrieved from myersbriggs.org/my-mbti-personality-type/mbti-basics/extraversion-or-introversion.htm. Accessed on April 1, 2019.

30. Cooper, B. B., "Are You An Introvert Or An Extrovert? What It Means For Your Career," *Fast Company* (August 21, 2013). Retrieved from fastcompany.com/3016031/are-you-an-introvert-or-an-extrovert-and-what-it-means-for-your-career. Accessed on April 1, 2019

31. Georgiev, S. Y. et al., "Ambiversion as independent personality characteristic," *Activitas Nervosa Superior Rediviva* **56**, 3–4 (2014).

32. Grey, S., "Why We Shouldn't Treat Introversion Like a Mental Illness," *The Mighty* (February 19, 2018). Retrieved from themighty.com/2018/02/introverted-not-mental-illness. Accessed on April 1, 2019.

33. Petrilli, L., "An Introvert's Guide to Networking," *Harvard Business Review* (January 25, 2012). Retrieved from hbr.org/2012/01/the-introverts-guide-to-networ. Accessed April 1 2019.

34. "Sensitive? Emotional? Empathetic? It Could be in Your Genes," *Stony Brook University News* (June 23, 2014). Retrieved from news.stonybrook.edu/news/medical/140623empatheticAron. Accessed on April 3, 2019.

35. Acevedo, B. P. et al., "The highly sensitive brain: an fMRI study of sensory processing sensitivity and response to others' emotions," *Brain and Behavior* **4**(4) (2014).

36. Ward, D., "How to Cope as a Highly Sensitive Extrovert," *Psychology Today* (August 9, 2014). Retrieved from psychologytoday.com/us/blog/sense-and-sensitivity/201408/how-cope-highly-sensitive-extrovert. Accessed on April 3, 2019.

37. Penderson, T., "Empathy," *Psych Central* (2018). Retrieved from psychcentral.com/encyclopedia/empathy. Accessed on April 3, 2019.

38. Davis, T., "What Is Self-Awareness, and How Do You Get It?," *Psychology Today* (March 11, 2019). Retrieved from psychologytoday.com/us/blog/click-here-happiness/201903/what-is-self-awareness-and-how-do-you-get-it. Accessed on April 3, 2019.

39. E. Teding van Berkhout and J. M. Malouff, "The efficacy of empathy training: A meta-analysis of randomized controlled trials," *J. Counseling Psychology* **63**(1) (2016).

40. Ferraro, P. J., "Know thyself: Competence and self-awareness," *Atlantic Economic Journal* **38**(2) (2010).

41. Luft, J. and H. Ingham, "The johari window," *Human Relations Training News* **5**(1) (1961).

42. "The Johari Window Model," *Communication Theory* (2013). Retrieved from communicationtheory.org/the-johari-window-model. Accessed on April 3, 2019.

43. Levenson, R. W., "Blood, sweat, and fears: The autonomic architecture of emotion," *Annals of the New York Academy of Sciences* **1000**(1) (2003).

44. Goleman, D., "How Emotionally Self-Aware Are You?," *Mindful* (March 30, 2017). Retrieved from mindful.org/emotionally-self-aware. Accessed on July 29, 2019.

45. Scott, E., "How Negative Emotions Affect Us and How to Embrace Them," *Very Well Mind* (June 18, 2019). Retrieved from verywellmind.com/embrace-negative-emotions-4158317. Accessed on July 29, 2019.

46. Giang, V., "The Surprising And Powerful Links Between Posture and Mood," *Fast Company* (January 30, 2015). Retrieved from fastcompany.com/3041688/the-surprising-and-powerful-links-between-posture-and-mood. Accessed on April 3, 2019.

47. Abraham, M., "Anxiety Often Causes Shallow Breathing," *Calm Clinic* (October 27, 2018). Retrieved from calmclinic.com/anxiety/symptoms/shallow-breathing. Accessed on April 3, 2019.

48. McNerney, S., "A Brief Guide to Embodied Cognition: Why You Are Not Your Brain," *Scientific American Blogs* (November 24, 2011). Retrieved from blogs.scientificamerican.com/guest-blog/a-brief-guide-to-embodied-cognition-why-you-are-not-your-brain. Accessed on April 3, 2019.

49. Dooley, R., "Why Faking a Smile Is a Good Thing," *Forbes* (February 26, 2013). Retrieved from forbes.com/sites/rogerdooley/2013/02/26/fake-smile/#131771d53676. Accessed on April 3, 2019.

50. Zolnierek, K. B. Haskard, and DiMatteo, M. Robin. "Physician communication and patient adherence to treatment: a meta-analysis," *Medical Care* **47**(8) (2009).

51. Levitt, S., "Why the Empathetic Leader Is the Best Leader," *Success* (March 15, 2017). Retrieved from success.com/why-the-empathetic-leader-is-the-best-leader. Accessed on April 3, 2019.

52. Sadri, G. et al., "Empathic emotion and leadership performance: An empirical analysis across 38 countries," *The Leadership Quarterly* **22**(5) (2011).

53. Alda, A., *If I Understood You, Would I Have This Look on My Face?*, Random House, New York (2018).

54. Eisenberg, A. et al., "Medicine as a performing art: what we can learn about empathic communication from theater arts," *Academic Medicine* **90**(3) (2015).

55. Bayne, H. B. and A. Jangha, "Utilizing improvisation to teach empathy skills in counselor education," *Counselor Education and Supervision* **55**(4) (2016).

56. "Social Intelligence Test," *Lab in the Wild*, socialintelligence. labinthewild.org.

57. Baron-Cohen, S. et al. "The 'Reading the Mind in the Eyes' test revised version: A study with normal adults, and adults with Asperger syndrome or high-functioning autism," *J. Child Psychology and Psychiatry* **42**(2) (2001).

58. Mascaro, J. S. et al., "Compassion meditation enhances empathic accuracy and related neural activity," *Social Cognitive and Affective Neuroscience* **8**(1) (2012).

59. Chiaet, J., "Novel Finding: Reading Literary Fiction Improves Empathy," *Scientific American Mind* (October 4, 2013). Retrieved from scientificamerican.com/article/novel-finding-reading-literary-fiction-improves-empathy. Accessed on April 3, 2019.

60. Thorndike, E. L., "Intelligence and its uses," *Harper's Magazine* (January 1920).

61. Goleman, D., *Emotional Intelligence*, Bantam, New York (1995).

62. Salovey, P. and J. D. Mayer, "Emotional intelligence," *Imagination, Cognition and Personality* **9**(3) (1990).

63. "About Daniel Goleman," *Daniel Goleman*. Retrieved from danielgoleman.info/biography. Accessed on April 3, 2019.

64. Gopen, G. D. and J. A. Swan, "The science of scientific writing," *American Scientist* **78**(6) (1990). Available at americanscientist.org/blog/the-long-view/the-science-of-scientific-writing.

65. Spolin, V., *Improvisation for the Theater: A Handbook of Teaching and Directing Techniques*, Northwestern University Press, Evanston, IL (1999).

66. Fisher, L., "The story behind 'The Eloquent Peasant,'" *Mail Tribune* (December 24, 2015). Retrieved from mailtribune.com/lifestyle/columnist-for-a-day/the-story-behind-the-eloquent-peasant. Accessed on April 5, 2019.

67. Perugini, M. et al., "The personal norm of reciprocity," *European Journal of Personality* **17**(4), 251–283 (2003).

68. Burger, J. M. et al., "The norm of reciprocity as an internalized social norm: Returning favors even when no one finds out," *Social Influence* **4**(1), 11–17 (2009).

Chapter 4
Conversational Principles

"The great gift of conversation lies less in displaying it ourselves than in drawing it out of others."

~Jean de La Bruyère (1645–1696), philosopher and satirist

4.1 The Importance of Conversational Skills

Conversation is an integral part of networking. Many networking opportunities involve social events where conversation is assumed, and other networking activities, including volunteering, mentoring relationships, interacting with coworkers, and personal meetings, also require it. Even if you do a lot of networking online and digitally, you still want to find opportunities to meet your online contacts in person when you can, which again requires conversation.

Beyond networking, your ability to make conversation affects most aspects of your life. You make conversation with friends, family, colleagues, teachers, clients, customers, when ordering food, buying groceries, or at the post office. You make conversation at networking events, during job interviews, and with your boss. Conversation can get you a job, a raise, a new networking connection, a new friend, advice, directions, or a date, and it's how you share information, praise, and feedback with others. Your conversational skills are like the marvelous, fictional sonic screwdriver, a tool wielded by the time-traveling title character of the British television show *Doctor Who*. The sonic screwdriver doesn't just loosen and tighten screws; it can hack, activate or deactivate electronics, open locks, perform medical diagnostics, light things on fire, and act as a flashlight, among others. In short, the sonic screwdriver can perform any function that the writers want in order to further the plot, and your conversational skills are just as versatile.

The good news is that making conversation doesn't require a lot of talent, just lots of practice, and opportunities for practice abound. This chapter explores what it means to be a good conversationalist and what constitutes a good conversation, and introduces some general conversational etiquette. The next chapter continues with this theme, but focuses more on the applications of these principles and includes suggestions for ways to improve your skills and upgrade your sonic screwdriver.

4.2 The Qualities of a Good Conversation(alist)

Conversations come in a wide variety. Short, long, serious, frivolous, entertaining, educational, emotional, technical, and more. Regardless of the format or content, a good conversation allows for the effective, mutual exchange of information. While most other factors are variable, this one is the core of good conversation. In a networking context, your exchange should allow you to learn something about the other person and share something about yourself in a way that is comfortable for all parties involved, and ideally, such that you are fondly remembered. In order to achieve this effective exchange of information, both parties need to spend time each speaking and listening.

Assumptions will be discussed at length in Chapter 6, but an important point to consider about assumptions as they relate to conversation is that they make it harder to hear what the other person is actually *saying*. Assumptions introduce a systematic error into your data collection. If you avoid assumptions about people (or keep in mind any assumptions may be erroneous), don't try to guess about the point they're trying make, and really *listen*, you will hear what your conversational partner is saying much better. It is not possible to avoid assumptions entirely, because many of them are subconscious, so using your self-awareness to remain cognizant of your biases will help you recognize faulty assumptions that can interfere with communication. Likewise, if you are just waiting for an opportunity to speak or thinking about what you want to say next, you won't really be listening either.

Listening is another key part of being a good conversationalist. It is about making an effort to understand what the other person is saying (or trying to say). The room may be noisy, they may be nervous, or they may not be speaking their native language; your job as a conversational partner is to do your best to interpret what they mean, even if they say it imperfectly. Avoid nitpicking your conversational partner's word choices, because it is a distraction that kills conversational momentum. If you make understanding the other person your primary goal and being understood your secondary goal, you will be really listening to them, which is something everyone appreciates. Everyone wants to be heard and understood.[1] A focus on listening and understanding will also help you to avoid the distraction of thinking about what you are going to say next, which prevents you from hearing what is being said.

Engage your whole body when you listen by making sounds or comments of agreement, nodding your head, smiling, facing the person, and making eye contact (more on eye contact in Subsection 4.4.1). Ask relevant questions that show you are listening and interested in hearing what the person has to say. Do your best to listen during introductions and remember the person's name. Focusing on the name and repeating it when you are introduced will help you to remember it. You can make statements such as, "Nice to meet you, Sunyu," or later, "How are you finding the conference, Adel?" The repetitions will help you remember the name (more on names in Section 5.3).

In addition to listening, being curious can help a lot in conversation. If you are curious about other people, what they do, who they are, etc., then asking questions and caring about the answers is much easier. Curiosity is what psychologists call a trait cluster; it is a combination of intelligence, persistence, and a hunger for novelty.[2,3] While some people are naturally curious, and most scientists and engineers are, you can also train yourself to be more curious by pursing topics you find interesting, talking to people, reading about a broad range of subjects, and asking lots of questions.[4,5]

A good conversationalist also recognizes that the purpose of a conversation isn't to make themselves look good but to make their conversational partners look, and by extension, feel good. To be a good conversationalist, you must be able to put your conversational partner at ease and make them comfortable, which is at the heart of etiquette as discussed further in Section 4.4. There is a good general principle that you can use to question and extrapolate whether saying or doing something is appropriate or not. If the answer to the question "Would it make this person uncomfortable?" is "Yes," "probably," or "I'm not sure," then don't do it.

It is important to be honest in your conversation and be your authentic self (as discussed in Chapter 3). But at the same time, recognize that some things that are honest would be too much information and could make your audience uncomfortable. This is about filtration and curation. The challenge is that the appropriate level of filtering is going to vary from person to person and situation to situation, and you have to spend some time calibrating based on the person and the circumstance. During an initial meeting, it is best to focus on safe and neutral topics while you acquire some data with which to make a calibration, and then adapt accordingly. As a general rule, it is easier to move from more formal to less than it is to go from informal to formal, so it is better to start off with a higher level of filtration and then gradually move to less as you gain familiarity with (data on) a particular audience.

Do not be afraid to allow some silence into the conversation. If you always talk to fill the silence, someone who may be less quick to speak or shy about asking a question may never have the courage to express it. Pauses also allow the other party an opportunity to make an exit from the conversation if they need or want to. If you act as the "host" of a conversation, it can be helpful for others who are shy or struggling with social engagement. Conversational hosting is a kind of facilitation: making introductions, welcoming newcomers to the conversation, or redirecting the conversation if starts to slow down or take a bad turn.

In short, being a good conversationalist means listening, being curious, asking questions, expressing yourself authentically while filtering appropriately, allowing for pauses, and keeping your conversational partner comfortable. A sincere interest in people is helpful. It doesn't have to be an interest of epic proportions, but it needs to be there, and it needs to be real. Treat everyone as though they have something interesting that you can learn from them, whether it's finding a potential job opening to apply for, an interesting piece of science or life experience, or a good local restaurant. And the things you learn from them can be useful for making conversation with others.

4.3 Conversational Style

Think about conversational styles as a spectrum from more talkative to less talkative. Depending on your style, you will need to pay more attention to certain aspects of conversation. Someone who is very talkative needs to attend to how much they talk and make sure they ask questions or leave pauses for the other party to interject. They also need to watch for signs that their partner is getting bored, such as looking around, glancing at their watch, etc. However, talkative individuals are also in a good position to take the burden of the conversation if the other person is less talkative, which may be a relief to an introverted person or someone less confident with conversational skills. A less talkative person needs to notice if they are only asking questions or avoiding sharing about themselves. It may be harder for a less talkative person to be in the spotlight, but a mutual exchange of information cannot happen if only one person talks. Ideally, a conversation will allow each party a roughly equal amount of talking and listening.

One of your goals in conversation should be to get your conversational partner to talk. If the person is talkative, this will be easy. Asking questions and follow-up questions (the best kind of questions) is how you get someone to talk, regardless of their talkativeness or level of introversion or extraversion. If you talk too much, you risk boring your conversational partner, which, while not explicitly rude, is undesirable as it discomforts them and leaves an unfavorable impression of you. On the other hand, people are rarely bored when they are talking, especially if they are talking about themselves or their work.

Some people, however, may be uncomfortable talking about themselves. They may be shy, there could be a language barrier, or they might simply be tired. There are plenty of reasons why someone might be happy to let you do more talking than them, but this is something you want to assess carefully. If you are talking a lot, make sure there is room for the occasional pause. If someone looks bored, you can always say, "I'm so sorry for keeping you so long, I'm sure you must have other people you need to catch up with." This gives them an opening to leave the conversation without interrupting you, which is gracious and avoids discomfort for both of you. If you were wrong and misinterpreted their demeanor as boredom, they might choose to stay and ask you a question.

Whether you are the sort of person who prefers to do more listening in conversations or you simply feel like taking a more passive role, it is important that you listen attentively. This means maintaining eye contact, nodding, and asking follow-up questions as appropriate. A pair of oft-quoted studies claim that 93% of communication is non-verbal (everything but word choice), but this was for the special case where word choice and non-verbal channels gave conflicting messages though in the study.[6,7] Another regularly cited study measured the informational content as 35% of the information conveyed coming from the words spoken.[8] Although social psychology has not identified the exact percentages, the point is that even when you are not speaking, you are still conveying information, and you need to think about what that information is, e.g., are you conveying boredom or disinterest? Or are you keeping your body language open and receptive (arms at sides, smiling, facing the person)? Listening attentively is just as important as speaking.

When trying to keep your conversational partner comfortable, assess their level or introversion or extroversion, shyness or talkativeness, and general social comfort. Should you find yourself in conversation with someone who is more comfortable listening than talking, it is okay to take a little more than half of the airtime, because it makes the other person comfortable. Your conversational partner should also make an effort to keep you comfortable as well, and they shouldn't leave you to struggle if you are having a hard time finding things to say. The conversation should be a friendly game of catch, not a tennis match where you are trying to avoid the conversational ball or fight for possession of it. Conversation is about cooperation.

Being aware of your own conversational style, and being able to assess the styles of those you converse with, will help you successfully navigate conversations. Knowing the strengths and weaknesses of your particular approach will also help you improve your skill set.

4.4 A Loose Guide to Conversational Etiquette

Etiquette is a codification of behaviors that are considered polite, intended to help people navigate social situations with grace.[9,10] Etiquette is nice when you are familiar with it for a given context, because you know what to do and how to behave, which dissipates a lot of the fear or anxiety over doing something wrong. Simply put, etiquette is an algorithm or decision tree that can be followed to determine the proper course of action.

The problem with etiquette is that it changes dramatically based on context. The etiquette that you observe in your home with your family is different than the etiquette observed by other families. The etiquette observed at your graduate school will be different than the etiquette observed at the company where you find your first job. There are different codes of etiquette for different kinds of social events, depending on their location or formality. Consider that all of this variation exists within a single region or country and that much greater variation exists across cultures and countries. Etiquette works very well within the confines of a specific context, but outside those limits it quickly falls apart.

While it is useful to learn aspects of etiquette in your home country, company, or university, it is impossible to learn etiquette for every context in which you will spend time. Even if you are in your own native context and know its etiquette, you will encounter others who are unfamiliar with it, which will force you to reevaluate how you interact with that person, because they may exhibit behaviors for which your etiquette decision tree does not have a defined response. So you need to learn how to operate when you are off the map, in territory that is new or not covered by your familiar etiquette protocols.

How is one to do that? The Golden Rule is a good place to start. But as discussed in Section 3.5, it has its own limitations, because it assumes that other people are just like you. Only they aren't, which leads to the Platinum Rule and attempts to treat other people the way *they want* to be treated. However, the

Platinum Rule is difficult to follow when you have just met someone or do not know them well. After all, it is easy to know how *you want* to be treated. There is no guesswork to treating other people accordingly with the Golden Rule, but the Platinum Rule relies heavily on your empathy and observation skills, which are in turn dependent upon your self-awareness.

Etiquette can be treated similarly to the Golden Rule: a good starting point or rough approximation that requires calibration based on observation. This is especially important when first meeting someone or when entering a new environment. The more data you collect and the more you observe and empathize, the better you will understand how you should act in that circumstance. So while the following suggestions will not hold perfectly across all contexts, like the Golden Rule, they will serve you well as a starting point in many networking circumstances. At its core, etiquette is about making social interaction comfortable, and if you act with kindness and try to set others at ease, you will succeed at being gracious in the moments when the rules would otherwise fail you.

4.4.1 Eye contact

When conversing with someone, you should dedicate the majority of your attention to them, and eye contact is the primary indicator of your attention. Letting your eyes wander around the room indicates that you are not paying attention, or it will likely be interpreted as such. Even if you are bored, don't scan the room looking for someone else to talk to; that will be obvious to your conversational partner and make them feel uninteresting, which is insulting and makes a bad impression.

However, you should not stare continuously, without a break, into the other person's eyes. This can be disconcerting or convey a message of *too much* interest in that person. The amount of eye contact that someone is comfortable with depends not only on culture but also individual preference. People from Western cultures tend find direct eye contact compelling and an indicator of confidence, but in some Eastern cultures, avoiding direct eye contact is considered a sign of respect and direct eye contact a sign of aggression.[11,12] A British study found that on average 3.3 seconds was the ideal duration of eye contact (subjects were visitors to the London Science Museum).[13] When direct eye contact is undesirable or when breaking eye contact momentarily to avoid staring, facing the person but gazing at their neck, ear, or shoulder will make it clear that they still have your attention. Some people may prefer to stand or sit side-by-side during a discussion or to occupy themselves with a task to avoid extended eye contact. If someone is not offering direct eye contact, try to determine whether this is a sign of disinterest or an adjustment they are making for their own comfort.

Starting out, make a point to make some eye contact, but don't let your eyes wander the room when not making eye contact. See how the person responds, if they look back at you or if they look down or away quickly, and then modify the amount of time you spend looking at them before glancing away accordingly.

4.4.2 Physical contact

It is important to be very careful with touching and personal space, especially with new acquaintances. In many countries, a handshake is acceptable, even between people of opposite genders, but this is not always the case. Any touching beyond a handshake is inadvisable if you are speaking with someone new to you and you do not know where they are from. If you extend your hand for a handshake and they do not respond in kind, move on without comment, and do not take it personally.

If you do shake someone's hand, it should be performed with a firm but gentle grasp. Do not squeeze the other person tightly; they may have arthritis or carpal tunnel syndrome, in which case pressure will hurt them. But don't use too little force, either. A limp handshake conveys the message that you are trying to avoid or dislike touching the other person, which is discomfiting. The covered handshake, in which a second hand in placed on top of the other person's clasping hand, should be avoided. It can be perceived as dominating or aggressive, and it makes it hard or impossible for the receiver to retract their hand (which is, again, discomfiting). Ideally, your hand should be dry for a handshake; hold any cold drinks in your left hand as they can condense and moisten your palm. Handshakes may also be performed while exiting an event or conversation.

The "no touching brand-new acquaintances" rule is especially important for men to observe with women. Women often receive unwanted attention or have their personal space invaded without invitation,[14,15] and being touched by a new acquaintance without being asked may provoke negative feelings from past difficulties. This is not to say that all women will respond with this way or that there aren't some women who would disagree with this statement. But there are enough women who *would* be bothered, and there is no way to tell in advance, that it is best to avoid the unnecessary risk of leaving a bad impression by not respecting her space.

That being said, once you develop a relationship with someone, you will get a better understanding of what they are and are not comfortable with, through observation and questions. Then you may expand the ways in which you make physical contact with them, such as pats on the back or shoulder, or hugs. However, as your relationship evolves, make sure to remember the principle of kindness, and avoid making anyone uncomfortable by making uninvited or unwanted physical contact.

4.4.3 How you speak

The manner in which you speak includes things such as volume, speed, and pauses. How you choose to speak to someone should adapt to or facilitate communication, and simultaneously keep your conversational partner comfortable.

The volume at which you speak will depend on whether you are speaking to one or many people and the level of ambient noise of the room. If you notice people leaning in or away, you may be speaking too softly or too loudly. It is also possible that you are speaking with someone with hearing loss, in which case make sure to look at the person when you speak so they can see your mouth and hear you better.

Speaking too quickly is a common mistake that makes it harder for your audience to understand you and is more likely to occur when you are nervous. You do not need to speak quickly to be a good conversationalist. In fact, speaking slower can give you the opportunity to choose your words more carefully, and avoid making filtering mistakes. If you notice that your audience or conversational partner seems to be having trouble following you, in addition to volume, note the speed of your words and see if you are out of breath. If you have been speaking too quickly, try to breathe deeply, relax, and carefully choose your words.

It is also good not to speak continuously for very long. One person speaking is a monologue, not a dialogue, and it can make the other person or people feel like they are being talked *at*, not talked *with*. Leave space and pauses between statements for them to agree, redirect, and ask questions. If you notice that you have been speaking uninterrupted for a while, end your story and ask the other person a question about themselves or their work. Should you find yourself conversing with someone who seems to want an audience for a monologue, avoid engaging in a verbal shoving match (interrupting); excuse yourself and find someone else to talk to. Graceful exits will be discussed further in Section 5.6.

4.4.4 Content, or what you say

Beyond being generally agreeable and considerate, your goal as a conversationalist is to be interesting. This means having something interesting to say. Of course, what people find interesting will vary, but if you are going to an event, then you know something about the people who are going based on the type of event. This is another instance when advance preparation will benefit you, and you can research and prepare some interesting topics of conversation before you attend.

You will occasionally be called upon to make conversation without an opportunity to prepare. To have things to talk about, paying attention to the news and knowing what is going on in the world, as well as reading and trying new things, will give you conversational material. This relates back to being curious, which will lead you to learn and seek information, providing you with many things to say. A superior conversationalist can speak with almost anyone, which requires knowledge of various topics and the ability to ask questions.

You want to avoid being interesting in the wrong way, e.g., by being a gossip. As social animals, it is human nature to gossip, and under some circumstances it can be helpful, such as warning a vulnerable person about another's antisocial behavior.[16,17] Even though not all gossip is bad, in many cases it creates a temptation to pass judgment on someone without affording them a chance to defend their self, and it is not kind behavior. If someone would not like to hear you say something about them or you would feel embarrassed to say it to their face, then it generally isn't a good idea to say it to someone else. If you find someone gossiping to you about information you don't need to know, you can cut them off politely with statements such as, "I don't need to know that," "That sounds like private information," or "Why don't we reserved judgment on that?" As a general rule, don't repeat hurtful things to the person they were said about; in most circumstances, it doesn't help.

4.4.5 People you find boring

Sometimes you will encounter people whom you find boring. As you become a better conversationalist and improve at asking questions, this will happen to you less, because everyone you meet has different life experiences and something that you can learn from them. The better you get at conversation, the better you will get at searching for these things or directing the conversation to subjects that are mutually interesting.

Should you find yourself in conversation with a person who talks too much (i.e., they aren't giving you a chance to speak), and they are expounding at length upon something you cannot bring yourself to care about, try redirecting the conversation. Do this by asking a question about something they may have opinions or thoughts on that you find interesting. That way, even if you can't have a proper conversation by getting to exchange ideas, at least you don't have to listen to commentary that bores you.

When you encounter someone who has less-developed conversational skills than you, remember always to be kind. If they are not being empathetic and adapting to you (which you should also be doing for them), they may seem boring or unpleasant; regardless, be courteous and give this person five minutes of your time. However, do not feel compelled to spend longer than that if you find the conversation unpleasant, especially if you are at a networking event, as they may prevent you from meeting other people. Give them your undivided and sincere attention for five minutes, then excuse yourself politely before departing. Never just wander off.

If for some reason you do not wish to or cannot leave a conversation because of obligations, then make an effort to engage the person about themselves or their research. Give yourself the challenge of getting them to talk about something that they are excited about, that you want to listen to, or that you can engage with fully as a listener.

4.4.6 Being a guest

When you attend an event that someone else has organized, even if it is a large event without a guest list or personalized invitation, thinking of yourself and behaving as a guest can be helpful. Being a good guest in a conversational context means having a relevant self-introduction and some conversational topics prepared, listening to others, making graceful exits from conversations, starting conversations with people standing alone, and paying attention to spouses and children. (The mechanics of *how* to do these things will be discussed in the next chapter.)

In a broader context, as a guest, make sure to RSVP promptly if you receive a personalized invitation. Greet the host or organizer when you arrive, and for large unhosted events, when afforded the opportunity, introduce yourself to the organizing staff. When you depart an event, thank the host or organizer; if it is an unhosted event, if possible, thank a member of the organizing staff. And when you are ready to leave, *leave*. Long goodbyes where you have to say goodbye to every single person you know are draining, time consuming, and awkward for everyone. Say good-bye, wave, and depart.

4.4.7 A special note regarding graduate students

Asking senior graduate students when they plan to graduate or what they intend to do after graduation can stir up difficult or unpleasant issues that they may not want to discuss. You can always ask them how things are going, and they can choose how far "into the weeds" (an American idiom that means to explore or immerse oneself in a high level of detail on a subject; see Section 9.4) they want to take you in describing the trials and tribulations of their quest to graduate. But they may have had a disagreement with their advisor, or a problem in the lab that is threatening their graduation date, and so it is best to avoid asking too specifically about defense dates and post-graduation jobs.

Remember that it is better to discuss positive subjects when first meeting someone, and therefore, asking too directly about a subject that may be fraught puts the other person in a potentially uncomfortable position. If they have good news, they will probably tell you about it, but if they are having a rough time, allow them to avoid or redirect rather than putting them on the spot.

4.4.8 Cell phones

Cell phone usage in social situations is a tricky subject, as we are still learning how to navigate the combination of the two. A good general rule is to stay off your phone as much as possible when at a social event. If you need to spend some time messaging or making a phone call, excuse yourself and do so away from the other guests or attendees. Standing amidst other guests and using your phone gives a bad impression; it makes it appear as though someone elsewhere is more interesting or important that those physically near you. It also makes you less approachable, so unless it's urgent, stay off your phone.

If you are trying to coordinate with someone to meet at the event and you are in the middle of a conversation, excuse yourself if you get out your phone to check your messages. In this case, it is also best to explain what's happening. Say, "I'm so sorry, I'm trying to tell my friend how to find me. When they arrive, I can introduce you, they work on ...." Getting out your phone and texting on it without an explanation in front of someone with whom you have been speaking is dismissive. It objectifies the other person, as though they are a TV show that you can pause and deal with at your leisure, rather than a person who has feelings.

Use kindness and the comfort of your conversational partner as your guiding principles when it comes to your cell phone use. Keep your phone in your pocket and out of sight as much as possible, and then excuse yourself or offer explanations if you absolutely must look at your phone. There are exceptions to this in the case of language barrier and translation apps (see Section 5.7.4).

4.4.9 Name tags and business cards

Common accoutrements of conversational networking are name tags and business cards, so having a strategy to deal with them is important.

While attending a networking event, at a conference, for example, if you have a name tag on a lanyard, it's a good idea to try and clip it to your lapel instead of letting it dangle at your stomach. It can be awkward if someone has to look down your body to your navel area to read your name, an especially sensitive issue for women, who may be uncertain of what you are looking at.

If you get to fill out your own name tag, do it! Be accurate, but don't feel confined to be dry. You can make yourself more memorable, and give people an easy conversation starter, by adding something interesting. You can include your job title or an "Ask me about _" statement, but be sure it's something you want to talk about. Also consider putting your preferred pronouns on your name tag, e.g., "she/her," "he/him," "they/them," etc. As will be discussed in Chapter 6, some people use pronouns you might not know to use without asking, so regardless of your gender identity, putting your pronouns on your nametag can reduce confusion and set people at ease.

There is no uniformly agreed upon side, right or left, for where to put a name tag, but if you put it on your right side, it makes for an easy line of sight when you shake hands (with your right hand). Regardless of the side, make it easy to see (near your lapels or collar bone).

Business cards are a common and useful part of networking that will be discussed at greater length in Chapter 9 in reference to conferences. They are a convenient way to share your contact information, and they are tangible objects you can leave with someone to help them remember you. That being said, you should distribute cards selectively. Only give them to people with whom you have made a connection and whom you want to encourage to follow up with you. If you want someone's card, it's good to offer yours first; people typically will offer their own in response. To be polite, look at the card when you receive it before you put it away.

If, after the fact, you cannot remember the person when you are looking at their card, throw it out and don't try and add them to your database of contacts. If you only get cards from people you have made a connection with, this shouldn't be a common problem. If you can't remember who it is, even after you've looked them up online, then you didn't really need their card anyway.

4.5 Grooming and Attire

There are certain aspects of your appearance that are beyond your control, and it is important to recognize that the people worth speaking with will not judge you based on things you cannot change. They will respond to you based on what you can control, such as what you do and say, and the part of your appearance that you have the most control over is your grooming and attire. Before you even speak, all of the information someone has about you is how you appear, so you want to do everything in your power to make a good impression. Your grooming and attire can also affect your conversational partner's comfort, so it is important to make sure that they are not a distraction.

When you first meet someone and they don't have any context with which to interpret you and your behavior, perception is truth. If you are disheveled, dirty, or aloof, this is all they know about you. While an especially generous and thoughtful person will take into consideration that you could be having an off-day, people will generally take your appearance at face value. And people tend to come to a conclusion based on appearance quickly: in about 100 ms.[18] This is why we strive to make good first impressions, because the shorter the time you have known someone, the more disproportionately represented you are by those few moments (this goes as a function of a/x, where a is an arbitrary, finite span of time, and x is the amount of time they have known you). You want to strive to make a positive and authentic first impression, so that what the person perceives as the truth *is* the truth about you. Also, some people will see but not speak with you, and your appearance will be their *only* impression of you.

It can be instructive to think of this issue in terms of signal-to-noise ratio. If your clothes are dirty, wrinkled, or inappropriate for the occasion, or if you are dirty or smell bad, these factors add noise to the message that you are trying to communicate. Bad odor is an especially potent form of noise on top of your signal, as it makes it hard for the person to listen to you over the discomfort of the smell. Only the most patient and determined of people will be able to find your signal. No matter how pleasant you are in other ways, if you have notably bad breath or body odor, it is going to make interacting with you unpleasant.

To that end, it is imperative that you bathe and use deodorant so that you do not have an unpleasant smell, and that you maintain good oral hygiene so that your breath is inoffensive. Avoid smelly foods, such as garlic and onions, before an event, or be sure you brush your teeth and have a mint before interacting again.

Body odor is largely a matter of genetics. Certain populations that possess a non-functional ABCC11 allele have fewer sweat glands that are associated with body odor and produce fewer of the compounds that cause odor, and this genetic tendency is predominant among East Asian populations.[19] So if your country of origin is in East Asia, you are less likely to need deodorant, but it's not a bad idea to consult on the matter with someone that you trust. And if your country of origin is outside of East Asia, you probably need deodorant.

It is important not to go overboard in the other direction and use too much scent. Aggressive use of perfume or cologne can be just as off-putting and distracting as body odor; furthermore, some people are allergic to perfumes, so if you use a scent, do so sparingly.

You do not need to have elegant, fashionable, or expensive attire, but apply the concept of signal-to-noise ratio to your clothes as well. Whatever you wear should be clean and pressed. Dirty, wrinkled, and inappropriate clothing can be distracting, and under most circumstances it is something you have control over. Further, being dressed appropriately for the event you are attending can ease anxiety and help you to fit in. Make sure that you feel comfortable as well, so wear comfortable shoes, as it is hard to be friendly and charming when you are in pain.

If you enjoy clothes and fashion, then by all means wear statement pieces that give people an opening to discuss with you. A colorful tie or an eye-catching pair of earrings or cufflinks can not only enhance your appearance but also give people an opportunity to start a conversation with you by asking a question about it or complimenting it. And if you wear a statement piece, be prepared for people to comment and have a reply that allows for conversation rather than just "thanks!" Conversely, some people may be wearing garments that are unfamiliar to you because of a different cultural or religious norm, in which case if you comment or make inquiries, do so with caution and a positive tone, recognizing that the person may not want or choose to answer your question. Diversity, culture, religion, and appearance are discussed further in Chapter 6.

Note that some events have an explicit dress code, in which case you should make sure to adhere to it. Professional networking events with requirements other than "business" or "business casual" are few and far between. But if you are invited to a formal black-tie or white-tie event, research the guidelines in advance and dress the part. As a general rule, it is better to be slightly overdressed than to be slightly underdressed (in terms of formality).

4.6 Common Conversational Pitfalls

Mistakes are inevitable, and conversation and networking are no exception. Even people who are master conversationalists make mistakes. Some mistakes are more common than others, and awareness will go a long way towards avoiding them. Some of these mistakes are discussed here to help you recognize them, but there is no way to prevent them entirely. When mistakes do happen, be forgiving with yourself and others, and use those valuable failures as data and feedback on how you can improve or change your approach. And keep practicing!

4.6.1 Interrupting

An interruption is when you interject your own commentary before the person currently speaking has finished. There are certain instances when this is necessary, such as an emergency, but interruptions should generally be avoided, because derailing another person's thought is disrespectful, and it is frustrating for the person speaking. You want to keep your conversational partner comfortable, so interrupting is a self-defeating practice that will likely leave a bad impression.

Studies have shown that the more important a person is, the less likely it is that others will interrupt them.[20] The corollary is that by interrupting someone, you are implying that they are not important. It has also been shown that women are typically interrupted more than their male peers,[21] betraying an unfortunate negative societal attitude towards women. Interrupting can be a hard habit to break, but do your best to notice if you are doing it, including soliciting feedback from friends and colleagues, and be extra attentive to the issue when addressing women, regardless of your gender. If and when you realize you have interrupted someone, apologize and return the floor to them. "I'm sorry, you were saying?" is a good, standard phrase.

Should you find yourself in conversation with someone who will not let you get a word in edgewise, then it's not actually a conversation. It is a monologue, and you should feel free to extricate yourself from the situation. Unfortunately, you may need to interrupt to do this, but do so politely and with an apology. For example, you can say something like, "I'm so sorry to interrupt you, but I just saw someone I really need to talk to now, in case they leave. Please forgive me, it was nice to meet you," and then make your exit.

4.6.2 Being negative

Colin: "Food?"
Nancy: "No, thanks."
Colin: "Yeah, a bit dodgy isn't it? Looks like a dead baby's finger. Oh, yeah, tastes like it too. I'm Colin, by the way."
Nancy: "I'm Nancy."
Colin: "Wicked. What do you do Nancy?"
Nancy: "I'm a cook."
Colin: "Ever do weddings?"
Nancy: "Yes, I do."
Colin: "They should have asked you to do this one."
Nancy: "They did."
Colin: "God, I wish you hadn't have turned it down."
Nancy: "I didn't."
Colin: "Right."

~Love Actually (2003)

As discussed in the section on grooming and attire, when meeting someone brand new, what you look like and first say are likely to be 100% of the information that your new acquaintance has about you. Due to this lack of context, your initial statements have a lot of impact and influence on how you are perceived. Therefore, the less you know of an acquaintance, the more you should limit the negative statements that you make. If you start out by saying something negative, such as, "This food is awful," what they know about you is that (1) you are a complainer or a picky eater, and (2) you have poor judgement in conversational topics. This person could be or know a member of the catering staff (as in the quote above), and you may have just insulted them.

An old friend, or a long-time acquaintance, who knows you well will interpret things differently than someone who has just met you and knows very little about you. If someone knows you well, they have a context for you as a person, and it can be good and healthy to share your negative feelings with them. If you have only just met someone or they are someone you don't see very often, play it safe and be positive at the beginning. Authenticity is still important, so if you are having a bad day or are going through difficulties, you don't need to lie about it, but keep in mind how your statements could lead to your conversational partner's comfort or discomfort. Becoming too personal too quickly can easily cause discomfort and in general can be seen as a warning flag by the other person, so do so with caution.

As discussed in Section 3.4, if you are tired or unhappy as you approach a social event, you have a few options. If you feel that you cannot perform in a satisfactory manner due to your mental or emotional state, it is perfectly reasonable and even advisable to take time to recover in private. You may avoid making a bad impression this way. However, studies have shown that socializing is good for your wellbeing and emulating happiness can improve your mood.[23,24] Your self-awareness can help you decide which course of action will be most beneficial.

4.6.3 Being invasive

When avoiding getting too personal too quickly, apply this in both directions, i.e., the types of question that you ask your conversational partner should not be overly personal, especially if they are a new or purely professional connection. Of course, asking personal questions is a natural part of many relationships, but this is a place where your personal life and your professional life play by very different rules. In a professional networking context, avoid comments on someone's weight or signs of stress, as well as inquiries about their relationship status, children, pregnancy, or medical conditions.

If you ask someone a direct question and get a vague answer, make a mental note of it, and don't pursue it. This can be hard for scientists and engineers, who like to understand things and are trained to ask questions, but unless it's an interrogation or a discussion about lab work, let it go. The person probably has a reason for being evasive, and in polite conversation they should be allowed to not answer. No one is obligated to offer information that they don't want to provide.

4.6.4 Becoming offended

Sometimes it will not be you who makes a mistake but your conversational partner. When this happens, do your best not to take such things personally. Typically, the person has made an error without realizing it; it is less common for someone to be intentionally rude or unkind. Don't let someone else's bad manners spoil your own by responding aggressively to a perceived insult. There is a possibility that you have misunderstood or suffered a miscommunication, in which case if you lose your temper you will be at fault. On the other hand, in the rare case that it was an intentional slight, you only give your insulter power over you by showing that they have affected you. You will also likely lose the sympathy of any bystanders if you lose your temper.

When a person is unaware of their error, you have several courses of action. Recognize that it is not your responsibility to educate the other person and that offering them feedback is an investment of your energy. Additionally, offering criticism to a new acquaintance can become socially awkward, so for smaller errors, it may be best to let it go. From there, you can either extricate yourself from the conversation or change the topic. If it is a more serious error, only address it directly if you can maintain your temper and keep it simple, such as, "That's not a very nice thing to say," or, "Please don't say (or do) that."

Note that you will generally get better traction with criticism if you offer it one-on-one rather than in a group, as embarrassing the person reduces their ability to listen and understand what you are saying.[25] If it is someone with whom you have regular contact, it can be useful to wait until you have the opportunity to speak in private. And if it is a friend who is in err, ask questions instead of taking offense, as it is entirely possible that you may have either misunderstood the situation or that you will receive an apology.

Ultimately, while keeping your temper and avoiding becoming offended is a benefit to you in many circumstances, you do not need to stay and subject yourself to bad behavior. More strategies for dealing with inappropriate comportment are discussed in Section 5.8.

4.6.5 How to address mistakes

When you realize that *you* have made an error, you should apologize briefly and then move on. Dwelling too long on an error or apology will derail the conversation and could possibly turn something that may have been minor into a big, more memorable deal. It is important to offer a succinct and direct apology when you realize you have said something inappropriate and to give the other party a chance to respond. After that, find a way to gracefully move the conversation along to another topic.

The focus of your apology should be on the other person, not on you. Do not lament about how bad you feel, because it's not about you, and it will make the other person feel more uncomfortable. Also, do not defend yourself, make excuses, or shift blame elsewhere. Keep it simple and to the point: "I'm sorry, I shouldn't have said that," "I apologize, that was a stupid thing to say," or "Please forgive me, that was a mistake. I'm so sorry" are good examples.

4.7 Patience, Forgiveness, and Judgment

Mistakes are bound to happen. Social interaction is anxiety inducing for a reason: it's hard. You will make mistakes, and so will others. Ideally, we all try to become more empathetic and self-aware conversationalists and networkers, and the errors that we make will decrease over time. Mistakes will never go away completely, and in those moments when we err, no one wants to be rejected and judged harshly. Human beings have a fundamental need for acceptance and connection, so do your best to be patient and forgiving of others' missteps. Kindness and generosity are core principles of sustainable networking; make sure to apply them to the mistakes, too. This is not to say that you should tolerate bad behavior or allow yourself to be mistreated, but most mistakes are simple errors in judgment or the result of ignorance, and being forgiving in those moments is the kind thing to do.

Exercises

(1)   Spend some time thinking or taking notes regarding your conversational style. Do you prefer to talk or listen? What are things that you can do to change your conversational style to allow for an equitable exchange of information with others?

(2)   Considering the section on etiquette, in as much as it is applicable to you and your context, what are the areas that you need to work on? Do you avoid eye contact because you are uncomfortable? Do you speak too fast or too quietly to be easily understood? Are there any topics that you know you should not talk about but that you can't seem to avoid? Try not to fall prey to the Dunning–Kruger effect as you do this self-assessment; everyone has something that they need to improve, and there is no shame in that. No one is perfect, and that is normal. [Author's note: And someone truly perfect would probably be insufferable.]

(3)   Think about your grooming and attire. Do you have clothes in your closet that are stained or in disrepair? Think about repurposing or donating them. Do you remember to bathe, comb your hair, and put on deodorant before social events or work? If you don't, consider updating your grooming routine and purchasing some new products as a treat to motivate yourself.

(4)   Regarding the section on pitfalls, take a moment to think about which of those mistakes you tend to make. Be honest and kind with yourself, as examining our mistakes is an unpleasant task that is necessary in order to change and improve. Just as we analyze our data and occasionally find errors in our methodology in the laboratory, so too can we examine the data that is our experience and explore ways to do things better. This task is challenging, so be patient with yourself as you try it.

References

1. Seltzer, L. F., "Feeling Understood - Even More Important Than Feeling Loved?" *Psychology Today* (June 28, 2017). Retrieved from psychologytoday.com/us/blog/evolution-the-self/201706/feeling-understood-even-more-important-feeling-loved. Accessed on March 28, 2019.

2. Berlyne, D. E., "A theory of human curiosity," *British Journal of Psychology. General Section*, **45**, 3, 180-191 (1954).

3. Kidd, C. and B. Y. Hayden, "The psychology and neuroscience of curiosity," *Neuron* **88**(3), 449-460 (2015).

4. Leslie, I., *Curious: The desire to know and why your future depends on it*, Basic Books, New York (2014).

5. Wai, J., "Seven Ways to Be More Curious," *Psychology Today* (July 31, 2014). Retrieved from psychologytoday.com/us/blog/finding-the-next-einstein/201407/seven-ways-be-more-curious. Accessed on March 28, 2019.

6. Mehrabian, A. and S. R. Ferris, "Inference of attitudes from nonverbal communication in two channels," *J. Consulting Psychology* **31**(3) (1967).

7. Mehrabian, A. and M. Wiener, "Decoding of inconsistent communications," *J. Personality and Social Psychology* **6**(1), 109 (1967).

8. Birdwhistell, R. L., "Kinesic Stress in American English," Chapter 18 in *Kinesics and Context: Essays on Body Motion Communication*, University of Pennsylvania Press, Philadelphia (1970).

9. Glover, R. B., "Understanding Etiquette and Manners," *The Spruce* (February 6, 2019). Retrieved from thespruce.com/definition-of-etiquette-1216651. Accessed on March 28, 2019.

10. Post, E., "The Definition of Etiquette," *The Emily Post Institute* (2019). Retrieved from emilypost.com/advice/definition-of-etiquette. Accessed on March 28, 2019.

11. Akechi, H. et al., "Attention to eye contact in the West and East: Autonomic responses and evaluative ratings," *PloS one* **8**(3) (2013).

12. Senju, A. et al., "Cultural background modulates how we look at other persons' gaze," *International journal of behavioral development*, **37**, 2 (2013).

13. Binetti, N. et al., "Pupil dilation as an index of preferred mutual gaze duration," *Royal Society Open Science*, 3, **7**, 160086 (2016).

14. Chatterjee, R., "A New Survey Finds 81 Percent of Women Have Experienced Sexual Harassment," *NPR National Public Radio* (February 21, 2018). Retrieved from npr.org/sections/thetwo-way/2018/02/21/587671849/a-new-survey-finds-eighty-percent-of-women-have-experienced-sexual-harassment. Accessed on March 28, 2019.

15. "Dress for Respect," *Ogilvy* (2018). Retrieved from ogilvy.com/work/the-dress-for-respect. Accessed on March 28, 2019.

16. Feinberg, M. et al., "The virtues of gossip: reputational information sharing as prosocial behavior," *Journal of personality and social psychology*, **102**, 5 (2012).

17. Beersma, B. and G. A. Van Kleef, "How the grapevine keeps you in line: Gossip increases contributions to the group," *Social Psychological and Personality Science* **2**(6) (2011).

18. Willis, J. and A. Todorov, "First impressions: Making up your mind after a 100-ms exposure to a face," *Psychological Science* **17(7)**, 592–598 (2006).

19. Martin, A. et al., "A functional ABCC11 allele is essential in the biochemical formation of human axillary odor," *J. Investigative Dermatology* **130**(2) (2010).

20. Jacobi, T. and D. Schweers, "Justice, Interrupted: The Effect of Gender, Ideology, and Seniority at Supreme Court Oral Arguments," *Virginia Law Review*, 1379–1485 (2017).

21. Kennedy, C. W. and C. Camden, "Interruptions and nonverbal gender differences," *J. Nonverbal Behavior* **8**(2) (1983).

22. Fratiglioni, L. et al., "An active and socially integrated lifestyle in late life might protect against dementia," *The Lancet Neurology* **3**(6) (2004).

23. Carter, C., "Fake It Till You Make It," *Greater Good Science Center at U.C. Berkeley* (February 17, 2009). Retrieved from greatergood.berkeley.edu/article/item/fake_it_till_you_make_it. Accessed on March 29, 2019.

24. Spector, N., "Smiling can trick your brain into happiness — and boost your health," *NBC News Better* (November 28, 2017). Retrieved from nbcnews.com/better/health/smiling-can-trick-your-brain-happiness-boost-your-health-ncna822591. Accessed on March 29, 2019.

25. Daum, K., "How to Give (and Receive) Positive Criticism," *Inc.* (May 24, 2013). Retrieved from inc.com/kevin-daum/how-to-give-and-recieve-positive-criticism.html. Accessed on March 29, 2019.

Chapter 5
Conversational Skills and Applications

"Boring conversation anyway."

~Han Solo (played by Harrison Ford),
Star Wars: Episode IV - A New Hope (1977)

5.1 From Theory to Practice

The last chapter discussed a number of theories and principles to use as a guide for conversation, to help you recognize what makes a good conversation and what can get you into trouble conversationally. Here, we discuss more specific applications and how to put these principles into practice in greater detail. This is where the rubber hits the road, or in other words, where theory gets put into practice. Keep in mind that like etiquette (discussed in Chapter 4), these suggestions will not apply equally well in all contexts or for all people. There is simply too much variation in the world to create absolute rules. But like the Golden Rule, this chapter should give you a useful starting framework that you can adapt to your personal style, culture, and circumstances.

5.2 Starting a Conversation

To have a conversation, someone has to start it. There are several ways that conversations can start, and many of them involve introductions. You can introduce yourself to someone or vice versa, someone may introduce you to a third party, or you can be the one introducing others. Facilitated introductions are nice, because they give you an easy starting place for your conversation, but they aren't necessary. You might strike up a conversation with a stranger with no introduction, as a result of an external event or object. Someone might ask you for directions or advice, or remark on the weather, or you may both be surprised by something that happens in your proximity and begin talking, only to realize later in the conversation that you haven't introduced yourselves.

Your most common conversational experience will likely be with someone you already know. Unless you have something difficult to discuss, these are the easiest kind of conversations to start, because (1) you already have precedent for speaking with that person, and (2) you have already collected experiential data about this person and so can predict to some extent how they will respond to you. This is what is hard about starting conversations with new people: not knowing how they will respond. But starting conversations involves overcoming the fear of rejection, and with practice the following strategies will make it easier.

5.2.1 Before you speak

An important part of starting a conversation happens before you ever say a word. This part is non-verbal, involving body language, eye contact, and observation. When you identify someone you want to speak with, begin by making eye contact. If they look back at you, that is a positive indication that they are open to conversing, and you should say hello and introduce yourself. If they do not look back or they quickly look away, then consider their body language and the circumstances. If the person displays discouraging body language, e.g., turning away, crossing their arms, or a facial expression that conveys negative emotions, this is an indication that they do not want to converse. Move on and see if you can find someone else who will engage in eye contact or displays encouraging body language such as smiling, arms at their sides, or turning towards you.

If the person did not make or broke off eye contact with you, but shows neutral or encouraging body language, next consider the social context. Are you at a social function or networking event that people attend for the purpose of making conversation? Or are you in an environment that does *not* assume interaction, such as a sidewalk, grocery store, or public transit? If you are in a situation designed for conversation, it is probably fine to greet the person and introduce yourself, remembering that cultural norms regarding eye contact vary and that the other party may not have meant to turn you away by not meeting your eyes or holding your gaze. However, if you are not in a place intended for conversation, and the person has been unresponsive to your attempt to make eye contact, even if their body language is not discouraging, it is probably best not to disturb them.

For starting a conversation with someone you already know, you should still check their body language to determine if this is a good time. If they meet your gaze and are displaying encouraging body language, you can greet them by name and ask them a question, such as how they are or how their day or work is going. If the person is a close friend and they are displaying discouraging body language, you can use your judgement and knowledge of them as a person as to whether it is appropriate to inquire if everything is okay. Under some circumstances, they may be focused or busy, and you will know based on experience that you should come back later. If you are uncertain, you can ask whether now is a good time. See Fig. 5.1 for a visual guide to opening a conversation.

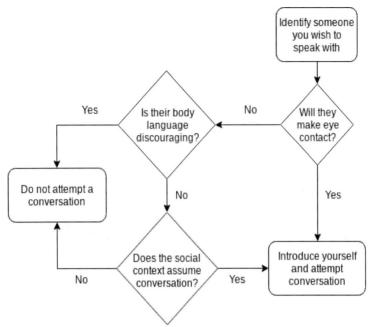

Figure 5.1 Flow chart for initiating conversations.

5.2.2 Introducing yourself

Being proactive about introducing yourself to people is a great way to start conversations. If you wait for others to introduce themselves to you, you will meet fewer people and risk being perceived as aloof, rather than shy. Fearing rejection and uncertainty is normal, but few people will be openly rude to you if you approach them, especially if they are at a networking or social event where conversation is expected.

To open the conversation, smile, make eye contact, and greet the person. If the circumstances merit it, you can extend your hand for a handshake. They will probably respond in kind with a greeting and shake your hand. What you say to open a conversation doesn't have to be perfect; it is far better to say something, even if it is imperfect, than to say nothing because of perfectionism and fear. A great move is saying, "Hello, I'm [Your Name]," and extending your hand for a handshake. You don't need a fancy opening line to start a conversation.

Next, you will want to give this person a bit of context about yourself. Having a short, topical introduction prepared for yourself in advance, that you can say in one or two sentences, can be helpful, especially if conversation makes you nervous. If you expect to attend a particular event, research the event, know its purpose, and look over the guest list if there is one available. Make it clear in your mind what you will have in common with the other people at the event and think of relevant information that you can share about yourself in a brief introduction. At a professional event, your introduction should include your name, what kind of work you do (without using much jargon), and where you work. But if you are at a social event, such as a wedding or a party, your work is less relevant than how you know the bride or the host. Remember: brevity and relevance are always important parts of your introduction, and relevance depends on the type of event.

The purpose of an introduction, self or otherwise, is not just to say who you are but to give your audience a positive experience or impression of you, and offer them information that they can use to engage and pursue conversation with you. You should be prepared to go into more detail about things you mention in your introduction, so don't mention things that you don't want to discuss. Make your introduction as relevant as possible to your audience. If it's a presentation, give information about yourself that pertains to the topic you are presenting. If it's a professional event, share information about what you do professionally. And if it's a planned, one-on-one meeting, research the person so that you can craft an introduction relevant to their interests and the purpose of the meeting (if you haven't done so already when you set up the meeting). Planning your introduction gets easier with practice and is something you will be occasionally called upon to do extemporaneously. Having different versions of your self-introduction prepared will help you improvise when necessary.

If you don't get a welcome reception when you attempt to open a conversation with someone, keep in mind that people who seem unfriendly may be preoccupied with other things. Their apparent disinterest may be related to a personal concern and have nothing to do with you. Or they might be feeling shy and uncomfortable. If someone seems like they don't want to talk, don't take it personally and just move on.

5.2.3 Being introduced

Conversations that start with an introduction from a third party are easier than introducing yourself. Instead of having to decide what information is relevant for your self-introduction, a third party who already knows you and the other person will do that for you. They perform the heavy lifting by providing the salient details you need for a conversational starting point. Subsequently, your introducer becomes a great topic of conversation, including how you each know them and any amusing or appropriate anecdotes about them.

Being introduced is also nice, because your introducer can say positive things about you that might appear pretentious if you said them yourself. It is appropriate to brag about your friends and colleagues, but it's not a good idea to do it about yourself. A third party can mention the awards you have won, your recent publication in a prestigious journal, or expound upon how you saved the world from an alien invasion, and it will generally be well received (except perhaps for that last one), but if you did the same things you might give an impression of arrogance.

When you are being introduced, pay attention to the name and the details offered about the person, smile, and shake their hand if appropriate. Thank your introducer and tell the other person that it is nice to meet them. If your introducer pronounces your name wrong, you can simply repeat the correct pronunciation when you perform the handshake, indicate yourself and say something like, "Christina. It's very nice to meet you, Kyoko."

You may be introduced to someone that you have met before, in which case "It's nice to meet you" is the wrong thing to say, as it implies that you have forgotten this person. "It's good to see you" is a good replacement if you are not certain if you have met them before or not. If you are on the receiving end of "it's nice to meet you" from someone you have met before, be forgiving. It's an easy mistake to make, and remember that your goal with your conversational partners is to make them comfortable. You can say, "I think we might have met before at…" if it makes sense to do so, but whatever you do, be gracious. Don't be the person who was memorable for being spiky or unforgiving.

5.2.4 The elevator pitch

The elevator pitch is named for a hypothetical encounter with someone important on an elevator, and you only have the duration of the ride to interest this person in your idea[1] (though the origin of the term is a point of debate). An elevator pitch needs to be clear and compelling enough that your audience wants your contact information or to buy your product before the brief ride is over. Concision, clarity, and targeted relevance are core to a good elevator pitch.

The elevator pitch is a construct that is most relevant for business people and entrepreneurs, but no matter your career type or stage, crafting one is a useful exercise. The ability to quickly state the value of your work and experience will help you when speaking with your boss or other decision makers, in meetings, at networking events, and when pursuing funding. It's also a good idea to have your pitch prepared for a variety of audiences, ranging from highly technical (an audience in your sub-field) to very general (one with no background in STEM).

It is especially difficult to explain complex ideas briefly, which is why practice and preparation are important. Write your elevator pitch down, edit it, and then say it out loud without speaking too fast; time yourself to see how long it takes. Then when called upon by surprise to introduce yourself or explain your work, you can do so in a concise manner that is appropriate to your audience.

Things to include in your elevator pitch are

(1) Your name,
(2) Where you work,
(3) Your specialty or skill set,
(4) Any special accomplishments, and
(5) Your goal(s).

The last three items on the list should be very carefully tailored (as best as possible) to your audience. How you describe your specialty to someone who has no science background should be materially different than how you describe it to someone who works in your field or sub-field. Be especially careful with jargon, which allows you to explain things more efficiently to those who already know the terms but will confuse your audience and obfuscate your message for those who do not. Jargon is noise, just like filler words, if your audience doesn't know the terms you are using.

With an eye towards sustainable networking, think about how to frame your elevator pitch in such a way that it explains how you can be helpful to your audience. For example, imagine that a engineer named Camelina is meeting someone who works in a research group she would like to collaborate with or join. She could say the following:

"(1) Hi, my name is Camelina. (2) I am a mechanical engineer at McGrover Inc., (3) with experience designing optomechanical systems for flight applications. (4) I recently worked on a system that was launched into a polar Earth orbit. (5) I'm very interested in your group's work on meteorite mining, and I think my skills would transfer very well to that area."

In this statement, Camelina knows she is talking to someone who has experience in her sub-field, so she can use more technical language. She gives (1) her name and (2) her place of employment, and then explains her (3) relevant skill set and (4) an interesting recent accomplishment. She ends with (5) a goal that is tailored to her audience that explains how she could be helpful.

However, if the person is the editor of a professional trade journal, who has experience with the field but no technical background, Camelina might say the following instead:

"(1) Hi, my name is Camelina. (2) I am a mechanical engineer at a defense contractor called McGrover, Inc. (3) I design mechanical parts for light-based systems that go on satellites, and (4) I recently worked on a system that is in orbit around the Earth. (5) I read your periodical regularly, and I have an idea for an article on satellite systems that I think your readers would enjoy."

Again, Camelina gives (1) her name and (2) her place of employment, but with more context. This time, she is talking to someone with minimal technical expertise, so when she explains her (3) relevant skill set and (4) recent accomplishment, she drops the technical jargon. She still ends with (5) a goal that is tailored to her audience and explains how she could be helpful.

5.2.5 Introducing others

If you are the one introducing two other people, there is standard etiquette for who to introduce to whom first in a formal setting, inasmuch as etiquette is applicable to your circumstances. Generally, you make the introduction by first presenting the junior person to the more senior person. This means introducing the younger person to the older person or the research scientist to the CEO. If the two people are very similar in age and rank, then you present first the person you are more familiar with to the person you are less familiar with. Present your old graduate school friend to the person you just met. The more informal the occasion, the less important it is to observe this standard, if at all.

When you introduce two people, you should offer information about each person to the other. This information should be complementary, relevant, and as interesting as possible, and it will act as a starting point for their conversation. It should be something that each person is happy to discuss. There may also be something that you know both parties have in common, such as being alumni of the same university or a shared interest in a sport or hobby, and this is good information to offer as well. You, as an introducer, can offer praise about each person in a way that they could not politely do about themselves, so if one of them has won an award or been featured in a new article, you can also offer that.

During the introduction, if you are unsure what title you should use for one of the people, make a point to ask during the introduction. You can say something like, "This is Dr. Boyd. Actually, do you prefer Dr. or Prof.?" and give them an opportunity to correct you.

The real trouble comes if you realize as you are making the introduction and you have forgotten a name. You have two options. The first option is to admit the memory lapse as you are making the introduction and then ask for the name. Second, which is risky, is to begin by introducing the first person and hope that the second person introduces themselves when you do not immediately. Whether or not you do this depends on the person. It is a gamble, but if they are the outgoing type, they will be more likely to jump in and introduce themselves, which will remind you of their name without having to admit you have forgotten it. However, this approach can backfire if the person expects you to say their name or feels shy about introducing themselves, so the first approach is generally the safer option. And you can combine the approaches: if the unnamed person hesitates to introduce themselves, you have given yourself a second opportunity to admit your memory lapse and ask for their name again.

If you are introducing someone to a group, you don't need to introduce everyone in the group if there are three or more. Simply give a general introduction of the new person to the group, sharing something about that person as a conversational starting point for the others.

5.3 Names and Address

Remembering people's names is a challenge. Research about names has shown that they are more difficult to remember than people's occupations[2] but that name recall improves by offering incentives through gamification.[3] Though it can be challenging to do so, most people appreciate it when you use their name. Saying someone's name increases the probability that they will comply with requests[4] and causes brain activation in a way other names do not.[5] It is possible to get better at remembering people's names, but it is important to make a conscious decision to do it.[6] In preparation for an event, mentally prepare yourself for remembering names. If there is a guest list and you can see who is attending ahead of time, spend some time looking it over and matching faces to names, especially for any people you are particularly interested in meeting.

Then, during introductions, make sure that you are *paying attention*. One of the biggest mistakes for name recall is performing introductions on autopilot and not paying attention when names are said. Hear the name and repeat it out loud when you say that it is nice to meet them and shake their hand. Look at them while you say their name to help associate it with their face. You can also come up with silly mnemonics or adjectives to help you remember the person, such as "Chemist Christie" or "Smiling Sameh." Just don't say it out loud. If it is a name you have not heard before, asking how it is spelled and if you are pronouncing it correctly can aid greatly with recall.

As you speak with the person, mentally repeat their name a few more times. If at some point you realize you have forgotten their name or that you weren't paying attention during introductions, apologize and ask for their name again at the close of the discussion. It can also help to get their card, if applicable.

If you have forgotten someone's name after your initial meeting, confess it as soon as you can with a *brief* apology. Don't elaborate or spend time explaining why you forgot; this only calls more attention to your mistake and implies that you feel you have done something wrong. An extended apology also puts the other person in a position of having to assure you they aren't bothered, whether it's true or not. Admit to and acknowledge it, and then quickly move on. And of course, be gracious and do not give someone a hard time if they have forgotten your name. You can help others avoid this problem by mentioning your name again when you see someone. Doing this may also spur them to say their own name, so you can easily move the conversation beyond what might have been an awkward moment. Avoid asking things such as, "Do you remember me?" It sounds accusatory, as though you assume that they will have forgotten you, and it makes the other person uncomfortable, especially if the answer is no!

If you find yourself facing someone whose name you can't recall but who looks familiar, it is safest to admit that you need a reminder. Pretending that you remember them and their name can backfire; it should only be done with caution. And if you see someone struggling to remember your name, assist them by introducing yourself.

When greeting someone by name, remember that it is rarely rude to be overly formal and to use someone's title, but it can be easy to be rude by being too informal. If you are uncertain about how you should address someone, use a person's title. With someone new, use their title initially unless instructed to do otherwise, and if you are not sure, ask. If they ask you to address them less formally, honor their request and treat them the way they are asking to be treated, following the Platinum Rule. Do not shorten someone's name or use a nickname that they have not asked you to use.

5.4 Maintaining a Conversation

Once you are past names and introductions, the possibilities multiply. There are so many things to talk about, but nerves may cause your mind to go blank, or you might suffer from analysis paralysis as to what you should say next. A good first point for a conversation is offering congratulations, if applicable. If you know that the person you are speaking with has recently been awarded a prize, published, received a promotion, taken on a new position, or received some other accolade, offering them praise and congratulations will make them feel good. If such things are mentioned during introductions, make a point to say something about it. And if you are on the receiving end, smile and thank the person for their compliment, even if receiving praise is a challenge for you.

The next step to develop the conversation involves asking questions, especially ones that are open-ended and about the other person or their work. Then there are follow-up questions. Open-ended questions require more than a yes or no answer and allow the other person to share information about themselves that you might not have been able to establish otherwise. It also allows them to decide how much or how little information they wish to share on the subject. It gives them the opportunity to include facts about themselves that they *want* you to ask about. Open-ended questions also elicit answers that give you more information for you to use to craft a follow-up question.

Questions about the other person are good, because people typically enjoy talking about themselves. It is unlikely that someone will feel bored when speaking about their self or their work. Asking someone questions about things that they like will not only make them happy and get them talking, it will make you more memorable in a positive way. Asking questions such as, "What was the highlight of your week?" or "What is your favorite aspect of your job?" gives the person something positive to talk about and gives you an opportunity to learn something about their work. If you run into someone whom you haven't seen for a while, be careful getting too specific about their personal details too quickly. They may have changed jobs or divorced, and you risk bringing up a sensitive subject. In general, do not ask questions that are overly personal in professional settings.

Follow-up questions take new information that you have learned from what the person has just said and go deeper into that subject or area. You can always use questions to direct the conversation intentionally, but follow-up questions are especially powerful, because you can use them to direct the conversation to a topic that *both* of you find interesting, and that is where *really* enjoyable conversations happen. If you direct the conversation with questions to topics that you find interesting, but not the other person, you will have a lackluster discussion and an unmemorable exchange. But if you pay attention to how someone answers a question and analyze it for possible further questions, you can steer towards something you both enjoy, creating a fun, memorable, and illuminating conversation. Good follow-up questions also demonstrate that you are paying attention and will make the person feel heard and understood.

Another flexible line of inquiry to pursue is, "How did you get here?" which could have several meanings. If you take the most literal interpretation, you are asking how they arrived at the event. They may have come from far away, and their answer gives you information you can ask about their hometown or travel habits. The question could also be understood to mean how the person arrived at their particular institute or field of study. Questions such as these afford a rich opportunity for people to respond to the interpretation they prefer and will yield unique answers.

Once you have asked a question, carefully listen to the answer. You can let the other person know you are listening by making eye contact, nodding, smiling, laughing (if appropriate), asking relevant follow-up questions, sharing similar stories, and keeping your body language open and receptive. Receptive body language includes facing the person, keeping your arms at your sides (not crossed), evenly distributing your weight on your feet, and smiling. If the answer to your question bores you or you can't find a way to invest yourself in the answer, then you have probably asked the wrong question.

If you are asked the first question, answer in a way that is comfortable, relevant, and appropriate. It is important to share information about yourself, but as discussed in the last chapter, you don't want to become overly personal or do so too soon. Some people respond well to unvarnished honesty and others do not, which makes it a gamble when you can't predict how a person will respond, because you just met them. You can use your answer to direct conversation just as much as you can with a question. You won't always answer the question exactly, but in polite conversation you are not required to do so, and the conversation benefits if you take a liberal interpretation of the question to give a more interesting answer.

Once you have answered, responding by asking the person the same question they have just asked you is a good way to continue. People often ask questions about things they are interested in and have good answers for, and sometimes they only ask a question because they want you to ask them! This has to do with the social norm of reciprocity (introduced in Section 3.6), meaning that people will typically respond in kind to how you treat or what you say to them.[7,8] The corollary to this is that you should only ask questions that you would be willing to answer.

Once you get good at asking questions, it can be tempting or even easy to keep the other person talking, but it is important that they get to know you as well. Remember that sustainable and effective networking relies on an equitable and mutual exchange of information, so speaking too little is just as ineffective as speaking too much. Make sure that you contribute your own information to the conversation. Conversely, if you notice that someone is only asking you questions, without making statements about themselves, make a point to flip some of the questions around and get to know something about them as well.

Author Anecdote

After reducing my tendency to monologue, I learned to ask a lot of questions. Out of fear of boring people, it became my default to ask more questions than I make statements. I discovered that some people will allow me to never speak about myself and happily answer the questions I ask. That can be relaxing if I am tired and don't want to speak much, but it is not effective networking if I don't share about myself and what I do.

As you are conversing, make a point to make statements that leave the other person some direction to take conversationally. If you discuss heavy social issues and find yourself unable to say much more than "That's too bad," then do your best to see this roadblock coming and find an exit for everyone. Whether you, another person, or the group in general, brought the conversation to this dead end, you can always help by finding a way to redirect. Finding something tangentially related that isn't so heavy or controversial will enable you to redirect seamlessly. Even if you can't find a smooth way to change the subject, everyone will appreciate the gesture when they don't know what to say.

Regarding humor, it is generally okay to laugh at yourself; it makes you warm and approachable. But don't take self-deprecating humor too far. Putting yourself down too much can cause your conversational partners discomfort. And do not put others down, even playfully, as this can easily go awry. Avoid any kind of negative humor, be it racist, sexist, homophobic, or based on religion or ethnicity. These jokes are unkind, convey a negative attitude, show poor judgment, and discomfit others. You can speak up if someone else uses inappropriate humor. Remain polite, or civil at the very least, and say something like, "I don't find that very funny, can we please change the subject?" or say you feel uncomfortable with that kind of humor and excuse yourself. Saying something may cause a slightly awkward moment, but it is important feedback and lets others know that you don't agree with the behavior. And maybe they will learn to change their behavior, which benefits everyone. However, don't feel obligated to speak up, especially if you feel unsafe doing so. You don't have to stay and listen to it, just excuse yourself and leave. More on dealing with bad behavior is discussed in Section 5.8.

As you speak, watch your audience for signs of boredom or disinterest. If they are fidgeting, looking around, or checking their watch, it might be best to bring the conversation to a close. However, it's always possible to misread these signs, so if you are interested in continuing the conversation, then leave the person a gap to speak. If they continue to talk with you even when you have given them a gap as an opportunity to excuse themselves, then they are probably still interested in talking with you.

Advance preparation is also useful for creating and maintaining interesting conversations. When attending an event or meeting, it is a good idea to have several potential topics of conversation in mind that can be tailored to the specific event you are attending. Spending time considering these topics of conversation and relevant questions before an event is especially helpful if you suffer from social anxiety when meeting new people, as it reduces the likelihood of a long pause as you search for something to say.

Finally, remember to treat people as people. Don't treat them like a celebrity, a doctor, a millennial, or a CEO, but as an individual with their own unique abilities, interests, and aspirations. Being seen and heard for who we are is important to us as human beings and is a kindness that you can offer others through conversation. Chapter 6 goes into further detail about interacting with a variety of people.

5.5 Entering an Existing Conversation

Sometimes instead of starting a new conversation, you may wish to join a discussion that is underway. This can be tricky to perform gracefully, but it is another skill that improves with strategy and practice.

When you identify a group or conversation you would like to join, just as you would assess the body language of an individual, take a moment to observe the participants. If they are laughing, joking, and appear to be having a good time, it is probably fine to attempt to join. The smaller the group, and the more serious and intense the conversation looks, the less likely it is that you should try to join, as it might be intrusive. In general, do not try to join a conversation between only two people, as the small number of participants increases the likelihood that they are discussing something particular or serious, and they may not welcome an interruption.

If circumstances indicate that it is a good time to join, move closer and try to make eye contact with someone in the group. This is a non-verbal request or statement that you would like to join. If someone makes eye contact, smile at them and ask, "May I join you?" or nod in the direction of the group to indicate the same question non-verbally, using an inquisitive facial expression as well. If they say yes or make room for you, move in closer to join the circle of discussion. You can also directly ask the group, "May I join your conversation?" even if no one has made made eye contact with you, but only do so if the conversation seems lighthearted. While it is unlikely that you will be refused in a networking situation, if the answer is no, accept it graciously and walk away.

Once you have joined a conversation, spend some time listening before you say anything. You want to make sure that your first comments to the group are on-topic to avoid being disruptive, and you can't do that if you don't know what is being discussed. When you speak, do not monopolize the conversation. It is also possible that you will be asked by someone to introduce yourself, so be prepared with a brief, topical introduction. If someone is especially alert and welcoming, they will give you a one- or two-sentence summary of what is being discussed (and if you are in a position to do this for someone who has just joined a conversation, it will typically be greatly appreciated).

Do your part to avoid serious and personal conversations in a space that is intended for people to circulate. Having a conversation that you do not want interrupted or joined into cuts you off from the standard flow of conversation, and it makes you unapproachable. If you need to have a serious or personal conversation immediately, then remove yourself and your conversational partner from the main social area so that you can have more privacy and reduce the possibility of interruption. If you find yourself on the receiving end of an unwanted interruption and your conversation is urgent, acknowledge the person and apologize, saying that you must finish your private conversation undisturbed. Acknowledge that you are breaking protocol under the circumstances, and do not rudely ignore them. Then move to a more private place or consider postponing the conversation, which is making you antisocial.

If you attempt to enter a two-person conversation and notice body language that indicates you are not welcome, such as lack of eye contact or backs turned to you, don't take it personally; just go find someone else who is more available.

However, sometimes there is a particular person you wish to speak with who is already in a conversation, possibly with only one other person. There are two methods for breaking into this conversation. If it is urgent, you can address the person's conversational partner with an apology and request to speak with the other person. The alternative method, which is less extreme, is to apologize for interrupting, let the relevant party know you are hoping to speak with them, then step away and let the two resume their conversation. You might say, "My apologies for interrupting, but I wanted to let you know that I am here, and I'd love to speak with you when you have a free moment." If the pair doesn't mind their conversation being interrupted or joined, they may invite you in. If not, you have greeted the person, and they know you are interested in speaking with them, so that they can come find you when their conversation concludes.

5.6 Making a Graceful Exit

Sometimes a conversation will end organically, but sometimes you will need to make an intentional exit, and there are several strategies for doing so gracefully. It can be difficult to execute, but this skill is important to practice and use in a social setting where you are expected to circulate. Your goal in exiting a conversation is to leave the other person with a positive impression and avoid making them feel like you are trying to escape. Even if you would prefer to keep speaking with this person, they may have other people whom they want to meet, and their departure is probably not about you (and vice versa). Note that you do not need to wait until you run out of things to say; in fact, it's better to end a conversation before that happens.

To make a graceful exit, wait until you have the floor and have made a statement, then initiate your departure by saying that it has been lovely to meet them (or some variation thereof), recap a part of your conversation to confirm that you were paying attention, and extend your arm to shake hands. For example, you could say, "It was lovely to meet you and hear about your fiber Bragg grating research," or "Great to see you again! It sounds like your talk is going to be exciting. Best of luck!" Then wish them a good evening and move to a different part of the room, ideally at least one quarter of the room away.

Other possible exit lines include:

(1) "It's been good to catch up."
(2) "I've enjoyed talking with you."
(3) "It was nice to meet you."
(4) "It's been great speaking with you. Can I get your card? Let's discuss this more next week."
(5) "Thanks for the chat. It was lovely to meet you."
(6) "I could monopolize you all evening, but I'm sure that other people want to meet you."

You can also say that there's someone you need to catch up with, but only do so if it's true. Otherwise, it may look like you're just trying to get away.

There are also ways to bring the conversation to a close without moving away from your conversational partner immediately. You can take them with you to get a drink or introduce them to others before excusing yourself. Based on the exchange you have just had with this person, you should have learned enough about them to be able to give them a thoughtful introduction to a third party. If the person you are speaking with seems shy, this is an excellent way to help them and yourself. Say, "Why don't I introduce you to a friend of mine?" and then once introductions have been made, you can excuse yourself without abandoning this person, and you get to circulate or take a moment to regroup.

If want to develop the relationship with this person further, make sure to get their contact information before you depart. This can be done by asking for contact information, offering your card (and they will probably respond by giving you theirs), suggesting that you meet for a coffee or a meal, or saying that you wish to continue your discussion. For the encounter to be a fruitful networking experience, the other party needs to remember you; following up is an important part of fixing yourself in their memory. You don't have to, and won't, turn every conversation into a new network connection, but you need their information if that is your goal.

At parties, receptions, and cocktail hours, the goal of the event is to circulate and speak with many people. Don't monopolize anyone's time for too long. If you enjoy their company, let them know you'd like to stay in touch, create a means to do so or a follow-up meeting, and then move along. There are exceptions to every rule, and if you think you have found a collaborator for your next project or some other profound thing, ask them if it's okay to take more of their time, acknowledging that this may be a break with social protocol.

5.6.1 Helping others make an exit

You may feel that the conversation is winding down or notice that your conversational partner is starting to fidget or showing signs that they are ready to move on, but at the same time, they are not making a move to end the conversation. This may be because they are unsure how to gracefully make an exit and do not want to offend you.

Don't be offended. There are many reasons the other person may need to leave that are not about you. Don't assume—unless you know that you have been disagreeable or committed a faux pas—that their departure is in any way a commentary on you. You can assist them in departing gracefully by making your own exit, as described above, or you can say something like, "I don't want to keep you if you need to be elsewhere, it was lovely to meet you," or anything that indicates that they are free to go without offending you.

Sometimes you may have misread their cues, and they may choose to stay and converse with you further. If you are happy to do so, stay and speak more, but if you are ready to move on, do so. But don't imagine that a conversation has been a failure if the other person wants to move on to speak with others. It is the goal of many networking events to meet many people, and it may not be that they don't wish to speak with you but that they have other people that they need to meet, and they have already given you a portion of their time. Since such events are finite, it is a necessary part of the process to have short conversations.

5.7 Language and Conversation

One aspect of conversation that is its own special issue is that of language. In our global STEM community, we are often called upon to either speak in a second (or third) language or communicate with someone speaking their second language—or both at the same time. Language barriers can make it more difficult to convey your message, but there are strategies to address them. Remember to be patient and empathetic, and to find ways to adapt to your audience.

5.7.1 Speaking in not-your-native language

Speaking in your non-native language, especially with native speakers of that language, can be challenging. Other non-native speakers will have many of the same issues that you have and will likely speak slower, but native speakers tend to speak at their natural pace, which may be faster than you can manage easily. If a native speaker is not familiar with speaking to non-native speakers, they may also use colloquial terms and idioms that are hard to understand.

If you are having trouble understanding someone, make sure to let them know that it is a language barrier. You can also ask them to speak more slowly or to repeat or explain words that you do not understand. Doing so gives them the information they need to adapt to your level of language ability. Likewise, try to be clear and enunciate as best you can to make it easier for the native speaker to understand you. Face them so that they can see your mouth as you speak, and use hand gestures to emphasize your points. Body language accounts for a lot of the information that is conveyed during conversation (as discussed in Section 4.3), so it is especially important to pay attention to it when there is a language barrier.

If you can anticipate needing to speak your non-native language, make a point to look up phrases that will be relevant to the setting at hand. Advance preparation is important for any networking event, and knowledge of as many of the relevant words and phrases as possible will make things easier as well. When speaking in a second language is challenging, conversing with a group of people can allow you to spend more time listening and reduce the amount of time you need to speak to keep conversation going.

Ultimately, if you expect to need to use this second language frequently, try to get as much practice as possible.

5.7.2 Speaking with a non-native speaker

When speaking in your native language with someone for whom it is a second or third language, recognize that as the more fluent speaker, the burden of adapting falls more heavily to you. Your fluency gives you more choices for adaptation, so make sure to exercise them as best you can and keep your conversational partner comfortable.

There are a variety of steps you can take to adapt to your audience. Speak a little slower than you normally do, using your empathy to gauge at what speed their comprehension begins to suffer. Make sure that you enunciate your words clearly, and use slightly more formal or textbook language, such as "yes" instead of "yeah," because slang will be less familiar and harder to understand. Also, make a point to avoid acronyms and idioms. Allow for greater pauses between your words and sentences to help the other person assimilate the information. This also means avoiding contractions if possible, saying "I will" rather than "I'll." You can also speak just a *little* louder than you normally do, especially if you are in a noisy room. Include more body language and gestures. You can also use props, such as a picture or object, to help convey your questions. Look for indicators that the person has understood you before proceeding. To avoid confusion, do not make abrupt changes to the topic of conversation. If your conversational partner's ability is more rudimentary, stick to more concrete questions.

There are many great conversations to be had and exchanges to be made, even with a significant language barrier, so don't give up when you discover one. As always, be patient, be kind, and adapt.

5.7.3 Both at once: two non-native speakers conversing

While two people speaking a language that is not native to either of them can be a challenge for both parties, there are also some advantages. Native speakers may speak quickly or have trouble with an unfamiliar accent on their language, but two non-native speakers may have an easier time understanding each other. They will speak slower than the native speaker, have fewer ingrained assumptions about pronunciation and sentence structure, and use fewer slang words or idioms.

Observe the strategies described above. Face each other, make eye contact, use gestures or props to emphasize your statements, and speak just a little louder than you would otherwise, especially if you are in a noisy environment.

5.7.4 Translation apps

A variety of smartphone applications can translate between different languages. When the language barrier is very great, or you simply need to look up a specific word, these apps can be very useful. Keep in mind that the translations are going to be inexact and error prone, and that the quality of translation will vary from language to language. You also want to avoid the trap of letting technology distract you from the human interaction. As discussed in Subsection 4.4.8, spending time on your phone when in a social networking context is undesirable, as it makes you unapproachable and distracted. But when the language barrier is such that you need the aid of a translation app to communicate, simply let your conversational partner know what you are doing and why. This lets them know that you are using your phone to converse with them, not someone else.

5.8 Disagreements and Bad Behavior

If you disagree with statements the other person is making, and you wish to make your disagreement known, how you go about that will determine whether what follows is an argument or a discussion. Using a neutral tone while politely saying, "I disagree," can foster a fruitful discussion, but if you lose your temper and tell the person they are wrong, there is no room for discussion. Statements such as,

"Do you really believe that?" or "Is that always true?" or "Are you sure? That's different from what I've heard," are non-combative ways to disagree with someone and foster a discussion. And if you want to try and change someone's mind on a given topic, you need to be ready to listen and give them the opportunity to try to change yours.

Beyond simple disagreements, you will sometimes find yourself in the presence of someone who is insulting or makes vulgar comments or unwanted advances. Should you decide to protest their behavior, only do so if you feel that you can do it safely. Also, recognize that offering someone polite feedback about their bad behavior is an investment of your time, patience, and energy. It can be good feedback for a person to know that their statements or behavior are troublesome, because otherwise this person may not learn to change their ways. But you don't know how your feedback will be received, and you are not obligated to educate them. So if you are uncomfortable providing critical feedback, then excuse yourself and leave. You don't have to endure their presence or bad behavior out of politeness, but don't let their bad behavior spoil yours. Make a point to excuse yourself and observe proper behavior. You can say, "Excuse me," "Good bye," or "Okay then," and go.

5.9 Improving Your Skills

Social and conversational skills are acquired and learned. You are not born with them, and regardless of your proficiency, you can improve them through learning and practice. It's a lot of work to change the way we do things, but there are many benefits to becoming a better conversationalist, including meeting job requirements, being more comfortable in social situations, and having easier, more enjoyable communication with colleagues, family, and friends. Upgrading your sonic screwdriver of social skills is worth it, because any improvements you make have a wide application.

A key aspect of improving your conversational skills is practice. Lots of practice will allow you to take the theory learned here and in your studies elsewhere, and learn how to apply it. Fortunately, it's easy to find opportunities to practice conversation.

Start by taking time to notice and observe the people around you. Strengthen your ability to empathize, and try to imagine or guess what people are feeling.[9] Next, start smiling and making short, simple conversations with people that you regularly encounter, perhaps the coffee shop barista or someone on your commute. These low-stakes, short interactions also allow you to practice your exit strategy, which can be especially challenging. Your coworkers are another great set of people to practice with by doing things such as asking about their weekends or how their day is going.

Conversation is also about vulnerability and overcoming the fear of rejection. This can be addressed in two ways: (1) reducing your general fear of rejection by practicing rejection therapy, as discussed in Section 3.2; and (2) becoming a more capable conversationalist, thereby reducing the probability of rejection. If you don't think that you will be rejected, you won't fear rejection as much.

Any kind of public speaking is also a great way to practice your communication skills, which will enhance your conversational abilities. You can participate in groups such as Toastmasters International, which is an organization centered around becoming a better speaker.[10] Public speaking is also considered an important skill in many workplaces[11] and can be a lucrative career.[12] More on public speaking is discussed in Chapters 7–9.

You can optimize the signal-to-noise ratio of how you speak. Do you use filler words? In English, these include "um," "like," "really," "you know," and "actually," though most languages have some kind of filler words, including sign language.[13] Overuse of certain words puts literal noise into the signal of the message you are trying to convey. It's actually, like, really, um, distracting if there's like, you know, lots of filler words in your speech. Just as typos can distract from the point of a written piece of text, so too can these verbal tics and filler words distract from your spoken message. It is not necessary to completely eliminate those words from your vocabulary, but you should strive to avoid their overuse. You may also have a personal word that you use in excess that isn't one of the commonly used ones. It may be difficult to recognize this kind of noise in your speech, so asking friends or making a recording of yourself can help. Practice with a friend who can make a gesture (without interrupting) to indicate that you used one of these words. After that, you will have to rely on your self-awareness to note when you are using them. Slowing down the speed at which you speak can also help you to filter these tics out.

Imitation is a great way to practice and improve. Think of someone that you know with whom you enjoy conversing, and consider what it is that makes them enjoyable to interact with. Begin to imitate those behaviors. Likewise, think of individuals who exhibit behaviors that you find disagreeable, and make mental notes of those behaviors, endeavoring to avoid repeating them.

After interactions or social events, it can be useful to ask yourself, "What could I have done differently?" It is important (and difficult) not to dwell on errors and let anxiety take over, but it is valuable to recognize them and think about how things could be improved should you encounter a similar situation in the future. This can be considered data analysis, and you can use it to develop theories and new methods.

Exercises

(1)   Review this chapter and note some conversational applications that you want to get better at. Once you've done that, select one and then find ways that you can practice it. Perhaps you want to ask more questions. In your everyday interactions with friends and colleagues, make a point to think about asking questions. Keeping practicing until this ability improves.

(2)   Do this exercise only after you have spent some time working on Exercise 1 and have seen some improvement. Review this chapter again, and reassess the list you made in Exercise 1, then update it if necessary, depending on what has changed since you made it. Take your updated list and select a new application to practice.

(3)   Do this exercise only after you have spent some time working on Exercise 2, then repeat Exercise 2 until you feel more comfortable at each of the applications in this chapter that interest you.

(4)   Recall the Dunning–Kruger effect (see Section 1.5). Ask a trusted friend or colleague—ideally, someone whose conversational style and abilities you admire—to help you assess yourself and what you need to work on. Also, refer to any self-assessments you made in Chapter 3, Exercise 1, to see the overlap between your answers and the applications given here.

[Author's note: Self-improvement is a never-ending process. Embrace it and acknowledge all that you have accomplished so far. This is not an easy task.]

References

1. Katen, L., "Perfect Pitch: How to Nail Your Elevator Speech," *The Muse.* Retrieved from themuse.com/advice/perfect-pitch-how-to-nail-your-elevator-speech. Accessed on March 30, 2019.
2. McWeeny, K. H. et al., "Putting names to faces," *British Journal of Psychology* **78**(2) (1987).
3. Festini, S. B. et al., "Assigned value improves memory of proper name," *Memory* **21**(6) (2013).
4. Howard, D. J. et al., "What's in a name? A complimentary means of persuasion," *J. Consumer Research* **22**(2) (1995).
5. Carmody, D. P. and M. Lewis, "Brain activation when hearing one's own and others' names," *Brain Research* **1116**(1) (2006).
6. Minninger, J., *Total Recall: How to Boost Your Memory Power*, Rodale Press, Eastern, PA (1984).
7. Perugini, M. et al., "The personal norm of reciprocity," *European J. Personality* **17**(4) (2003).
8. Burger, J. M. et al., "The norm of reciprocity as an internalized social norm: Returning favors even when no one finds out," *Social Influence* **4**(1) (2009).
9. Alda, A., *If I Understood You, Would I Have This Look on My Face?* Random House, New York (2018).
10. Toastmasters International, toastmasters.org.

11. Santana, Y., "Why Is Public Speaking Important? 11 Solid Reasons Why Public Speaking Is Important In Your Life," *LinkedIn* (January 5, 2016). Retrieved from linkedin.com/pulse/why-public-speaking-important-11-solid-reasons-your-life-santana. Accessed on March 30, 2019.

12. The Oracles, "The Secrets to Becoming a High-Income Public Speaker," *Entrepreneur* (February 7, 2019). Retrieved from entrepreneur.com/article/327610. Accessed on March 30, 2019.

13. Inglis-Arkell, E., "Every language needs its, like, filler words," *i09 Gizmodo* (April 8, 2013). Retrieved from io9.gizmodo.com/every-language-needs-its-like-filler-words-466993943. Accessed on March 30, 2019.

Chapter 6
The Strength and Challenge of Diversity

"It's not the things you don't know that trip you up. It's the things you think you know, but you don't. You fail to ask a certain question because you believe you know the answer. Separating your information from your assumptions can be very tricky business."

~Claudia Gray (1970-), author, on the topic of research

6.1 Why Diversity Can Be Hard, or Your Brain Is Lazy

Research has shown that when you do something repeatedly, your brain creates habitual neural pathways that allow you to complete the task without paying much attention to it.[1,2] This is an evolutionarily adaptive tendency, because it allows you to think about newer, more interesting things while you complete a familiar task, but at the same time, it allows you to mechanically go through the motions without paying attention to what you are doing.[3] The more you do something, the more habitual it is and the better your brain gets at automating it, conserving processing power for other things.

This sort of neurological efficiency is also what tends to keep us doing familiar things instead of trying new ones. New activities are hard and require a lot more processing power than ones that are familiar, for which we have already built convenient and efficient neural pathways.[4,5] This can lead us to avoid things that are new or too unfamiliar. When it comes to diversity, we naturally gravitate towards people who seem familiar.[6,7] We already know them personally, they look like us, or they look like other people we know well. This tendency can lead us to spend networking events with our existing friends and colleagues rather than make connections with new people, and it is the enemy of both networking and diversity.

Developing your self-awareness and recognizing this tendency within yourself will help you choose when to avoid it and when to follow it. If you had a stressful day and only want to be in a familiar place with familiar people to comfort yourself, following the impulse towards familiarity is probably a good thing. However, if we repeatedly choose to spend time in spaces or with people that are already familiar, we miss opportunities to expand our network and grow in both our personal and professional lives. Just like science, we stagnate when we do not acquire new data and new experiences.

The uncertainty of not knowing how someone will respond to us contributes to the challenge and discomfort of meeting new people of another culture, gender, or company. Fortunately, the process of meeting new people becomes easier with practice, and once the neural pathways are formed, they remain. Just as practice can improve your empathy and conversational skills, practice meeting new and different people will make it easier. But you have to practice and repeatedly do something to make it habitual and form those neural pathways,[11] an investment that makes you more flexible and pays off for a long time.

One of the challenges that we face with respect to diversity is the subconscious assumptions that we make. Humans are very good at making snap decisions based on a very limited amount of information, something that has enabled our species to survive in life-and-death scenarios. This behavior (sometimes called "thin slicing") is a valuable skill, but it operates on subconscious assumptions and biases, which can wildly skew the results.[8] As scientists and engineers, we pride ourselves on being rational and logical, but it is only possible to be rational and logical when we make *conscious* decisions. One cannot be reflexive and rational simultaneously; unchosen and unexamined behaviors or responses are inherently irrational. With respect to diversity, many people do not operate in an intentional fashion and thus rely on subconscious assumptions and stereotypes.[9] People of different backgrounds, origins, and genders can experience the same environment differently because of how people interact with them. Confusion or disagreements may be caused by this assumption, so ask questions.

Our subconscious assumptions and biases are a potential problem because they are typically based on stereotypes that we have about people who are different than us, whether that is gender, age, culture, or country of origin. While we may consciously embrace the idea of diversity, it is possible for our words and actions to betray negative subconscious beliefs about others and to impact them negatively, even if only subtly. It is important for us to examine our words and actions, identify their origin, and make an effort to act consciously so that we can choose our course of action rather than react without thinking.

A common assumption is that everyone experiences the same things that we do. This is normal thinking, but it is often inaccurate[10] and can lead to misunderstandings and miscommunications. For example, one person may walk down a street and get chased by a dog, leading them to declare that they felt unsafe walking there. This might confuse another person who had a relaxing walk down the same street and did not encounter the dog. Unless they compare their experiences (the data they collected) and recognize the differences (dog versus no dog), they may misunderstand each other and never resolve why one person enjoys walking down that street and the other does not. This is a simplistic example, but it illustrates how the same things can be very different based on the person experiencing them.

Navigating diversity successfully requires us to consciously examine our behavior and its subconscious roots, and make intentional decisions about what we say and how we behave. This takes mental effort, self-awareness, and empathy, and it is not easy. But it is not only the right thing to do in order to treat other people fairly; it strengthens us as individuals, and it strengthens our communities. Being self-aware allows us to speak mindfully and intentionally so that we can mitigate the subconscious biases that we have, and our empathy allows us to gauge how we are doing. We all have biases[12] (assuming that you are human; if you are an alien or deity, it may not apply), but only some people do the work to become aware of it.

6.2 The Importance of Diversity

Diversity is strength. Just as networking is a problem-solving tool, so is diversity. If you imagine assembling a tool kit to do work in lab, you would not stock your toolbox with ten of the same tool. Neither would you want a homogeneous investment portfolio,[13] gene pool,[14,15] or ecosystem.[16] An individual who experiences a diverse range of emotions is a healthier person than someone who rejects other emotions in the dedicated pursuit of happiness.[17] Studies have shown that diversity in the workplace enables more productivity and creativity.[18] In short, diversity is almost always a good thing and benefits everyone.

In reference to networking, a lack of diversity will hinder your efforts. For example, if you only know people in your own sub-field, you are likely to miss interesting, multi-disciplinary solutions to your research problems. The broader and more diverse your network, the more multi-dimensional it is as a problem-solving tool, and the more it will help you to expand and grow as a scientist or engineer. To diversify your knowledge and create a strong network, you should meet and connect with people from various backgrounds, including but not limited to education, employer type, color, gender, ethnicity, and country of origin.

Author Anecdote

The benefit of a highly diverse network was impressed upon me by an experience I had that was totally unrelated to STEM or my research. I enjoy writing fiction, and I received a critique on a story that suggested I use the text-to-speech function to locate typographical errors. At the time, I was also preparing essays for fellowship applications. This advice turned out to be incredibly useful in finalizing my essays. If I hadn't been involved with networking via the critique website I was using, it would never have occurred to me to use the text-to-speech function to typo-check my fellowship applications.

Everyone has a different set of experiences, which makes diversity highly valuable for problem solving; diversity increases the collective intelligence of a group. Studies show that a group composed of high-IQ individuals who have the same profession, has a lower collective intelligence than a group of people who have a greater diversity of backgrounds.[19] No matter how smart the *individuals* are in a group, homogeneity reduces the measured group intelligence, but diversity increases it. Diversity matters *more* than individual intelligence when it comes to group settings.

A network's strength has more to do with its diversity than its size. Aim to incorporate people of different ages, backgrounds, specialties, and walks of life into your network. In addition to attending events relevant to your specialty, also attend events with subjects that are adjacent to your work to add diverse and relevant connections in your network. Allow for serendipity to strike and occasionally participate in events that seem far afield. Planning and strategy are important, but leaving a little space for randomness can be beneficial by giving you interesting connections and valuable lessons you might not otherwise encounter.

6.3 Cultural Differences

Science is a global community, and over the course of your career in STEM you will encounter people from many different backgrounds. This is a good thing, because diversity fosters creativity, but it requires caution with the assumptions that you hold when meeting someone new. Foremost in your mind should be that the way you do things in your culture may differ from the way someone from another culture does things. Assuming that you can always do things your way or that your way is the only correct one can lead to confusion or discomfort during cross-cultural interactions.

For example, different cultures have different standards when it comes to touching, such as shaking hands, and the amount of appropriate personal space.[20] In some cultures, any kind of physical contact between members of the opposite sex is inappropriate, whereas in other cultures kissing is the standard way to greet or bid farewell to someone regardless of gender. Therefore, when meeting people for the first time, be aware that their standard method of greeting could be different than yours, and respond in a way that keeps both of you comfortable. If the other person seems uncomfortable with your culturally appropriate greeting, change your approach and don't take it personally. In such situations, being observant and empathetic, as well as asking questions, will help you navigate these potentially tricky issues.

Author Anecdote
When I came to the end of the year that I lived in Japan, I wanted to hug people good-bye, which is typical of American culture. To my surprise, some of my Japanese friends refused to hug me—even members of my karate team who were willing to kick and punch me during practice! It wasn't because they didn't like me; it was because hugging is not a part of Japanese culture the way it is in the United States. What to me, an American, seemed perfectly normal was odd and uncomfortable to some of my Japanese friends. Should you ever find yourself in similar circumstances, accept refusal gracefully, do not push, and move on.

Cross-cultural interactions can benefit from advance preparation. If you know that you will be spending time with someone from another culture, or in another culture, do some research on cultural norms. If you are attending an event in a culture that is not your own, read up on etiquette in terms of social behavior and attire. You are likely to find a wealth of information with a simple web search. However, given the amount of erroneous information that exists on the internet, use this research as a rough guide; do not assume it is perfectly accurate. Even if the information is accurate, there are so many variations amongst people within cultures that it may not apply to the person with whom you are speaking. While it's important to do this kind of research, it is also important to rely on your empathy and ask questions. Observation and questions will help you get to know the person better, and to observe the Platinum Rule (introduced in Section 3.6), much better than any assumption.

When asking questions, recognize that a person may not always want to explain their culture to you. They may get these sorts of questions often or not want to be a spokesperson for their community, so if they change the subject, accept that and move on. You can always preface questions with statements such as, "If you don't mind me asking…," or "If you get this question too often, please ignore it, but I am curious about…," which indicates that you understand that they may not want to explain and gives the other party a chance to change to a different topic, if so desired.

Being a visitor in another culture also requires you to adapt to your audience in ways you may have never done before, and there is an important balance to be struck. On the one hand, adopting local customs will help you to communicate better with others and keep them comfortable, but there is an important distinction between doing something that is uncomfortable because it is new and forcing yourself to do something that is against your personal code. Recognizing the difference and honoring your personal beliefs when necessary requires both courage and self-awareness. But when it does not disturb your personal ethics or beliefs, pushing yourself get out of your comfort zone and try new things will allow you to connect more deeply with others and benefit you both personally and professionally.

As you speak and interact with people from different cultures, you may notice habits of speaking that are strange to you based on your own cultural context. For example, in American English it is common to ask, "How are you?" as a form of hello, without expecting or waiting for an answer. This can be considered as a "ritual question," where the literal meaning of the question is not the one intended. To those who have not encountered this particular ritual question before, it may seem rude to ask a question without wanting an answer. Alternatively, the question may seem invasive or overly familiar to other people. However, it is simply a ritualized way of saying "hello," and many cultures have these types of ritual greetings and questions. In China, "Have you eaten?" is used in a similar way,[21] as is "Where are you going?" in the Philippines.

When you encounter these kinds of statements for the first time, it may seem odd, but try to reserve judgment. Typically, these types of questions are not meant to be taken literally, and attempting to interpret these statements through our own cultural filters can result in erroneous translations of the gesture's original intent. In these cases, it is useful to stop and ask the meaning of the question and what sort of response, if any, is customary.

If someone you meet behaves in a way that strikes you as odd, especially in a professional or networking context, there are several possible explanations. It is possible that the person is being odd, even for their own cultural context. It is also possible that they have different culturally acceptable ways of doing things than you do. (It could be both.) Furthermore, scientists and engineers are often not average representatives of their own cultures. Either let the odd behavior pass or ask questions to understand it, so long as the questions do not cause discomfort.

Beware the tendency to call things that are unfamiliar "weird" or "strange." Simply because something is different doesn't mean it is wrong or bad. For many things, there is no one right way to do it. Ours is not the only way, so calling others' ways "weird" sounds derogatory and betrays a lack of familiarity with the other person's culture. Keep an open mind, ask questions, and try to understand the reason for the person's behavior.

6.3.1 Taboos

Taboos are topics of discussion or behaviors that are prohibited by social custom. Every culture has taboos; some are nearly universal, but many are not. This variation in taboos makes interacting in our global culture more complicated, as there is no fixed set of universal rules for what you should not talk about.

Taboo subjects tend to have strong emotions attached to them, and they are usually a subject about which a person is unlikely to change their mind. Thus, if you begin to speak on a taboo subject, and you do so with someone who has an opposing opinion, you may end up in a heated argument with neither side willing to budge. Not a recipe for a pleasant or successful networking exchange. If you want to hear someone's opinion on a taboo subject and are willing to ask questions and listen, you may avoid an argument, but if you broach a sensitive topic in an attempt to change someone's opinion, you are more likely to create an argument. Thus, it is best to avoid taboo topics with people you do not know well.

Part of the reason to avoid taboos and cursing during a conversation is as a demonstration of your good judgment. You may be speaking with someone who would not be offended by discussing these types of things, but by avoiding taboo topics under professional circumstances, you are demonstrating your restraint and good judgment. Even if you don't offend them, bringing up a taboo subject may give your conversational partner the impression that you do not know how to change your comportment to match your surroundings.

Topics that are commonly considered taboo include money, sex, politics, religion, questions about family or marital status, and commenting on a person's physique.[22,23] However, there are more taboos beyond this set, and in some places, not all of these will be considered taboo. When first meeting people or learning about a new culture, it is best to err on the side of caution. There are many interesting and professionally relevant things that you can discuss, and questions you can ask, that are not taboo, so there is rarely a good reason to bring up a potentially taboo subject. As you get to know someone better, you can broaden your topics of conversation to include taboo subjects, but that should be done with caution, if at all, and with the comfort of your conversational partner at the fore.

6.3.2 A brief note on American culture

The presence of this section is not intended to imply, in any way, the primacy or importance of American culture. American culture is simply the home culture of the author, who has spent time living and traveling in cultures outside of the United States, giving her a unique perspective on it. The purpose of this subsection is to explain or demystify some aspects of American behavior for a non-American audience. Of course, people from any given culture vary wildly, Americans included, so "your mileage may vary." These are intended to be useful generalizations, but they won't apply uniformly to every American you meet.

As a general rule, Americans tend to place a high premium on individuality and audacity, or the willingness to step outside of their comfort zones.[24] This may be speaking to your boss's boss, asking the question that everyone is afraid to ask, or "telling it like it is." Being audacious means taking some level of risk, and those who are willing to set aside their fears of rejection and make a bold move are considered to be brave, often leading to rewards, though not always (otherwise it wouldn't be a risk). Americans also tend to value independence.[25] They may imagine that they can "make it on their own," an attitude that can make it difficult for them to reach out when in need.

Participation is also something that the American school system values, and students can be penalized for not speaking and offering their opinions in the classroom.[26] This can make things challenging and difficult for introverted students or foreign students from less outspoken cultures, who would rather not speak in front of the group. This relates to the idealization of extraversion that is common in many Western countries, as discussed in Chapter 3.

6.4 Women, STEM, and Networking

Historically, women have been unwelcome in STEM fields and higher education,[27–29] and though numbers vary from country to country, women are consistently underrepresented in STEM fields worldwide.[30] While much has changed, many women today are regularly confronted with the attitude that STEM fields are the realm of men. This attitude is less explicit today than it used to be (in many places), but women still face bias, both conscious and subconscious, that makes it hard for them to advance their careers, receive pay equal to their male peers, and have their work and accomplishments recognized.[31] Negative subconscious bias against women is so culturally ingrained that both men and women are responsible for discriminating against women.[32]

With that in mind, regardless of your gender, pay attention to the kinds of assumptions you make about women. It is possible to consciously (rationally) welcome women in STEM fields and make subconscious (irrational) assumptions that are not welcoming. For example, have you ever met a woman at a professional networking event and assumed that she must be either an administrator or the spouse of a scientist or engineer at the event? While it might not be intentional, making a comment to that effect or saying, "You don't look like a scientist/engineer/etc." is unwelcoming, because it implies that women do not belong in those roles.

Also, make a point to examine the assumptions that you make about women and their relationships. Inquiries about a person's relationship status, whether they are male or female, are best avoided, because they can bring up painful issues (what if the person is recently divorced?) or feel invasive (what motivates your interest in their availability?). If you know that a woman is married, do not automatically assume that she changed her name to that of her spouse. If she has earned a doctorate, married, and kept her name, but you address her as Mrs. Smith instead of Dr. Singh, the implication is that her role is only relevant with respect to her spouse, not due to her work and merits. She may have chosen to change her name, in which case she should be addressed as Dr. Smith, and doing so is honoring her choice. A longer discussion on how to address others can be found in Section 5.3.

As to the subject of children, again, avoid assumptions. While you want to do this regardless of the gender of the person with whom you are speaking, women are often subjected to assumptions about children and caregiving. There are many subjects to discuss that are professionally relevant that have nothing to do with a woman's reproductive choices, so leave it up to her if she wants to discuss it. Just like relationship questions, reproductive questions can bring up strong emotions or feel invasive. Some people have physical or economic reasons preventing them from having children, some may have lost a spouse or a child, and some people don't want children, so it is important to remember that reproduction is not a foregone conclusion. If a person, regardless of their gender, wishes to talk about their children, let them bring the subject up; do not force it upon them.

Numerous studies show that women are interrupted more frequently than men.[33,34] Sometimes interrupting is necessary, but it is the verbal equivalent of shoving; it should be avoided unless there is a problem, because being interrupted is a frustrating experience, regardless of gender. Make a point to raise your awareness of how often and when you interrupt, and be especially attentive when interacting with women. Interrupting is about power and social dominance[35] more than it is an innately gendered issue, and the fact that women are interrupted more than men is largely due to cultural power imbalances.

Women are also often the recipients of unwanted sexual attention from men. If you are a man, as a rule, avoid making advances of a sexual nature towards women in professional networking situations. Stick to the topic at hand: career and research. Women often face discrimination and struggle to be taken seriously as scientists and engineers,[36,37] and if you flirt or make overtures to a woman in a professional environment, it does her disservice as a scientist or engineer.

As a woman, should you be the recipient of unwanted interest, it can be difficult to choose how to respond in a professional setting. In the interest of our professional network, people tend to avoid confrontation or making a scene, but you do not have to tolerate bad behavior. When faced with actions that make you uncomfortable, excuse yourself and leave. If you choose to address the behavior, do so in a way that maintains your safety. You can be direct and say, "No, thank you," or you can choose to be subtle. Behaviors such as reducing the amount of eye contact you make, turning away slightly, or increasing the physical distance are all subtle cues to indicate disinterest, which, ideally, your conversational partner will have the empathy to notice. You can also invite a third or fourth person into the conversation as a deterrent, and heavy use of formal titles such as "Sir," "Doctor," or "Professor" instead of a first name will help to clarify a lack of interest. See Section 5.8 for more strategies on dealing with bad behavior.

Unfortunately, sexual harassment of women in STEM fields is a pervasive and recurring problem, but as of this writing, there are a number of efforts to address it.[38] Codes of conduct have become common at many technical conferences, so do not be afraid to contact conference staff, get help, and report any individual who is making you uncomfortable. Organizers can and will intervene, even to the point of ejecting or banning transgressing attendees from events. If you are not a woman, it is important to recognize that part of the problem is the frequency with which women face bias and unwelcome behavior and that the daily burden of it can be discouraging. Do your best to be self-aware, empathetic, and examine your assumptions in order to be kind, conscious, and welcoming.

Being supportive of your female colleagues (regardless of your gender) is not just the kind thing to do; women are an important part of diversity. A study of S&P firms (the top 500 largest, publicly traded companies in the United States) showed that firms with women in top managerial positions are more successful.[39] And in general, studies show that gender diversity is good for fostering creativity.[40] However, inclusivity in STEM fields remains a struggle the world over, with many cultural and institutional biases against women making it hard to achieve gender equity. But a culture is the sum of many individuals, and if we use our self-awareness to recognize sexism in ourselves, subconscious or otherwise, regardless of our own gender, we can work towards eradicating these attitudes and achieving equity.

6.5 The Negative Effects of Stereotypes

Stereotypes are widely held, oversimplified images or ideas of a type of person or thing. They are useful in that they allow us to respond quickly by categorizing something or someone that we encounter. Our ability to "thin slice" and rapidly assess someone without conscious thought relies on stereotypes. Again, this is an adaptive behavior for life-and-death situations where the speed of your response will determine your survival. However, in a modern professional and networking context where life is not on the line, stereotypes—especially ones that we hold subconsciously—cause us to ignore individual differences and make mistaken assumptions about others, leading to miscommunications, discomfort, and possibly unfair treatment.[41]

Think about the following stereotypes that you may have encountered:

- Germans have no sense of humor.
- Women and Italians are too emotional.
- Asians are quiet and good at math.
- Millennials are entitled and unfocused.
- Middle-aged people are technologically inept.
- Overweight people are lazy.
- Americans are fat and loud.

These are examples of stereotypes propagated through culture and media, and even if we do not believe them consciously, they can influence how we treat others. Stereotypes, even when they are positive, box people in and fail to acknowledge a person's individuality. When you stereotype someone, you treat them like a demographic, not a person, which is unkind. This applies whether or not the person fits the stereotype. If they do fit the stereotype, you are effectively telling them that they are not special; personal choice has nothing to with it because that's "just how they are." If they do not match the stereotype, then you imply that they are abnormal or "doing it wrong." Worse, stereotyping is often subconscious, and therefore irrational, which requires self-awareness and analysis to recognize it.

After repeated exposure to a particular stereotype, confirmation bias can start to take effect, where we only notice experiences that confirm our existing beliefs and ignore contradictory experiences.[42,43] Confirmation bias is something that the scientific method helps us to avoid when we are doing experiments, but it is harder to notice and eradicate when interacting with people. As discussed in Chapter 3, self-awareness is key to becoming conscious of our stereotypes and biases so that we can avoid reinforcing them—an important step in embracing diversity and welcoming people who have historically been marginalized.

Another negative impact that stereotypes have is how they can shape people's expectations of others. People tend to react negatively when a person does not behave in a manner that fits their expectations, and expectations are often based on stereotypes. This effect is called "cognitive dissonance," meaning that the mental conflict created by reality not meeting expectation results in a negative emotional response and a rejection of the conflicting information, or the backfire effect.[44] For example, when a man is assertive, he is considered confident, but when a woman is assertive, she may be considered unlikeable or pushy. The man who behaves to stereotype by being assertive is often rewarded, and the woman who does not behave to stereotype (because being assertive is stereotyped as a male trait) is often punished.[45,46] This punishment for not conforming to stereotype is typically subtle and social, but the punishment enforces stereotypical behavior in the person who is "misbehaving."[47]

"Stereotype threat" is another issue, one that affects individuals who identify with the stereotyped group. It is the fear of performing in accordance with a negative stereotype about oneself, i.e., a fear of proving the stereotype correct.[48] The anxiety created by stereotype threat has been shown to reduce performance, creating a sort of self-fulfilling prophecy.[49]

Dismantling stereotypes will help to improve equity in many arenas. It is especially important for dominant-group members to examine how stereotypes about members of non-dominant groups affect their behavior. The dominant group can be defined as one that has historically been overrepresented in positions of power.[50] Group dominance is highly context dependent, differing from country to country, and even company to company, and it can be based on almost any characteristic, including gender, race, body type (height or weight), country of origin, or whatever else might constitute a majority in a particular environment. Because the dominant group by definition has more power, negative attitudes that the dominant group holds about non-dominant groups have an especially negative impact on members of the non-dominant group.

On the grand scale, stereotyping leads to inequity. On the individual scale, it prevents you from knowing and adapting to your audience. And adapting is one of the most important things you can do to be better understood and improve your networking.

6.6 Diversity and Sensitivity

Whether you are presenting to a large group or speaking one on one, adapting to your audience is key to effective communication, as discussed in Chapter 1. This means watching their reactions and adjusting your content, way of speaking, physical movements, and proximity in a way that allows you to be better understood. The more diverse your audience is, the more you need to pay attention and adapt in order to effectively convey your message and connect.

In terms of networking, there are two ways to consider diversity. First, as a scientist or engineer in our global community, you can expect to interact with a variety of people from different backgrounds, so be sensitive to how these differences inform your interactions. Second, a diverse network of connections is valuable, as it makes your network stronger and more useful for you and your connections. The stronger your network is, the greater your ability to help others.

The following subsections provide suggestions to consider when meeting and conversing with people of varying backgrounds. Beyond these suggestions, additional research and advance preparation can make interactions less daunting.

6.6.1 Appearance

When first meeting people, appearance plays a special role. How you present yourself gives the other person a lot of information about you before you even have a chance to say your name. But there are things about your appearance that you can control and other things that you cannot. Your height, skin tone, and to some extent your weight and your accent, are outside of your control. This applies to everyone, so avoid making assumptions about someone based on immutable aspects of their appearance.

Just like stereotyping, it is human nature to make snap judgements of other people based on their appearance.[51] For example, it has been shown that people have a subconscious bias about height, with male CEOs of companies being disproportionately tall, despite the fact that there is no empirical evidence that tall people make better leaders.[52] Likewise, people tend to associate sloth or a lack of moral fiber with people who are overweight, which is an unfair and unsubstantiated. Avoiding these sorts of erroneous assumptions will help you avoid social gaffes, treat other people more fairly, and allow you to get to know people better than you would have otherwise.

As a topic of conversation, only comment positively on aspects of the person's appearance that they can control. Things such as height, beauty, skin color, and weight are not things that a person chose for themselves, and if it is not something they can easily change, avoid commenting on it. Things that they can change relatively quickly, such as their attire, haircut, or accessories, are acceptable things to compliment, but do not criticize someone's appearance. If you are a man, complimenting a woman on her appearance beyond, "You look nice," or that you like a particular accessory she is wearing, is generally inadvisable, as women regularly get unwanted attention for their appearance, and you do not want to add to it and make them uncomfortable.

Even aspects of appearance that are mutable are somewhat fraught, as money and background play a role. Wealth, socioeconomic status, culture, and gender all play into what are considered acceptable or professional attire, accessories, and haircuts. Unfortunately, racism and sexism can result in different standards of appearance for different people, making it important that we scrutinize our subconscious assumptions about appearance. Wealth and socioeconomic status are discussed later in Subsection 6.6.9, but for now, remember that what a person wears in terms of flash, trends, and brand names, is far less important than things like their clothing being clean and and whether they are well groomed. Grooming is an important aspect of networking, and it was discussed in Section 4.5 in the context of in-person conversation.

Finally, don't make assumptions about where someone is from based on their appearance. Simply because someone may look Chinese *to you* doesn't mean they speak Chinese or are from China; they could have grown up in New Jersey or Mexico City! So if you ask where someone is from and are surprised, do not follow up by asking where they are "really from." This question is based on erroneous expectations about what a person *should* look like if they are from a certain place. Asking it implies that they don't belong or fit into the place they call home, and it sounds as though you are questioning their truthfulness.

6.6.2 Age

There is a lot to be learned from people younger and older than ourselves, but generational and age differences can make it feel difficult to relate across the gap. Generation-based behaviors are a common thing to poke fun at but should be avoided.[53] "Those entitled millennials" or the tired idiom "kids these days" will alienate a younger conversational partner. This principle also means that younger people should not make derisive statements about older generations, such as mocking them for being unable to adopt new technologies or considering older people as less relevant.

There is a lot to be learned on both sides of an age gap. A younger person may give you a fresh perspective on something that is already familiar to you, and an older person will probably have a much broader set of life and career experiences to share with you. If you are uncertain what to talk about, ask the person questions about their experiences of things you both may have done, such as graduate school and work. Discussing the ways that things that you both experienced have evolved over time can be interesting and fruitful, as you will find some similarities as well. Of course, some people would prefer to avoid the topic of age altogether, in which case you can focus on other subjects.

If you are the older person in the conversation, remember what it was like to be the younger person's age. Recognize that this young person has the potential to become the leadership of tomorrow, and they will remember if you were kind and helped them when they needed it the most. Taking time for people younger or less senior than you is a great way to help them at a point in their career when they are most needful. You never know what kinds of roles and responsibilities they will take on in the future, and how you might be able to shape or change that. Being a mentor can be very rewarding (see Section 7.4).

6.6.3 Religion

In many cases, it is not possible to identify a person's religious preferences by looking at them. Some religions prescribe certain modes of attire or grooming, such as wearing a hijab or yarmulke, but many do not have such identifiers; some followers don't observe these attire prescriptions; and some people do not practice religion. Religion is considered a taboo discussion topic in polite conversation, because it tends to be very personal with strong emotional elements and the improbability of changing one's views.

It is therefore generally best not to inquire about someone's religion or make statements about religious groups to which you do not belong. Doing so risks discomfiting or offending your conversational partner. If they bring up the subject of their own religion and you feel comfortable talking about your beliefs, then it is probably okay to ask them further questions on the subject. Always be careful to ask questions, watch your assumptions, and avoid making generalizations.

If religion is an important part of your life or the life of someone who is a close connection, it can be good to discuss it to get to know them better, so long as you are trying to improve your mutual understanding, not for the purpose of changing the other person's mind. Debating religion and religious views can lead to healthy and interesting conversation, but it falls far outside the professional networking context and should generally be avoided under such circumstances.

6.6.4 Politics

Political affiliation is another issue of diversity that is largely impossible to know based on someone's appearance, unless they are holding a sign at a protest. Like religion, it tends to be very personal, emotional, and entrenched, and is therefore also a taboo conversation topic in many cultures. It is a good policy not to make negative statements about political groups or affiliations, as you risk offending or discomfiting your conversational partner; even if the person agrees with you, it demonstrates questionable judgment.

If your conversational partner mentions their politics, they are signaling a willingness to discuss the subject. If you want to reciprocate in a respectful, calm fashion, focus on asking questions and understanding their perspective rather than engaging in debate. Overall, politics can be a thorny issue, and it is the safer course of action to avoid the subject entirely unless it is relevant to your business purpose.

6.6.5 Sexual orientation

Sexual orientation specifies the gender (or genders) to which a person is sexually attracted, including but not limited to heterosexual (opposite-sex attraction), homosexual (same-sex attraction), and bisexual (attraction to more than one gender). The majority of people are heterosexual, though the survey and reporting of non-heterosexual identity has its challenges due to social pressure.[54] The acronym LGBTQ (Lesbian, Gay, Bisexual, Transgender, and Queer), is used to refer to the community of people who are not heterosexual and cisgender (more on gender and cisgender in the next section). Sometimes the acronym is written as LGBTQ+ or LGBTQIA to include other demographics, such as people who are intersex or asexual, people who do not identify with either male or female gender, and more.[55]

Sexual orientation is an especially tricky subject, because in our global community there are many places where it is unsafe to be openly part of the LGBTQ community; some have laws against homosexuality. And like politics and religion, it is not something that you can identify visually.

In a professional setting, sexual orientation will rarely be discussed, because the subject of sex is taboo. However, it is important to not assume that everyone you meet is heterosexual and to refrain from making disparaging commentary or using offensive slang regarding the LGBTQ community. Disparaging any group or demographic is unkind, and you risk offending or discomfiting your conversational partner whether or not they are a member of that group, and it exhibits poor judgment.

As with politics and religion, do not begin asking questions about a person's sexual orientation unless they first volunteer information on the subject. If they do bring it up and you choose to ask questions, watch your assumptions and keep your tone positive, focusing on understanding them better. And if they change the subject, accept that and move on even if you did not get the answers you wanted.

6.6.6 Gender

When the subject of gender arises, many people generally think of men and women. This is called the "gender binary;" however, there are many aspects to gender that fall outside the traditional binary.[56] Modern biology has shown that gender is more of a spectrum than a binary, with many variations.[57,58]

An important concept relating to gender is that of *cisgender* and *transgender*. Most people are cisgender, which means that the person's gender identity is matched with the sex they were assigned at birth. People who are transgender have a gender identity that does not match the sex they were assigned at birth.[59] A trans woman is a person who identifies as a woman but whose assigned sex is male, whereas a trans man is a person who identifies as a man but whose assigned sex is female. And beyond cis and trans, there are people who are intersex, meaning that their bodies exhibit aspects of both male and females sexes; people who are gender fluid, i.e., their gender identity may be dynamic; and people who are non-binary or genderqueer, who do not identify as either a man or a woman.

If you are cisgender and heterosexual, you are in the majority and may not feel a lot of motivation to understand the complexities of gender outside the binary. This relates to the discussion on neurological pathways and habits in Section 6.1, about how learning and adapting to new information takes effort and processing power. However, being misgendered (having their gender mis-identified by others) is a common experience for trans people and those with non-binary gender identities, and it can be very disheartening. As discussed in Chapter 4, your job as a good conversationalist is to keep your partner comfortable, and to do that you must use the pronouns (he/him, she/her, they/them, etc.) that they want or ask you to use. If you are unsure what gender a person is, do not ask, "Are you a man or a woman?" or worse, "What are you?" (human, the answer to that question is always *human*, and perhaps *affronted*), but do ask, "What pronouns do you prefer?"

While things such as accent and skin tone are aspects of a person's appearance that they cannot control, much of gender presentation is a matter of choice (within limits related to wealth and socioeconomic status; see Subsection 6.6.9). The way a person styles their hair and the clothes they wear, as well as any make-up or accessories (or lack thereof), can indicate gender.

As always, strive to treat a person as an individual and not a demographic, so if someone has non-traditional gender presentation, ask them about their preferred pronouns. If you are in a group, ask for everyone's preferences to avoid singling anyone out. If it is not possible to inquire about pronoun preferences, use the pronoun that seems consistent with their gender presentation or use the non-gendered, singular pronouns they/them. Putting pronouns on nametags can make this easier and is valuable for cis people as well, because it makes it more comfortable for trans and non-binary people to do so.

For more information on gender, gender identity, and appropriate transgender terminology, refer to the Planned Parenthood article, "Gender and Gender Indentity"[60] and the GLAAD Media reference guide on transgender terms.[61]

As a final consideration for gender, avoid stereotyping members of a different gender. Don't assume that they are interested in certain topics that are "male" or "female" simply because they are a man or a woman, or that they would not be interested in things that you do not associate with their gender. Historically, STEM fields were considered the realm of men, but not all men are interested in a career in STEM, and many women are. The more assumptions you make, the fewer questions you will ask and the less you will learn about your conversational partner.

6.6.7 Disabilities

As you network, you will encounter people who have disabilities such as blindness, reduced hearing, and physical or neurological differences. There is, and has been, a lot of stigma and confusion concerning people with disabilities,[62] and discrimination against such people is referred to as ableism.[63] This prejudice can cause people to avoid interacting with those with disabilities and thus miss engaging exchanges and fruitful networking connections. When interacting with a person with a disability, do not use the word "normal" to refer to people who do not have disabilities or imply that people with disabilities should be pitied. Because a disability is a part of someone that they cannot change, much like the immutable aspects of a person's appearance, it is best not to make it a subject of conversation.

As with any difference, there are ways to adapt your communication style to make conversation easier and more enjoyable for both of you. If you are speaking with a blind person, you will not receive any information via eye contact, so pay more attention to body language and tone of voice. Imagine that you are talking on a phone and adapt your behavior accordingly.

When speaking with a person who is hard of hearing, the techniques described in Section 5.7 regarding non-native speakers can help. Face the person so that they can see your mouth and understand better if they can read lips. Looking at someone while you speak also increases the volume at which they hear you versus when you look away. Do not mumble; adjust your volume; and maintain eye contact.

If someone is a wheelchair user and you expect to converse with them for more than a few moments, sit down so that they do not have to look up at you. Treat their chair as an extension of their personal space, and do not invade their space by touching or moving it. Don't assume that people who use a wheelchair are not intelligent or interesting people, or that they have an intellectual disability.

Author Anecdote

A friend of mine injured her foot on the way to a conference and spent the event in a wheelchair with her foot in a cast. She noticed that many people spoke to her more loudly and slowly than before. It surprised her to discover that many people assumed that she couldn't understand them because she was using a wheelchair. This is an illustration of the subconscious stereotypes many hold.

If you are interacting with someone who has a speech impediment, such as a stutter, it may become more noticeable if they are nervous, e.g., during social events and in-person networking. Don't mention it or complete their sentences.

You may also encounter people who are neurodivergent, including but not limited to Attention Deficit Hyperactivity Disorder (ADHD) and autism. These conditions can make it more challenging to interact or converse in certain social settings. If someone you meet avoids eye contact or fidgets, remember that it may not have to do with you but with their neurological state. Be patient and ask questions if you are not sure what is happening. People with autism often have trouble noticing nonverbal social cues, so questions or clarifying statements help.

This is a brief and simplified overview of a complex topic, and you are encouraged to educate yourself further on the subject. Some suggested reading on disabilities can be found in the article, "The best books on disability recommended by Tom Shakespeare."[64]

Regardless of your conversational partner's type of disability, use your empathy: note if the person seems uncomfortable and adapt your behavior to make them more comfortable. As with all forms of diversity, carefully examine yourself and your behavior, and avoid subconscious actions or assumptions that may be unproductive.

6.6.8 Industry, academia, and government

This is a difference that is more superficial, because the person chose where to apply for their job, but it is an important aspect to notice in a professional context. Someone who works for a company that sells a product is going to have different pressures and goals than someone who is a professor at a university where publishing journal articles and writing grants is the priority. Having someone be part of your network means knowing them professionally and understanding their goals, accomplishments, and motivations; the sector in which they work has a significant impact on that.

Because employment is largely a conscious choice, it makes for a good topic for conversations at professional networking events. Asking people what they like about their job and discovering their concerns and projects will generally be welcome.

6.6.9 Wealth and socioeconomic status

A person's wealth and socioeconomic status can have a large effect on how they present and express themselves. There are ways of speaking and dressing that we associate with different status levels, and it is important to be aware of these associations. It is unfair and unkind to judge people who we perceive to be from backgrounds of lesser means or a lower educational level.

Many of these ideas may be subconscious and require self-examination to note. For example, a strong southern United States accent is often stereotyped as belonging to people with lower income or lesser intelligence, which is an unkind and unsubstantiated assumption that judges a person by the sound of their words as opposed to their content. However, people's behavior can be subconsciously influenced by such negative stereotypes, which is why self-awareness is important for recognizing such biases.

People who are wealthier also have more disposable income to spend on their appearance, whereas people of lesser means may not be able to update their wardrobes, haircuts, or accessories as frequently, or present themselves as fashionably. This puts wealthier people at an advantage when making first impressions. While it is human instinct to judge appearances, do your best to evaluate a person based on substance rather than how trendy or expensive their clothes appear, because wealth is not equitably distributed, and many interesting and incredibly talented people come from backgrounds of lesser means.

This is only a brief sampling of some significant topics relating to diversity; it is by no means perfect or all inclusive. The goal of these sections is to help you consider ways in which people may differ from you, and how you can adapt your approach to interacting with them to enable better communication and more effective, sustainable networking. Ideally, this subject should be an ongoing topic of learning and growth.

6.7 The Culture of Science and Engineering

No matter a person's walk of life or history, as human beings we have far more in common than not. Don't shy away from getting to know people who are different than you. They can teach you a lot, and as scientists and engineers, we have a large repository of knowledge and shared life experiences to discuss. A conversation is as much about finding common ground as it is about learning, and so speaking with any and everyone, no matter their appearance, can be incredibly rewarding.

When you are networking professionally with other scientists and engineers, they will be able to relate to you on subjects that other people cannot. This includes topics such as your area of study, the nature of laboratory work, modeling and analysis, data collection, publications and technical presentations, and likely a desire to explore and understand the nature of the universe. It gives you a huge pool of potential conversational subjects and ways to connect and learn.

As humans, and as scientists and engineers, our variations and permutations make life more interesting and enable us to solve bigger problems than we could if we were a homogenous group. Diversity is strength—it makes things interesting, and it helps us to grow.

Exercises

(1)   Consider your existing network. In what ways is it diverse? In what ways does it lack diversity? Make a list based on the examples given above. Analyze the notes you just made to identify a pattern of certain types of people who are not represented in your network. Is it because there are not many of those types of people in your company or school? Or are those people present, but you haven't connected with any of them? If so, use your self-awareness and ask yourself why.

(2)   Look for opportunities to diversify your network and take small actions to do so. Find a local networking or social event to attend, join a LinkedIn or Facebook group, or find a volunteering opportunity where you can meet people who are different from you or who are not currently well represented in your network.

(3) Imagine a scientist or engineer who is very different than you, in one or many of the ways discussed above. What might you also have in common? What are good topics of conversation, or questions you might ask this person, to get to know them better? Write them down. This exercise will help you have appropriate things to say when you meet people who are different from you.

References

1. O'Hare, J. K. et al., "Pathway-specific striatal substrates for habitual behavior," *Neuron*, 89, **3**, 472-479 (2016).

2. Comaford, C., "The Truth About How Your Brain Gets Smarter," Forbes (November 7, 2014). Retrieved from forbes.com/sites/christinecomaford/ 2014/11/07/the-truth-about-how-your-brain-gets-smarter. Accessed on April 1, 2019.

3. Duhigg, C., *The Power of Habit: Why We Do What We Do in Life and Business*, Random House, New York (2012).

4. Sadtler, Patrick T., et al., "Neural constraints on learning," *Nature*, **512**, 7515 (2014).

5. "Flexing the brain: Why learning tasks can be difficult," *Press Release: Carnegie Mellon University* (August 27, 2014). Retrieved from eurekalert.org/pub_releases/2014-08/cmu-ftb082014.php. Accessed on April 1, 2019.

6. Peskin, M. and F. N. Newell, "Familiarity breeds attraction: Effects of exposure on the attractiveness of typical and distinctive faces," *Perception* **33**(2) (2004).

7. Ward, D., "The Familiarity Principle of Attraction," *Psychology Today* (February 10, 2013). Retrieved from psychologytoday.com/us/blog/sense-and-sensitivity/201302/the-familiarity-principle-attraction. Accessed on April 1, 2017.

8. Bengtsson, S. L. et al., "Extensive piano practicing has regionally specific effects on white matter development," *Nature Neuroscience* **8**(9) (2005).

9. Gladwell, M., *Blink: The Power of Thinking without Thinking*, Little, Brown, and Company, New York (2005).

10. Hinton, P., "Implicit stereotypes and the predictive brain: cognition and culture in "biased" person perception," *Palgrave Communications* 3, 17086 (2017).

11. Ross, L. et al., "The "false consensus effect": An egocentric bias in social perception and attribution processes," *J. Experimental Social Psychology* **13**(3) (1977).

12. Paul, A. M., "Where Bias Begins: The Truth About Stereotypes," *Psychology Today* (First published May 1, 1998, last reviewed on June 9, 2016). Retrieved from psychologytoday.com/us/articles/199805/where-bias-begins-the-truth-about-stereotypes. Accessed on April 1, 2019.

13. Lioudis, N. K., "The Importance of Diversification," *Investopedia* (March 29, 2019). Retrieved from investopedia.com/investing/importance-diversification. Accessed on April 1, 2019.

14. Frankham, R. et al., *Introduction to conservation genetics*, Cambridge University Press, Cambridge (2002).

15. Joshi, P. K., et al. "Directional dominance on stature and cognition in diverse human populations," *Nature* **523**, 7561 (2015).

16. Cleland, E. E., "Biodiversity and Ecosystem Stability," *Nature Education Knowledge* **3**(10) (2011). Retrieved from nature.com/scitable/knowledge/library/biodiversity-and-ecosystem-stability-17059965. Accessed on April 1, 2019.

17. Quoidbach, J. et al., "Emodiversity and the emotional ecosystem," *J. Experimental Psychology: General* **143**(6) (2014).

18. Grillo, G., "Diverse workforces are more innovative," The Guardian (March 27, 2014). Retrieved from theguardian.com/media-network/media-network-blog/2014/mar/27/diversity-innovation-startups-fortune-500-companies. Accessed April 1, 2019.

19. Hong, L. and S. E. Page, "Groups of diverse problem solvers can outperform groups of high-ability problem solvers," *Proc. National Academy of Sciences* **101**(46) (2004).

20. Sorokowska, A. et al., "Preferred interpersonal distances: A global comparison," *J. Cross-Cultural Psychology* **48**(4) (2017).

21. Wang, J., "Why do Chinese people always ask 'Have you eaten?'" TutorMing Mandarin Learning Tips Blog (September 1, 2016). Retrieved from blog.tutorming.com/mandarin-chinese-learning-tips/why-do-chinese- people-ask-have-you-eaten. Accessed on April 1, 2019.

22. Samovar, L. A. et al., *Communication between Cultures*, Nelson Education, Toronto (2015).

23. Batista, A., "The Things You Should Never Talk About," *Elite Daily* (August 27, 2012). Retrieved from elitedaily.com/life/culture/talk. Accessed on April 1, 2019.

24. "Key American Values," *International Student and Scholar Services University of Missouri-St. Louis* (July 17, 2013). Retrieved from umsl.edu/~intelstu/Admitted%20Students/Visitor%20Handbook/keyvalues.html. Accessed on April 1, 2019.

25. "'So you're an American?' A Guide to Answering Difficult Questions Abroad," U.S. Department of State. Retrieved from state.gov/m/fsi/tc/answeringdifficultquestions/assets/m/resources/DifficultQuestions-AmericanValues.pdf. Accessed on April 1, 2019.

26. Miller, B. M., "Teaching - Should Class Participation Be Graded?" *Perspectives on History* **47**(8), 33 (2009).

27. Schiebinger, L., "Women in science: historical perspectives," *Women at Work: A Meeting on the Status of Women in Astronomy* (1993). Retrieved from stsci.edu/stsci/meetings/WiA/schieb.pdf. Accessed on April 1, 2019.

28. "Lise Meitner (1878 - 1968)," *Atomic Archive* (2015). Retrieved from atomicarchive.com/Bios/Meitner.shtml. Accessed on April 1, 2019.

29. Lewis, J. J., "A Brief History of Women in Higher Education," ThoughtCo (March 25, 2019). Retrieved from thoughtco.com/history-women-higher-ed-4129738. Accessed on April 1, 2019.

30. "Women in Science," *UNESCO Institute for Statistics*, Fact Sheet No. 51, FS/2018/SCI/51 (June 2018). Retrieved from uis.unesco.org/sites/default/files/documents/fs51-women-in-science-2018-en.pdf. Accessed on April 1, 2019.

31. Williams, J. C., "The 5 Biases Pushing Women Out of STEM," *Harvard Business Review* (March 24, 2015). Retrieved from hbr.org/2015/03/the-5-biases-pushing-women-out-of-stem. Accessed on April 1, 2019.

32. Reuben, E. et al., "How stereotypes impair women's careers in science," *Proc. National Academy of Sciences* **111**(12) (2014).

33. Kennedy, C. W. and C. Camden, "Interruptions and nonverbal gender differences," *J. Nonverbal Behavior* **8**(2) (1983).

34. Hancock, A. B. and B. A. Rubin, "Influence of communication partner's gender on language," *J. Language and Social Psychology* **34**(1) (2015).

35. Farley, S. D., "Attaining status at the expense of likeability: pilfering power through conversational interruption," *J. Nonverbal Behavior* **32**(4) (2008).

36. Wenneras, C. and A. Wold, "Nepotism and sexism in peer-review," *Nature* **387**, 6631 (1997).

37. Funk, C. and K. Parker, "Women and Men in STEM Often at Odds Over Workplace Equity," *Pew Research Center, Social & Demographic Trends* (January 9, 2018). Retrieved from pewsocialtrends.org/2018/01/09/women-and-men-in-stem-often-at-odds-over-workplace-equity. Accessed on April 2, 2019.

38. Hill, C., "Why So Few? Women in Science, Technology, Engineering, and Mathematics," *American Association of University Women (AAUW)* (2010). Retrieved from aauw.org/research/why-so-few. Accessed on April 2, 2019.

39. Dezsö, C. L. and D. G. Ross, "Does female representation in top management improve firm performance? A panel data investigation," *Strategic Management Journal* **33**(9) (2012).

40. "Innovation, Creativity and the Gender Gap," *World Intellectual Property Organization (WIPO)* (2018). Retrieved from wipo.int/ip-outreach/en/ipday/2018/innovation_creativity_gender_gap.html. Accessed on April 2, 2019.

41. Zhang, S. and D. Deng, "Stereotypes Communication," *International Education Studies* **2**(4) (2009).

42. Nickerson, R. S., "Confirmation bias: A ubiquitous phenomenon in many guises," *Rev. General Psychology* **2**(2) (1998).

43. Moskowitz, G. B. and D. Carter, "Confirmation bias and the stereotype of the black athlete," *Psychology of Sport and Exercise* **36** (2018).

44. Shermer, M., "How to Convince Someone When Facts Fail," *Scientific American* (January 1, 2017). Retrieved from scientificamerican.com/ article/how-to-convince-someone-when-facts-fail. Accessed on April 2, 2019.

45. Brescoll, V. L., and E. L. Uhlmann, "Can an angry woman get ahead? Status conferral, gender, and expression of emotion in the workplace," *Psychological Science* **19**(3), 268–275 (2008).

46. "Infographic: The Double-Bind Dilemma for Women in Leadership," *Catalyst,* New York (August 2, 2018).

47. Jhangiani, R. and H. Tarry, "Influencing and Conforming: Person, Gender, and Cultural Differences in Conformity," Chapter 6 in *Principles of Social Psychology*, 1st International Edition, The B.C. Open Textbook Project (2014). Retrieved from opentextbc.ca/socialpsychology/chapter/ person-gender-and-cultural-differences-in-conformity.

48. "Stereotype Threat," *National Institutes of Health (NIH)* (June 30, 2017). Retrieved from diversity.nih.gov/sociocultural-factors/stereotype-threat. Accessed April 2, 2019.

49. "Stereotype Threat Widens Achievement Gap," *American Psychological Association* (July 15, 2006). Retrieved from apa.org/research/action/ stereotype. Accessed April 2, 2019.

50. Dandy, J. and R. Pe-Pua, "Attitudes to multiculturalism, immigration and cultural diversity: Comparison of dominant and non-dominant groups in three Australian states," *International J. Intercultural Relations* **34**(1) (2010).

51. Willis, J. and A. Todorov, "First impressions: Making up your mind after a 100-ms exposure to a face," *Psychological Science* **17**(7) (2006).

52. Kaul, V., "The necktie syndrome: Why CEOs tend to be significantly taller than the average male," *The Economic Times* (September 30, 2011). Retrieved from economictimes.indiatimes.com/the-necktie-syndrome-why-ceos-tend-to-be-significantly-taller-than-the-average-male/ articleshow/10178115.cms. Accessed April 2, 2019.

53. Chamberlin, J., "Overgeneralizing the generations," *Monitor on Psychology, American Psychological Association* **41**(6) (2009).

54. Coffman, K. B. et al., "The size of the LGBT population and the magnitude of antigay sentiment are substantially underestimated," *Management Science* **63**(10) (2016).

55. Gold, M., "The ABCs of L.G.B.T.Q.I.A.+," *New York Times* (June 21, 2018). Retrieved from nytimes.com/2018/06/21/style/lgbtq-gender-language.html. Accessed on April 2, 2019.

56. Blair, K. L., "Has Gender Always Been Binary?" *Psychology Today* (September 16, 2018). Retrieved from psychologytoday.com/us/blog/inclusive-insight/201809/has-gender-always-been-binary. Accessed on April 2, 2019.

57. Ainsworth, C., "Sex redefined," *Nature News Feature* (February 18, 2015). Retrieved from https://www.nature.com/news/sex-redefined-1.16943#/spectrum. Accessed on July 23, 2019.

58. "Gender and Genetics," *World Health Organization Genomic Resource Centre* (2019). Retrieved from www.who.int/genomics/gender/en/index1.html. Accessed July 23, 2019.

59. Mayo Clinic Staff, "Transgender Facts," *Mayo Clinic* (September 1, 2017). Retrieved from mayoclinic.org/healthy-lifestyle/adult-health/in-depth/transgender-facts/art-20266812. Accessed on April 2, 2019.

60. "Gender and Gender Identity," *Planned Parenthood* (2019). Retrieved from plannedparenthood.org/learn/sexual-orientation-gender/gender-gender-identity. Accessed on July 23, 2019.

61. "Glossary of Terms - Transgender" GLAAD Media Reference Guide - Transgender. Retrieved from glaad.org/reference/transgender. Accessed on July 23, 2019.

62. Buljevac, M. et al., "The stigma of disability: Croatian experiences." *Disability and Rehabilitation* **34**(9) (2012).

63. Smith, L., "#Ableism," *Center for Disability Rights*. Retrieved from cdrnys.org/blog/uncategorized/ableism. Accessed on July 23, 2019.

64. "The best books on Disability recommended by Tom Shakespeare," *Five Books* (2019). Retrieved from https://fivebooks.com/best-books/tom-shakespeare-on-disability. Accessed on July 23, 2019.

Chapter 7
Networking Activities for Anywhere

"It's a dangerous business, Frodo, going out your door. You step onto the road, and if you don't keep your feet, there's no knowing where you might be swept off to."

~Gandalf,
The Lord of the Rings (1954), by J. R. R. Tolkien

7.1 Networking Opportunities Abound

Now that we have discussed a lot of theory and skills relating to networking, it is time to discuss applications, activities, and venues. Networking is an activity that we tend to envision happening at certain times, such as at conferences or events labeled "networking." Those are valuable opportunities, but networking can occur almost anywhere. The activities described here can be practiced in your company, town, online, at conferences, while traveling, and beyond. They are introduced here are concepts in a general sense, with specific applications discussed in the chapters on local networking (Chapter 8), conferences (Chapter 9), and online and digital networking (Chapters 10 and 11).

7.2 Volunteering

Volunteering is one of the best possible opportunities for sustainable networking. It is about generating mutual success, which is what makes it such a powerful tool. Volunteering your time and energy benefits the organization that you are helping, and the event or activity you are volunteering for is typically designed to benefit a particular community. Time spent volunteering is also rewarding on a personal level,[1] as you get the satisfaction of helping your community, and you will typically learn new skills in the process.

It also creates great opportunities to meet people. Working side-by-side with like-minded people on something that you all care about can create a strong contact or bond. Interactions that involve a shared struggle or accomplishment of a common goal have been shown to create trust and bonding,[2,3] and volunteering can generate this type of interaction. For some volunteering engagements, you will have direct contact with the community and get to meet people that way. You will also have contact with the organizing staff, and if you are helpful and reliable, they

115

will remember you and probably contact you for additional volunteering opportunities, generating Opportunity Momentum (introduced in the Preface and discussed in Chapter 2).

Many organizations and events look for volunteers, so as you search for opportunities, whether they are close to home, at a conference, or online, look for organizations whose goals and interests align with yours. When you find such an organization, look for any volunteering-related information on their website, and look for events that they are hosting in your area or any conferences they hold. Even if they don't explicitly advertise a need for volunteers, contact the organization, introduce yourself with an appropriately tailored elevator pitch, say that you want to get involved, and ask about volunteering opportunities.

Some volunteering opportunities will be available to you as a new attendee or member (entry-level roles), but others will only become available once you have established yourself as reliable. Higher-level volunteering roles will generally have a greater time commitment and more responsibility, but they can be prestigious or involve leadership positions, which is why they require established trust. They can include being an event organizer or helping with administrative aspects of the organization, such as committee membership or serving on the board of directors. Committee and board membership are amazing sustainable networking opportunities, because as you dedicate your time and energy to serve the organization better, you take on a decision-making role that puts you in touch with other decision makers, and it gives you greater visibility within your community.

The types of volunteering opportunities offered by an organization will depend on its goal, size, structure, and location. Events and conferences will have a variety of in-person roles (see Subsection 9.8.2); for example, serving on the the welcoming committee allows you to meet and assist many other attendees. In addition to in-person events, many organizations will have remote opportunities, such as being a journal reviewer, writing articles or blog posts, and moderating or facilitating discussion in online forums.

When searching for volunteering opportunities, don't be afraid to try something new. Everyone is new when they first get started, and doing new things will teach you skills, make you more adaptable, and stimulate your mind.[4-6] Volunteering can be rewarding professionally and personally, and venturing into unexplored territory will diversify your network and create both personal and professional growth.

7.3 Meetings with Colleagues

Whether you are in your hometown or traveling for leisure, work, or a conference, you can create networking opportunities by making meetings and appointments with colleagues. You can have something specific you want to accomplish, but you don't need to have a defined agenda to set up a meeting. At a minimum, the goal of your meeting should be to get an update on your contact's current situation so that you can assess ways that you might be able to help them, and to share your relevant progress with them as well. Meetings can be done in person in your hometown, such as over coffee, in your company break room with a coworker, at conferences, or remotely via phone or video call.

To cross-pollinate your network and offer new connections to your existing contacts, you can arrange meetings and gatherings with multiple people who you think will blend well and be interested in meeting each other. This gives you a chance to maintain your existing relationships and help others expand their networks. It can be an informal social event, based on pairings or groupings of people that you think will enjoy each other's company, or it can be a more formal professional event where you introduce colleagues based on their common work and professional interests. It can save time (e.g., at a conference), because instead of having separate meetings, you can meet multiple people at one event, potentially with the sum being greater than its parts. See Sections 7.9 and 7.10 for more details.

7.4 Mentors and Mentees

The mentor–mentee relationship is a special and valuable networking relationship. Finding a mentor within your university or company can be a great help for your career and professional development. A mentor can advise you on things you need to know, including ways to advance your career and be a better, more productive employee, which also benefits your company. Acting as a mentor is an excellent way to give back to your network, and teaching others is the best way to cement and deepen your understanding of the information that you already possess. And when a mentee matures in their career and becomes successful with your assistance, they can and likely will offer assistance in return.

A mentor–mentee relationship should follow the same rules of equitable exchange, authenticity, and sustainability as other networking relationships. Mentees should seek ways to help their mentors, even as they also seek career guidance. Mentors will look to help people who they think have promise and for whom their guidance will make an impact; they want to see their advice applied and their mentees succeed. And a big way that a mentor can help their mentee is by providing access to their more expansive and developed network. A mentor wants a committed, hardworking mentee, because they will be vouching for their mentee and putting their reputation behind the endorsement.

Like other networking partnerships, mentor–mentee relationships are not exclusive. You can have multiple mentors or mentees at any given time, and it is especially useful if you are pursuing multiple specialties or interests. Diversity in your mentor–mentee relationships is good for the same reason a diverse network is good: it exposes you to new information and ideas.

When considering mentoring, reflect on the importance of diversity and our subconscious behaviors. It has been shown that effective feedback improves performance, because the recipient is given the opportunity to strengthen their weaknesses.[7,8] Feedback offered by a mentor can make a big difference in a person's career and job satisfaction.[9] However, as humans we naturally gravitate towards relationships, including mentoring relationships, with people who feel familiar, which can make it especially challenging for underrepresented groups to find mentors,[10] but mentoring has been shown to be especially important for those same underrepresented groups.[11] Women and minorities are most likely to say that mentoring has been "extremely important" in their career development.[10]

This issue is compounded by our discomfort with giving critical feedback. For most, giving critical feedback is difficult, but it is especially uncomfortable to give to people whose response we are less able to predict. This feeling produces a strong aversion to giving feedback to people who are unfamiliar.[12] For example, a white male manager will be less likely to give critical feedback to an employee who is female or a person of color, as opposed to another white male, which gives a subtle but powerful advantage to workers who are demographically similar to their bosses, given how important critical feedback is for advancement. If we can overcome our subconscious tendency to gravitate towards the familiar and mentor not only those who look like us but also those that don't, we will improve the diversity of our STEM community and make it stronger.

As a mentee, you can help your mentor in the same ways you help other networking connections: by connecting them with others in your network, circulating their work on social media or LinkedIn, notifying them of articles or awards that are relevant to them, and otherwise assisting them in their endeavors. In turn, you should implement their advice and follow up to let them know the outcome. Do your best to learn their communication style so you can fully absorb what they are telling you and potentially recognize advice that may not be explicit.

To find a mentor or mentee, you can either go through formal mentoring programs, or you can invite someone you know to be a mentee or ask if they would consider being your mentor. How your mentoring relationship functions will depend on the guidelines given by the matching program, if you used one, and the tastes and preferences of the people involved. At the beginning, you should discuss what the mentee is hoping to accomplish through the relationship, what types of subjects you will cover, types of requests that are acceptable, how often you will speak or write, and what mediums you will use to communicate. It is also important to observe the principle of equitable exchange, so that the mentee can know what is going on in the mentor's professional life, such that they can offer relevant assistance as possible. Mentoring relationships have been shown to be more productive when a solid relationship based on mutual understanding exists between mentor and mentee.[13]

Being specific and concrete with goals and requests can help define a mentoring relationship. The more specific and tangible an offer or request for help is, the more likely it is to be accepted or given. For example, a vague offer of, "Let me know if you need anything" is much less likely to get a response than, "I can help you go over your resume." As a mentee, think about specific questions and goals to discuss with your mentor, as well as thoughts about the format and frequency of your meetings. There is a vast amount of advice on mentoring available online, so spend some time researching the subject and then consider who in your network could be a good mentor (or mentee).

Note that it is possible to be both a mentor and a mentee at the same time. No matter where you are in your career, there are always going to be people more and less advanced than you; filling one role can help you to perform the other.

7.5 Applying for Awards and Scholarships

In addition to the honor and excitement of winning an award or getting the support of a scholarship, applying for these kinds of honors is a great form of networking. Whether you are chosen for the honor or not, the selection committee gets to see your name and information, bringing you to the attention of decision makers. If you are selected, the public announcement and receipt of the honor affirms your abilities, benefits your reputation, and raises your visibility. It also offers people a chance to contact you and congratulate you—a valuable form of passive networking. Winning an award also makes it easier to win more awards later (Opportunity Momentum). And when someone you know wins an award, that is a great moment to send them a message to connect or reconnect.

There are various awards to apply for, offered by numerous organizations. As you research awards, consider what is offered by your current organization or company, the college or university you attend or attended, and any professional societies to which you belong. In addition to annual awards, many societies also have Senior and Fellow member status to which you must be nominated as an honor. There are awards for research and innovation, small business, teaching, outreach, presentations, community service, and more. Competitions—such as *The Flame Challenge*,[14] where you explain a complex scientific subject to an 11-year-old audience, and *Dance Your Ph.D.*,[15] where you explain your dissertation in dance form—offer interesting communication challenges for scientists and engineers. Share relevant awards with your colleagues, mentees, or mentors. And if someone involved in the award, or a mentor, suggests that you apply for something, do it. They probably either think you have a high likelihood of success or they know something that you don't that is in your favor.

The process of writing an application for an award or scholarship is valuable practice in communication. It is like an extended elevator pitch, where you are required to assess your abilities and accomplishments, and showcase them in a persuasive manner. The more prestigious the award is, the longer the application process is likely to be. Be strategic with your time and how much you should commit to an application, and don't pour too much of your time into a low-level award. It is a good idea to contact the spokesperson for the award with questions and make sure that you are targeting the content of your application appropriately.

If you cannot nominate yourself for an applicable award, then you can ask a friend or colleague to do so. If you need letters of recommendation for your application, make sure to supply your recommenders with as many relevant details as possible, such as your current CV, drafts of the other materials you are planning to submit, details received from asking the award spokesperson questions, and the deadline and letter submission method. In the U.S., it is common for the applicant to furnish their recommender with a draft recommendation letter, covering the relevant details for the award. The recommender can then modify and personalize the letter.

Requests for nominations and recommendations should be made as early as possible, and make sure to send timely reminders. Then always follow up with your recommenders to send them thanks and let them know the results. For something like a recommendation letter, a written thank-you note in the mail is culturally appropriate in the United States.

If you win the award, it's not just a line on your CV. You can and should share it via your online accounts, through member and alumni networks, and any other applicable venues. Do so with gratitude. For example, you can make a post on LinkedIn stating that you are grateful to have won the award, thanking your recommenders, the selection committee, the organization sponsoring the award, and any other relevant actors. It's good publicity for everyone involved, and it's excellent networking. If there's an awards ceremony, attend it, give a speech if applicable, and offer your thanks in person.

Finally, for any award you do not win, ask the spokesperson if the committee had any feedback on your application, so that you can improve subsequent applications. Also, do not be afraid to apply for the same award multiple years in a row. Sometimes multiple deserving candidates apply in the same year, and not getting it is a matter of who else applied, as opposed to your application being lacking.

7.6 Writing

Written publications allow you to share a useful message or information with others, which is a benefit to the community, and it brings you to the attention of others in a positive light, making it an excellent sustainable networking activity. A written document has longevity, allowing others to find your message long after it has been published, which is why it is one of the best forms of passive networking. This allows people to see your message and contact you without additional effort on your part. It also helps with Opportunity Momentum, as you may be contacted with more writing opportunities because of a particular piece, well after it was published.

If you are interested in writing, you can produce content for technical journals, trade journals, popular science periodicals, membership periodicals, alumni magazines, news outlets, and blogs (including creating your own blog). The venue you choose will depend on your goals and the type of writing that interests you.

At first, to find opportunities to write, you will need to look over the website of the publication and find their submission guidelines. You may need to contact the publisher and pitch them your story, or in the case of peer-reviewed journals, you will need to write your paper according to house guidelines before submitting it. If you already have another publication of similar type, your pitch can reference or share it to boost your credibility as a writer. You can also aim to publish a few articles or papers in lower-profile publications to start and, like higher-level volunteering opportunities, gradually build up to higher-profile publications. [This last point does not apply to peer-reviewed technical journals, where it is the impact of your research, not your writing history, that will determine your paper's acceptance.]

7.7 Public Speaking

Public speaking, like volunteering, is a premium sustainable networking activity, the primary goal of which is to share something that will benefit the community. Delivering a presentation or speech requires you to exercise your communication skills, including planning and conveying a clear, audience-appropriate message, and you will get better at it the more you do it. Public speaking brings you to the attention of others in a positive way, which benefits your career and network, and results in future speaking opportunities.

However, there are several barriers of entry to public speaking. Most people find public speaking to be an unpleasant, anxiety-inducing enterprise, which has roots in our fear of ostracism and the historical need to collaborate to protect ourselves against predators.[16] The next barrier is finding venues for speaking. As a person in STEM, conferences are likely to be one of your most accessible public speaking opportunities, as it is a part of STEM culture to present your research in such a forum. This puts you in front of an audience of your peers, so any resulting network connections will be relevant to your work. There are also opportunities to speak at workshops, through society visiting-lecturer programs, and programs such as Pint of Science and Nerd Nite (discussed further in Chapter 8). Opportunity Momentum applies to speaking engagements as well, so the more public speaking you do, the more such opportunities will present themselves to you.

Author Anecdote

I have improved my public speaking and communication skills by taking related workshops at conferences. Dr. Jean-luc Doumont of Principiae[17] has been very influential for me and regularly works with SPIE, including offering online courses that are available for free with SPIE membership.[18] Communications specialist Christine E. Haas[19] also regularly works with SPIE, and I have found her instruction very helpful. Whether you take an in-person workshop, an online course, or read a book, study followed by application will help you acquire the skills you need to become a public speaker.

Then there is what might be considered the epitome of terrifying public-speaking experiences: stand-up comedy. Even if you are not interested in a career in comedy, standing in front of an audience and trying to make them laugh is great practice for learning to be comfortable on stage and in front of a microphone. Many places allow people to sign up for an open-mic night and get five minutes on stage. While it is an adrenaline-inducing experience, it is a low-stakes endeavor. If you do poorly (which is not rare in amateur comedy), you have only bored people for five minutes in setting unrelated to your career. You should try to be amusing without being offensive, but if you don't make people laugh, you can try again.

Although improvisational comedy is more performance art than public speaking, joining an improv troupe is another way to improve your communications skills and develop comfort in front of an audience (as introduced in Subsection 3.4.1).

7.8 Sharing STEM with Non-specialists

As a scientist or engineer, you will occasionally find yourself in a situation where you want to share your work with someone who has limited knowledge of STEM fields. This may occur in a casual, personal environment or at a networking event; you may even seek it out, as in science policy and advocacy events where you could be speaking with policy makers. Being prepared to explain and discuss complex technical subjects with a non-STEM audience is important for you and your career, because not everyone with whom you network (even those in decision-making roles) has a technical background.

When speaking about a technical subject with a non-technical person, you don't need to them everything; you only need to tell them enough to make them interested. You may be tempted to explain it so that they can fully understand the subject, but if you do so, you risk overwhelming them. People tend to say "no" when they don't understand something, so communicating in a clear and understandable fashion is incredibly important. Accordingly, don't spend a lot of time on details or caveats. Talking in too much detail is referred to as "getting into the weeds" in American English, and it is tempting because that is where scientists and engineers spend most of their time working: on the details. However, you will lose a non-technical audience in the weeds, so get to the main message right away.

Emotion makes things memorable, so getting people excited about your message will help them remember it,[20] e.g., sharing information in the form of a story with personal or emotional context. Lectures can be boring and hard to remember, because they often answer questions that have not been asked (by the audience). Presenting information in a way that causes your audience to ask themselves the questions that you are going to answer draws them in and avoids boredom to a great extent. According to Aristotle, dramatic action occurs when a hero tries to achieve something of great personal importance but has to overcome obstacles.[21] Creating a sense of drama by introducing an obstacle can keep a non-technical audience attentive and make the message more memorable, because we as humans tend to identify with someone who has to struggle to achieve a goal.

Here again, adapting to your audience is key. Much of communication depends on the listener already knowing something about what the presenter or storyteller is saying, which means knowing your audience and their background knowledge. What the audience already understands is the foundation upon which the rest of the communication is built. Whether it is a presentation you are preparing for a large group or a one-on-one conversation, you should think about what knowledge your audience (probably) already has and use that to guide your word choice, examples, and comparisons. Jargon should be limited and *conscious*; it can make communication efficient when everyone involved understands it, but it is a major barrier to communication if someone doesn't. Moreover, it can be hard to drop the habit of using jargon all the time if you do it subconsciously, so begin to pay attention to how and when you use it, and practice using it in an audience-dependent fashion.

A significant issue that scientists and engineers encounter when addressing a general audience is "the curse of knowledge." Studies on this effect have shown that knowledge can be a detriment to communication,[22] because when you have deep knowledge of a subject, you often can't remember what it was like to acquire that information or to be without it, which makes it hard to relate to an audience that doesn't possess that knowledge. If you can't relate to your audience or imagine how they think, adaptation becomes difficult. But empathy, observation, asking questions, and practice can help you to combat the curse of knowledge.

7.9 Organizing and Hosting

Organizing and hosting events is a great way to do sustainable networking. You gain organization skills, meet people, and provide a valuable service to participants. It allows you to create the type of networking opportunity that you want but doesn't already exist or isn't accessible to you.

Creating your own networking opportunities takes more work than participating in those created by others, but as the architect of an event, you get to choose the theme, subject matter, venue, who gets invited, and the format. It gives you an amazing amount of parameter space to play around in. Your event can be small or large scale, formal or informal, focused on the latest developments in your STEM area or simply on socializing and community. The event can be in a reserved space in a formal venue or hosted at your home. You don't have to be the sole organizer; you can ask other people to collaborate with you.

Communication with guests in and around an event can help you create a successful event and make improvements in the future. Depending on the style of the event, especially if it's more formal, it is a good idea to let guests know who else is on the guest list. Ryan Paugh and Scott Gerber, the authors of *Superconnector*, use the app Groupme to create a group message thread that allows guests to interact before the event (a Facebook event or Whatsapp group would serve the same purpose; see Chapter 11). Continue the communication after your event by following up with people to thank them for attending and get feedback. Incorporate their suggestions for your next event.

It is a big paradigm shift to begin thinking about how to craft networking events not just for yourself but for others as well. Organizing and hosting is something that you can do at any stage of your career, including as a student. It will result in many valuable experiences and networking opportunities, and it is an excellent way to serve your community and help your local network connections to succeed.

7.10 Community Building

Community building is an extension of organizing and hosting but on a larger scale. It is about finding and meeting a need in your community. This can often start with organizing and hosting small events, either in person or online, and from there it can grow into a larger community of people and even expand to other locations. There are numerous examples of large organizations and communities that started small and grew because they met a greater need. The women's professional network Ellevate, formerly 85 Broads, started as a network for alumnae of Goldman Sachs, created by one such alumna.[23] The non-profit TED, which shares ideas about technology, entertainment, and design, was originally a small, invitation-only event.[24]

The events and the community that you want to create can be in-person, online, or both. Like individual networking relationships, a symbiosis of both real-world and online activity can help a community to flourish. An online space associated with the event makes it easier for people to follow up with each other and allows them to continue interacting between events. As will be discussed in Section 11.1, the online space that you use for your activities should be tailored to the type of event or community you are building, in terms of content and formality level.

Community building takes work, but it is also one of the best ways to network sustainably. It has all the benefits of volunteering, and the same freedom of vision as hosting, but at a larger scale with commensurate learning and expansion of your skill set and network. You don't need to aim to start a company or a large community, but recognizing ways in which your smaller event can expand gives it the potential to become something big. If what you want doesn't exist yet, build it yourself, and do not be afraid to think big.

7.11 Accidental Encounters

Any time you leave the house, unless you live in true isolation, it is possible for you to meet people and to network. You might encounter someone you already know, or you may converse with a stranger. These people can bring new and valuable ideas and to your awareness. Traveling to new places or conferences is a great way to invite these new ideas into your life.

A study at MIT showed that productivity and innovation are positively correlated with population growth.[25] Other studies have shown that novelty (often generated by accidental encounters), creativity, and the neurotransmitter dopamine are interrelated, with creativity and dopamine also being positively correlated,[26] and novelty seeking being positively correlated with dopamine, as well.[27] Additionally, openness to new experiences is a strong indicator for scientific success and achievement.[28] The book *Heart, Smarts, Guts, and Luck* qualifies certain people as "luck dominant" and notes that 86% of such people attributed this to being open to new experiences.[29] It follows that being open to new experiences, novelty, and serendipity can benefit you through inspiration and diverse network connections. Getting outside of your comfort zone, or what is familiar, causes growth.

To some extent, you can engineer serendipitous encounters by where you go. You can meet people anywhere, but if you have a goal in mind, you can find clubs, events, and businesses that attract the kinds of people who you want to meet and who share a common interest with you. Public transit and airplanes are great places to meet people, but remember to respect other people's time and space.

Looking for statistically probable coincidences can also pay off. For example, if you are traveling to a conference and notice another attendee on your flight or when you arrive at your destination, you can introduce yourself and offer to split a cab. Also, take advantage of accidentally running into people you recognize from other professional events by saying hello and introducing yourself. But do so in a brief and gracious fashion; don't attempt to monopolize them for very long. This can be particularly fruitful if it is an otherwise important person whose attention is ordinarily hard to attract (more on interacting with celebrities in Section 9.7).

7.12 Following Up

Following up is an essential aspect of networking, and it is something that should be done no matter the networking activity. It can transform an interaction, such as an accidental encounter, into networking when it would not have been otherwise. Because sustainable networking is about building reciprocal, beneficial relationships based upon a mutual understanding of needs, the follow-up is a crucial and necessary step. Meeting someone once is not enough to add them to your network—you need to have multiple contacts with a person to establish a relationship. Following up with someone after meeting them is the first indicator that you intend to stay in touch and are serious about building a relationship.

While a follow-up after a first-time encounter is especially important, follow-ups become no less important once you have an established relationship with someone. Letting someone know it was nice to see them again is good practice, but follow-ups can also be used to recap meetings and highlight action items if you are working on a project together. A follow-up can document the material you covered in case you need to refer to it later.

Follow-ups are typically performed electronically after an in-person meeting, but not necessarily. They can be a phone call after an initial electronic exchange, a text after a phone call, or a handwritten note after a meeting. The typical modern follow-up would be an email after an in-person interaction, whether it was the first, third, or hundredth time you have spoken.

As you prepare to send an initial follow-up, look to see if the person has Twitter, LinkedIn, or other social media, and follow them if you like their content (more on these platforms in Chapter 11). What platform or medium you use to perform a follow-up presents the issue of adapting to your audience. When you meet someone, you can ask if they prefer email, LinkedIn, or a phone call as a follow-up. If you don't know their preference, take your best guess, and if you don't hear back, try a different medium. See Chapter 10 for more on composing follow-up messages and what medium to use.

If you have been given an offer of time, advice, or assistance by someone who is advanced in their career, in a position of power, or otherwise important, *do not fail to follow up*. This is an incredibly valuable opportunity that you should seize immediately.

The timing of follow-ups is a matter of strategy and preference. If it is someone important or whom you only met briefly, you want to do everything you can to ensure that they remember you, then the sooner the better. A follow-up the next day is ideal, but do not wait more than a week; otherwise, you may fade in their memory. If you failed to send a follow-up in a timely fashion, it is still okay to do so later; if someone remembers you after several months and replies, then you know you made a good initial impression. However, you risk people forgetting or ignoring you if you take a long time. More on the timing of message is discussed in Section 12.6 in reference to cold emails.

Exercises

(1)   Think about your professional relationships and whether any of them qualify as a mentor–mentee relationship, formal or otherwise.

(2)   If you have such a relationship already, whether you are the mentor or mentee, take a moment to reassess ways in which you can help them in their professional life, and make a point to do so. You may need to review their professional information or ask them questions, but it is important to find ways to be kind and helpful to this person.

(3)   If you do not have such a person, think of who in your school, company, or network is in a position to be a mentor for you or who could benefit from your mentorship. Once you have identified ways in which you can be helpful, set up a meeting with them. You do not need to make it formal; in fact, it is probably better to arrange an initial informational interview (more on this in Section 10.5) to see how you two get along before mentioning the idea of mentoring.

(4)   Research awards for which you are eligible within your school, company, professional societies, local organizations, and beyond. Apply for something. Even if you don't get it, the process of researching and applying are good learning opportunities, and if you do get it, then you have won an award!

(5)   If you enjoy writing, or the idea of public speaking intrigues you, start thinking about what kind of message or content you could offer and to what audience. Do you have technical information to share with a STEM audience? Professional development information to share with a student audience? Interesting science to share with a general audience? Once you have an idea for your message, you can find suggestions for how to pursue it in Chapter 8.

(6)   Because it is an important skill that you will likely have to exercise at various points in your career, find opportunities to practice explaining your work to people who are not in STEM. Your family, and your friends outside of work, are good candidates and can give you feedback. Consider volunteering and doing outreach or science advocacy in order to practice this skill and apply it towards bettering your community.

(7)   If you enjoy hosting and organizing events, think about starting a dinner club, happy hour, lecture series, or similar event. You can start with friends and colleagues who share a similar interest and hold small events until you get comfortable before expanding to include more people.

(8)   Think of ways that you can change your routine and engineer serendipitous encounters with others and add novelty, whether that is walking a different way to or from work, joining a new activity group, shopping in a new grocery store, or any other way that you can expose yourself to new people and environments.

References

1.   Thoits, P. A. et al., "Volunteer Work and Well-Being." *J. Health and Social Behavior* **42**(2) (2001).

2.   Bastian, B. et al., "Pain as social glue: Shared pain increases cooperation," *Psychological Science* **25**(11) (2014).

3.   Wolf, W. et al., "Joint attention, shared goals, and social bonding," *British J. Psychology* **107**(2) (2016).

4.   Schweizer, T. S., "The psychology of novelty-seeking, creativity and innovation: neurocognitive aspects within a work-psychological perspective," *Creativity and Innovation Management* **15**(2) (2006).

5.   Bunzeck, N. and E. Düzel, "Absolute coding of stimulus novelty in the human substantia nigra/VTA," *Neuron* **51**(3) (2006).

6.   Tierney, J., "What's New? Exuberance for Novelty Has Benefits," *New York Times* (February 13, 2012). Retrieved from nytimes.com/2012/02/14/science/novelty-seeking-neophilia-can-be-a-predictor-of-well-being.html. Accessed on April 2, 2019.

7.   De Stobbeleir, K. et al., "Self-regulation of creativity at work: The role of feedback-seeking behavior in creative performance," *Academy of Management Journal* **54**(4) (2011).

8.   "Performance Management, Performance Management Cycle," *United States Office of Personnel Management*. Retrieved from opm.gov/policy-data-oversight/performance-management/performance-management-cycle/monitoring/feedback-is-critical-to-improving-performance. Accessed on March 27, 2019

9.   Smith, B. L., "The lifelong benefits of mentoring," *gradPSYCH American Psychological Association* **12**(4) (November 2014). Retrieved from apa.org/gradpsych/2014/11/mentoring-benefits. Accessed on March 27, 2019.

10. Emrich, C. et al., "Creating a Culture of Mentorship," Heidrick & Struggles (December 27, 2017). Retrieved from heidrick.com/ Knowledge-Center/Publication/Creating_a_culture_of_mentorship. Accessed on March 27, 2019.

11. Thomas, D. A., "The truth about mentoring minorities. Race matters." *Harvard Business Review* **79**(4) (2001).

12. Liswood, L. A., *The Loudest Duck: Moving beyond Diversity while Embracing Differences to Achieve Success at Work*, John Wiley & Sons, Hoboken, New Jersey (2009).

13. Mincemoyer, C. C. and J. S. Thomson, "Establishing effective mentoring relationships for individual and organizational success," *J. Extension* **36**(2) (1998).

14. "The Flame Challenge: Explaining Science to an 11-year-old," *The Alan Alda Center for Communicating Science.* Retrieved from aldacenter.org/outreach/flame-challenge. Accessed on March 28, 2019.

15. "Dance your Ph.D.," *Science by AAAS.* Retrieved from sciencemag.org/projects/dance-your-phd. Accessed March 28, 2019.

16. Croston, G., "The Thing We Fear More Than Death," *Psychology Today* (November 29, 2012). Retrieved from psychologytoday.com/us/blog/the-real-story-risk/201211/the-thing-we-fear-more-death. Accessed on March 28, 2019.

17. *Principiae: Structuring Thoughts,* principiae.be.

18. Doumont, J.-L., "Making the most of Your Presentation" *SPIE Online Short Course.* Retrieved from spie.org/education/courses/coursedetail/ WS897?f=Online. Accessed March 28, 2019.

19. *Christine Haas Consulting*, christinehaasconsulting.com.

20. Buchanan, T. W. and W. R. Lovallo, "Enhanced memory for emotional material following stress-level cortisol treatment in humans," *Psychoneuroendocrinology* **26**(3) (2001).

21. Aristotle, *The Poetics.* Retrieved from classics.mit.edu/Aristotle/poetics.1.1.html. Accessed March 28, 2019.

22. Heath, C. and D. Heath, "The Curse of Knowledge," *Harvard Business Review* (December 2006). Retrieved from hbr.org/2006/12/the-curse-of-knowledge. Accessed on March 28, 2019.

23. "Welcome to Ellevate, the leading network for professional women," *Ellevate.* Retrieved from ellevatenetwork.com/about. Accessed on March 28, 2019.

24. "History of TED," *TED.* Retrieved from ted.com/about/our-organization/history-of-ted. Accessed on March 28, 2019.

25. Pan, W. et al., "Urban characteristics attributable to density-driven tie formation," *Nature Communications* **4** (2013). [doi: 10.1038/ ncomms2961]

26. Zabelina, D. L. et al., "Dopamine and the creative mind: individual differences in creativity are predicted by interactions between dopamine genes DAT and COMT," *PloS one* **11**(1) (2016).

27. Costa, V. D. et al., "Dopamine modulates novelty seeking behavior during decision making," *Behavioral Neuroscience* **128**(5) (2014).

28. Kaufman, S. B., "How to Cultivate Your Creativity [Book Excerpt]," Scientific American Mind (January 1, 2016). Retrieved from scientificamerican.com/article/how-to-cultivate-your-creativity-book-excerpt. Accessed on March 28, 2019.

29. Tjan, A. K. et al., *Heart, Smarts, Guts, and Luck: What It Takes to Be an Entrepreneur and Build a Great Business*, Harvard Business Press, Cambridge, Massachusetts (2012).

Chapter 8
Networking Locally

"There's no place like home."

~Dorothy (played by Judy Garland),
The Wizard of Oz (1939)

8.1 In Your Own Backyard

Procrastination is a common human inclination,[1,2] and without a deadline or scarcity to force us to action, we tend to put things off.[3] There are likely many interesting tourist destinations in your hometown that you have either never visited or did so only with a visitor. In a similar vein, we tend to ignore or neglect networking events in our own backyard, but this is a mistake!

Many networking events, venues, and activities exist close to home. This chapter lists various opportunities that are probably available to you every day through work or your local community. Such a long list may seem overwhelming, so remember to focus on consistency rather than intensity. Find a networking opportunity on this list that fits your goals and preferences, whether small or large, and make participating in it a habit. Effective and sustainable networking does not require a huge time commitment, but a consistent or regular commitment will make your networking strategy fruitful and effective. Regularly doing a networking activity in your local community will benefit everyone involved.

8.2 Your Workplace

One of your most important sources of networking opportunities is where you currently work or study. It is your most available networking area, one that provides opportunities daily. Don't neglect networking where you are right now because you can put it off until tomorrow. Developing relationships with your colleagues will not only make your work life more enjoyable but also improve your job performance. No one works with complete independence. If you know about the skills, talents, and interests of those around you, when you hit a roadblock with a project, need an extra pair of hands, or want to brainstorm ideas, you will know who to turn to for assistance. And your projects and company will benefit as a result.

People in your company will be more motivated to help you than those outside of it, because supporting you means supporting the success of the company and employees such as themselves. Remember the principles of sustainable networking, and make yourself available to help your coworkers equitably. Things are a little different with close, longer-term relationships such as work colleagues, because you have more opportunities to respond in kind for assistance rendered. Regardless, seek out ways that you can offer help even when not asked.

The equal exchange of information is important for this kind of networking. In addition to knowing your co-workers' interests and strengths, make sure they know yours, too, including your ongoing projects. If your colleagues and your boss have a clear picture of your interests, skills, and talents, they are more likely to include you in new, relevant projects. Networking within your company is also a great way to generate new ideas for projects and find areas where your company can improve. If you develop rapport vertically with management, as well as laterally with your peers, it will be easier to share those ideas and get them implemented.

Begin networking or expand your existing networking efforts by having more conversations with your colleagues and boss/supervisor. A water cooler or break room is one of the best places to develop rapport with your colleagues, because so long as you do not speak for long, you are not interrupting their work (because they are already taking a break) and they will be more receptive to conversing. These so-called "water cooler" moments encourage the sort of informal collaboration that will help you address your work challenges.[4,5] You can also stop by other people's offices, but be observant and use your empathy to ascertain if the other party has time to talk. During your conversation, watch their body language to assess when they are ready to get back to work; as a general rule, keep these conversations brief.

If you consider the extent of your company, unless it is very small, there are likely to be people whom you don't know but see regularly; you might not know what they do. In addition to networking with your immediate co-workers, get to know these others who are outside of your direct area. If you are a scientist or engineer, get to know your fellow scientists and engineers, but also the administrative staff, the business development staff, facilities staff, and the management. The same applies if you are in a university: whether you are a student, a post-doc, faculty, or staff, get to know the people in the other demographics.

This network expansion can be done gradually. If you take small steps, such as checking in with two people you already know and introducing yourself to one new person each week, over time you will accrue a lot of information. This is another instance where taking notes is useful, either in a notebook or spreadsheet, to help you remember details about the people you meet.

It is also helpful to attend social events hosted by your organization. Holiday parties or happy hours are important ways to get to know co-workers and build your relationships with them. You may even build some enduring friendships that continue long after you have changed jobs. However, if the events demand too much of your time, and you are already well acquainted with the colleagues who attend, don't feel compelled to attend each one. Instead, maintain consistent but less frequent attendance, in accordance with your schedule.

Your office holiday party is a great opportunity to get to know your co-workers and management better, and to celebrate and acknowledge their successes. If it is an event where spouses and family members are invited to attend, introduce yourself and be welcoming. Spouses may feel uncomfortable because they don't know many people, especially if they do not work in the same field as their spouse. Being welcoming is a kindness that will make them feel better. On the flipside, if you make a negative impression by being cold or unfriendly, it will get back to their spouse, who may be a boss or upper management. It's not just good manners to be kind and inclusive; it can affect your job and job prospects.

Even though it is a party, it is still a business function. Your behavior there can have an impact on your job. It is a great opportunity to get to know your colleagues better, but mind your manners and don't overindulge if alcohol is served (a special note on food and alcohol can be found in Subsection 9.5.4).

Depending on the size of your organization or university, there may be clubs, chapters of professional organizations, associations, or diversity and professional development groups, all of which provide networking opportunities. This is especially true at universities, where student groups and clubs proliferate. Explore which of these options match your interests and goals to find one or more to attend as your schedule allows. Even if you are busy, don't skip this—instead, attend regularly with low frequency. Consistently showing up to the same event, even if it is not often, will still make you familiar[6] and open up network connections and friendships.

As discussed in Section 7.9, creating or hosting your own event is an excellent way to create social and networking opportunities within your workplace. For example, you can organize a journal club, a running group, a happy hour, or a monthly event where people summarize their current work projects. Depending on the space you want to use and the level of formality of your workspace, you may need to get permission and make reservations to hold an event on your company's or university's property.

Some companies create organized volunteering opportunities within the community. Participating in this way is a great sustainable networking opportunity that benefits the local community and your company, and allows you to learn new skills and engage with your co-workers. It is easier to sign up for this kind of volunteering opportunity than it is to seek out your own, because someone else is organizing it, so it requires less upfront investment of your time.

The connections and friendships that you develop with your classmates or colleagues will remain an important part of your network even after you graduate or change jobs. It is easiest to create enduring connections when you are in close proximity to people. You have the most opportunities and the fewest logistical challenges to get to know them. Not developing those relationships is like ignoring your company's offer to match your retirement contributions; don't leave these opportunities on the table.

8.2.1 For remote workers and telecommuters

Being physically removed from your co-workers presents different challenges to networking within your work "place." If possible, go to your office in person at regular intervals, be strategic with your visits, and optimize the face-to-face interaction that you get when you are there. Create a routine so that people know when to expect you to be in the office, and observe the principles described above about getting to know your co-workers and management. Try to participate in office social events, parties, and volunteering opportunities. Also, not being in the office every day doesn't preclude you from being an organizer.

When you are not in the office, or if you are a completely remote employee, telephone and video calls will be an important substitute for face-to-face interaction. You can still build relationships with your colleagues, but it will take regular maintenance and intentional effort. Chapter 10 describes helpful strategies for maintaining your network with digital and online methods. It will also benefit you to find geographically local networking opportunities.

8.3 Professional Organizations

Professional organizations offer networking opportunities not just at conferences but also in your local area and remotely. If you are not already a member of a professional organization relevant to your work life, do some research and find one that aligns with your interests. The society's mission makes membership a process of self-selection for people, so the advantage of joining a professional organization and participating in events that they organize is that you know you have a lot in common professionally with the other members. Some professional organizations have local chapters and sections with regular meetings, and most will have remote ways to get involved.

Membership in a professional society also gives you access to the member directory, society awards, professional development courses and materials, and career services. Filling out your profile in the member directory is a great way to increase your visibility, and allows you to browse other members' profiles. Societies often offer awards, scholarships, and prizes that you can apply or be nominated for, a great form of passive networking discussed in more detail in Section 7.5. Some societies have online course offerings that you can use to learn more about technical or professional development subjects. There may also be a career services section where employers can post opportunities, and job seekers can post their resumes.

Non-profit professional societies often have a committee and governance structure that is run by volunteers sourced from, and elected by, the membership, including executive positions and the Board of Directors. Access to those kinds of volunteering roles requires you to establish yourself as a reliable volunteer and passionate about the society. This kind of service is an excellent sustainable networking opportunity. You are serving the society and your community, while networking with other volunteers who may be decision makers in their own careers, learning about governance and leadership, and getting greater visibility for yourself and your company. To learn about this structure, you can typically find governance information on the society's website to see who is currently serving in what roles, and how the election process works.

Societies often also have member news sites, periodicals, and social media accounts. These are great ways to stay aware of events and activities within the society and its related fields. And if you enjoy writing, you can contact the society to pitch stories for publication related to your research or other professional matters. Writing and participating in the society's social media are great passive networking opportunities, as discussed in Section 7.6.

Public speaking is another excellent form of sustainable networking (see Section 7.7) that can be pursued through society involvement. Many professional societies offer a visiting lecturer directory, through which member groups can request a lecturer to visit and give a presentation. Often, there is funding provided by the society to the lecturers to cover travel expenses. If you have a topic that you can speak about, whether it is technical or related to career development, and public speaking is something you are interested in, check the eligibility requirements for your society's visiting lecturer program.

8.4 Local Alumni Clubs and Chapters

Many colleges and universities will have alumni associations with a chapter or a club in your area. These groups typically host social and educational events, which are valuable networking venues because you have two things in common with the other attendees already: your alma mater and your geographic location. But unlike a professional organization, the career types represented in this group will be diverse, so it's a rich opportunity to diversify your network. You will probably find volunteering and leadership opportunities, as well. Like professional societies, alumni associations often have a directory, giving you visibility through your profile and the opportunity to browse others' profiles.

You can learn about alumni associations on your university or college website, or on social media such as Facebook or LinkedIn. If you went to graduate school at a different place than undergraduate, look up both of your alumni associations. There may be alumni groups for fellowships you have received, your high school, or workshops that you attended.

There is likely also an alumni newsletter, social media, or periodical interested in updates and accepting story submissions. As with professional societies, if you are interested in writing or moderating, these are great forms of passive networking (see Chapter 7).

8.5 Science Museums and Other STEM Events

Local science museums are great places to patronize, support, and find volunteering opportunities. They typically offer memberships with perks such as free guest passes or member-only events, and depending on the museum, volunteering opportunities may include serving as a docent and helping with outreach events, including organizing. Many science museums are child-oriented, but they sometimes host adult-only events in the evening after normal business hours, where you can enjoy the space in a different atmosphere, possibly with refreshments. While not formal networking events, these special events offer a way to meet other people with an interest in STEM and to practice your conversational skills.

Organizations such as Nerd Nite,[7] Pint of Science,[8] and Cafe Scientifique[9] look for speakers to share their research for a general audience in a casual atmosphere. While formats vary, they typically involve one or more speakers giving presentations formatted for a general audience that may not have STEM backgrounds; for example, Nerd Nite does not confine itself to STEM topics. Attending these events and meeting other attendees is a great way to learn new things, meet people in your community, and network with others who are curious about the world. There is the possibility of volunteering to give a talk, which can be intimidating but also helpful in terms of raising your visibility in the community, sharing your work, and teaching others about STEM.

Author Anecdote

I gave a talk at Washington D.C.'s Nerd Nite titled *How do frickin' 'lasers' work? And do they really go 'pew pew pew'?* It was so exciting to share the history, physics, and pop-cultural aspects of lasers with a large, enthusiastic audience, and I highly recommend speaking at Nerd Nite or similar venues.

8.6 Local Science Fairs

Local science fairs are competitions where students present science projects in which they have performed an original experiment that is shared by a poster board presentation and a model, demonstration, or report. Competitions are typically open to elementary-, middle-, and high-school students, and winners can progress to regional, national, and international competitions, such as the Intel International Science and Engineering Festival.[10] As a scientist or engineer, you are equipped to judge such competitions, and organizers are often looking for volunteer judges. Some science fairs pair students with mentors, and if you are willing to make the commitment, mentoring is a sustainable networking relationship that can make a huge difference in a student's future career[11] (see Section 7.4 for more on mentoring relationships).

8.7 Public Libraries and Community Centers

If your country has a public library system or your town or neighborhood has a dedicated community center, these are excellent spaces for local networking. They may already have activities arranged that you can attend and meet others who live near you, and they often also have spaces that you can rent to host activities if you want to start a group or do outreach. Refer back to Sections 7.9 and 7.10 for more on hosting and organizing activities.

8.8 Festivals, Expos, and Trade Shows

Festivals and expos are typically large events that are open to the public, where there may be panels or presentations, and vendors and organizations have booths. Festivals tend to be more educational and focused around a subject area, whereas expos are typically associated with an event, such as an athletic competition, and are more focused on vendors selling products or services. A trade show or fair is similar to an expo but they focus more on the state of the art or latest products.

Each of these events brings together a variety of vendors and organizations (much like conferences), and they can be great ways to meet representatives and ask questions. These events do a lot of heavy lifting for you, like professional organizations or conferences, in terms of bringing together people interested in a particular topic. If you are part of a local organization or society, you can volunteer to exhibit or staff a booth and meet a lot of people.

8.9 Advocacy

The term "advocacy" here refers to the process of representing the needs of a community to policy makers in the government. This is a form of volunteering and community service that can be done on an individual basis, but advocacy efforts are often arranged by an umbrella organization. This organization will typically advocate for something relating to the needs of the community it serves, a message that volunteers will carry to policy makers. Volunteering in this way also puts you in contact with other volunteers and organizers. What makes advocacy different is that you are brought into contact with policy makers, which gives you the opportunity to network and create connections with them as well. This makes advocacy a high-impact, sustainable networking opportunity in terms of service to the community, an organization, and the potential connections that you can create.

The form advocacy takes depends on how your local government operates. If the government is an electoral democracy (63% of countries (123), as of 2017[12]), you may have elected representatives who want to hear from constituents. Some professional societies organize events and meetings where members attend a training and meetings where they can advocate for the STEM community to policy makers. However, in some governmental structures around the world, advocacy may not be welcome or advisable based on the current political climate.

It is beyond the scope of this book to explore this topic in much detail, and due to the extensive variation between countries and governments, there is no one resource with answers that are applicable everywhere. Your knowledge of your home country and some online research using "STEM advocacy + your country/region" as search terms will help you find ways to advocate for STEM funding and education locally. If you are part of a professional society, see what kind of advocacy efforts they support. For one example, see SPIE's site describing its advocacy efforts at spie.org/about-spie/advocacy. Even if your professional society does not currently have advocacy activities in your country, staff should be able to give you advice about how to find, pursue, or create local advocacy opportunities.

8.10 Entrepreneurial Groups and Industry Clusters

There are typically local organizations that concern themselves with the economic development of your geographic region, including entrepreneurial groups, industry clusters, and your local chamber of commerce. Local economic development groups often try to attract as many STEM professionals and companies as possible to their area because of the growth they promote. Universities will also often have entrepreneurship programs; even if you are not an entrepreneur, local entrepreneurs are valuable people to know. These organizations and programs may offer networking and volunteering opportunities, and getting involved is an excellent way to support your local community and meet other locals with similar interests and goals. You can find these organizations by performing searches online using your city or region's name along with terms like "cluster," "industry association," "entrepreneurship," "start up," "chamber of commerce," and "venture capital."

8.11 Philanthropic Organizations

There are probably multiple philanthropic organizations in your region, and volunteering for and participating in their activities is a great way to support your community, meet people, and diversify your network. So long as it is an organization whose mission you care about, it doesn't need to be a STEM-related field for you to participate. It could be health, diversity and inclusion, or charity, and it will still be rich in networking opportunities and ways to expand your knowledge base and local network. Charity organizations will often host fundraising events that you can pay to attend, such as foot races or balls.

You can find such groups by searching online using your city name and terms like "philanthropy," "non-profit," "community service," "charity," and "volunteering." If you already know of a philanthropic group that you like, you can look them up and see if they have any local branches or chapters. Asking your connections in your local geographic network for recommendations is also a good way to find groups that host good events or have volunteering opportunities.

8.12 Maker, Hobbyist, and Social Groups

Most communities will have social and hobby groups, including Maker groups and spaces that focus on giving people the tools they need to build and create, including projects in the areas of electronics, machining, chemistry, sewing, photography, gardening, and beyond. Maker groups often have a strong emphasis on STEM subjects and offer memberships for access to tools and space, as well as competitions, outreach, and educational events. Maker fairs are local events that you can attend to shop, take classes, and network. Maker spaces often rely on donations and volunteers to stay open, and so if you like making things and you have the time, getting involved will help the group, give you access to a lot of interesting tools and classes, and provide you with a wealth of networking opportunities.

There are also typically lots of hobbyist and social groups available in any given city. Websites such as Meetup.com[13] are great places to look for activities in your area, as well as event calendars at your local library and community centers. You can find anything: tabletop gaming, athletics, writing groups, language exchange, and more. Especially if you are new to a city or region, local hobbyist and social groups can help you get established with a new social group and do some local networking that can yield diverse connections and friendships.

Exercises

(1) Assuming that you are currently employed or a student, find one or more ways to network within your organization or school. Attend a social event organized by your department or help to organize it. Identify people whom you see regularly but don't yet know, and make a point to meet them. Whatever it is, it doesn't need to be big; it should be achievable, quantifiable, and something you can make a habit to expand and strengthen your network in your place of work or study.

(2) If you are not already a member of a professional organization, spend some time researching and see if there is one that fits your interests and goals, and offers services that interest you. If it is economically feasible for you to do so, join the organization that best suits you, and take advantage of the services they provide in terms of networking, career development and services, and volunteering opportunities.

(3) Considering the possible ways to network and get involved locally, spend some time online researching local groups or activities that interest you. Find a few that seem promising, attend some of their events or meetings, and pick one that suits you. It should be either in-line with your career goals or something that you enjoy personally. Begin to attend consistently, if not frequently. If you are a member of a professional society, see if it offers local sections or events.

(4) Consider finding ways to volunteer locally, whether it's judging a science fair, giving a talk at a Nerd Nite, helping at a Makerspace, or staffing a charity event. Try it out, and see what you learn and how you respond.

(5) Consider all of the above to be experiments, and if they don't work, try something else. If you are so inclined, keep a journal or lab notebook, and note down what you did or didn't like about a certain event. As you try out different things, see if you find a pattern. Not all groups, events, organizations, or volunteering opportunities will resonate with you, and that discovery process will teach you things about yourself and improve your self-awareness so that ultimately you can find the right fit.

References

1. Ferrari, J., "Psychology of Procrastination: Why People Put Off Important Tasks Until the Last Minute," *American Psychological Association* (April 5, 2010). Retrieved from apa.org/news/press/releases/2010/04/procrastination. Accessed on April 2, 2019.

2. Jaffe, E., "Why Wait? The Science Behind Procrastination," *Association for Psychological Science* (April 2013). Retrieved from psychologicalscience.org/observer/why-wait-the-science-behind-procrastination. Accessed on April 2, 2019.

3. Heshmat, S., "The Scarcity Mindset," *Psychology Today* (April 2, 2015). Retrieved from psychologytoday.com/us/blog/science-choice/201504/the-scarcity-mindset. Accessed on April 2, 2019.

4. Wu, L. et al. "Mining face-to-face interaction networks using sociometric badges: Evidence predicting productivity in it configuration," *The 2008 Winter Conference on Business Intelligence*, University of Utah (2008).

5. Pentland, A., "The Water Cooler Effect," *Psychology Today* (November 22, 2009). Retrieved from psychologytoday.com/us/blog/reality-mining/200911/the-water-cooler-effect. Accessed on April 2, 2019.

6. Fournier, G., "Mere Exposure Effect," *Psych Central* (2018). Retrieved from psychcentral.com/encyclopedia/mere-exposure-effect. Accessed on April 2, 2019.

7. Nerd Nite, nerdnite.com.

8. Pint of Science, pintofscience.com.

9. Cafe Scientifique, cafescientifique.org.

10. Intel International Science and Engineering Festival (ISEF), intel.com/content/www/us/en/education/competitions/international-science-and-engineering-fair.html.

11. Smith, B. L., "The lifelong benefits of mentoring," *gradPSYCH American Psychological Association* **12**(4) (November 2014). Retrieved from apa.org/gradpsych/2014/11/mentoring-benefits. Accessed on March 27, 2019.

12. Freedom House, "Populists and autocrats: The dual threat to global democracy," *Freedom in the World Report* (2017). Retrieved from freedomhouse.org/sites/default/files/FH_FIW_2017_Report_Final.pdf. Accessed on April 2, 2019.

13. Meet Up, meetup.com

14. Gerber, S., and R. Paugh, *Superconnector: Stop Networking and Start Building Business Relationships that Matter*, Da Capo Lifelong Books, Boston (2018).

Chapter 9
Networking at Conferences

"Turning a conference into your own turf and setting goals ahead of time is what shifts a casual conference attendance into a mission."

~Keith Ferrazzi and Tahl Raz,
Never Eat Alone (2005)

9.1 The World of Networking in a Nutshell

Technical conferences are an amazing place for professional networking, as they represent almost every kind of networking opportunity at one time in one location. There are presentations, poster sessions, courses, workshops, plenary talks, receptions, exhibitions, panels, product demonstrations, coffee breaks, cocktail hours, volunteering opportunities, and more. Because a conference can bring together hundreds or even thousands of people with related professional interests, it is one of the richest possible places to network in terms of the density and variety of related professionals that you might meet. This chapter focuses on the mechanics of conference attendance and the types of events and networking opportunities you will encounter there.

9.2 The Importance of Advance Planning

The value of planning before conferences cannot be overstated. And the larger the conference is, the more value you will get from advance preparation. Unless the conference you are attending is small, there will typically be parallel sessions and events, so you will not be able to see everything. If you bounce randomly about, you will probably miss something specifically relevant to you, and you will not be networking as efficiently as you could towards your goals. If you do advance planning and have a strategy in place for which talks, booths, networking events, and meetings you will attend, as well as the people you want to meet, you can use your time and expend your energy more effectively. This advance plan will also allow you craft event-specific self-introductions and topics of conversation, ensure that you have eaten, and make sure that your attire is appropriate. The more you make advance preparation a reflexive part of your conference routine, the easier it will become and the smoother the event will go.

> **Author Anecdote**
> The first conference I attended as a graduate student was Photonics West, and other than preparing and practicing for my talk, I did no advance preparation. As a result, I spent much of the event bewildered, or following the more senior graduate students from my group, instead of pursuing my own interests. Afterwards, I realized there was a student paper competition I could have entered, but I had missed the deadline. The experience taught me that advance preparation lets you find and take advantage of more opportunities.

9.2.1 Planning and self-care

The first stage of your conference planning is registering and booking your travel. As much as possible, schedule your travel arrangements to give yourself time after arrival to organize yourself and rest. Self-care is an important investment at conferences, because both travel and crowded spaces increase your chances of getting sick.[1,2] In addition to washing your hands regularly,[3] following your usual routine as much as possible, eating healthy, and exercising can help to prevent illness.[4] Getting sick and being trapped in your hotel room is unpleasant and hampers your networking and productivity. On the other hand, being rested and healthy allows you to be a more relaxed and engaging person. This applies to your return home from the conference, as well. Ideally, you should allow yourself time to rest and recuperate before returning to work.

This may not be possible or practical, depending on your restrictions and the variety of things that you need to accomplish. But any small acts of self-care that you can practice during the conference, such as drinking plenty of water and regularly washing your hands, are valuable. Maintaining your health and demeanor makes you feel better, and it is an investment in your ability to network with others and have a productive meeting.

For your next stage of preparation, you will want to examine the conference agenda and see which presentations, courses, and events you wish to attend. Continuing with the theme of self-care, while you are planning what to do, also plan the appropriate amount of downtime for yourself. As best you can, ensure that you have enough time to rest, organize your thoughts, send follow-up emails, and de-stress if social interaction is difficult for you. Conferences are very stimulating, and taking time to accommodate your comfort level with that amount of stimulation is important. Just as networking is a very personal process, so is conference attendance. Use your self-awareness and learn to recognize if you are letting social anxiety and fear prevent you from engaging in certain activities. Avoid making decisions out of fear, but recognize the difference between that and taking the downtime and personal space that you need, when you need it.

The acronym FOMO stands for "fear of missing out," and it can be a problem at conferences. There can be so many things going on at once that it is impossible not to miss *something* that interests you, and FOMO can drive you to wear yourself out. Peer pressure to socialize, stay up late, and drink can be a factor, but don't let

FOMO win if you know that what you really need is to do is go back to your room and spend time alone recuperating and preparing for the next day.

If you want to stay up later than you would normally to take advantage of catching up with friends or getting to know new contacts better, then do so, but as a *conscious* choice. Examine yourself and your options, and choose a course of action based on you, not on perceived obligations or peer pressure. This is about remaining self-aware and using your time in the way that is best for you. Airline safety videos instruct you to put on your oxygen mask before helping others, because you are better able to help others if you are functioning well,[5] and this is equally applicable to conferences.

Author Anecdote

Conferences bring out many of my extravert tendencies: there's so much to see, so many new people to meet, and so many friends to catch up with! I love it, but the reality is that social interaction requires a lot of energy from me. After socializing, I can become very tense and anxious, largely focused around my perceived failures (called "rumination"). It can be so bad that it keeps me from getting good rest, creating a negative cycle. Knowing this about myself, and strategically planning around it, helps me to get better rest, keep a positive mood, and be productive at conferences. So I practice self-care by planning time alone and doing things such as drinking tea and practicing yoga or breathing exercises before bed to help me relax. It is an essential part of my conference strategy.

9.2.2 Conference content: what you attend

As a general rule, you want your conference preparation and the events that you select to attend to contribute to a goal (discussion of goals can be found in Section 2.1). This goal should relate to your career and current work goals, which will shape what you hope to get out of the event. The goal does not have to be big or long-term. For example, you could be interested in learning more about a subject because you want to work on more of that type of project at your company. That goal then informs which related courses, demonstrations, and presentations you will attend, as well as which vendors to visit at the exhibition. Or you might want a new job, or a job at a specific company, and can plan to attend presentations by employees of that company and visit their booth at the exhibit or job fair, if they have one. Your goal could be as simple as seeing what is new in your sub-field by attending the relevant presentations, poster sessions, and receptions, and looking at new products at the exhibition. Whatever your goal, it focuses your efforts and provides a metric for assessing the value of attending any given event. It will allow you to prioritize, prevent yourself from becoming overwhelmed, and get more out of the conference.

Make a plan, but be flexible. Circumstances often interfere, and you may show up to an event that isn't what you thought it was or has been canceled, or something else that requires extemporaneous decision making. To account for this, leave space in your schedule for spontaneity and be flexible, as there are some excellent opportunities that you may only encounter in the moment. Be ready to adapt your plan. There will be more discussion on serendipity and spontaneity in Subsection 9.8.6.

Advanced preparation isn't just for high-level planning; it also applies to individual events. Plan in advance how you will introduce yourself in a way that is specific to that event, whether it is a general-purpose introduction for people you might bump into during a coffee break or a course where the professor asks students to share their reason for attending. Also, take time to think of good topics of conversation. This can be specific to the conference, where it is held, the recent weather, and any major news items that might be of interest to the other attendees, in addition to your work and research. This kind of preparation can save you from drawing a blank when looking for something to say.

On an even finer level of detail, prepare by researching individuals you might want to meet and who you know will be at certain events. If you have a particular person in mind, look up their CV, company website, LinkedIn profile, etc. That will give you insights on what they do and what interests them, which can give you things to say and talk about once you meet them. You can pick people to meet simply because you find them interesting or because you have similar work experience, research projects, or other goals. When strategically planning to meet people, keep the principles of kindness and sustainable networking in mind, and consider not just why you want to meet them but why they might want to meet you and what kind of assistance you might be able to offer.

You may also have existing contacts who are geographically distant but will be at the conference. Reach out to them in advance to ask about their schedule. And if you have been corresponding online with anyone in advance of an event, but you have never met them in person before, make a point to look them up online so that you know what they look like. Matching a face with the correspondence will save you from potential awkwardness if you encounter that person unexpectedly. Likewise, if you anticipate old classmates or former colleagues will be present, contact them in advance so that you can set up a meeting about what is going on in their work and personal lives.

Use the conference app if available! It can help you to stay on top of your schedule without the necessity of a big conference booklet. Staying actively involved on social media and following the conference hashtags can also alert you to social events and happenings that you might not otherwise find.

One final step of advance preparation before entering an event is to check your appearance. If possible, go to the bathroom and confirm that your shirt is tucked in, your fly is zipped, your hair is tidy, and there is nothing stuck between your teeth.

9.2.3 Business cards

At conferences, it is typical and culturally acceptable to exchange business cards to get people's contact information, but there are a few things to consider before ordering cards and handing them out. First, business cards aren't absolutely necessary. Most people can type your email directly into their phone, or your name into the LinkedIn app, to connect with you quickly. However, not everyone has a smartphone, not all rooms have good mobile or wifi connections, and so on, and thus the business card remains useful.

Author Anecdote

Some people insist that you *have* to have business cards at a conference, and I used to share this attitude. It caused me a lot of stress, because I was terrible at remembering to bring them with me. Then I went on extended travel, leaving my job to do so, and I had no business cards, even though I was still attending conferences through my volunteer roles with SPIE. Did the world end? No. In fact, no one even commented that they thought it was odd. Even though I did a lot of networking, it was easy to exchange email and other contact info without cards. So don't let business cards stress you out. They are nice to have, and they are useful, but they aren't a necessity. And if someone judges you for not having one, that says more about them than it does about you.

If you want business cards but don't have them already, order them in time for the conference, as well as some kind of case for storing them (including cards you receive from others). Whether you or someone else in your department designs your cards, make sure that all of your information is accurate and spelled correctly. If you are designing your card, use a small number of colors and fonts. Apply the principle of signal-to-noise ratio to your card design; you don't want the design to distract from the contents.

There is some debate about whether to put your degree on the card with your name. Some people think that it looks conceited to include "Name, Ph.D.," whereas others consider it standard practice.[6] It is a personal choice that will depend on the other contents of your card and the signal-to-noise ratio. If you have a job title, such as Professor, it is likely redundant to state that you have a Ph.D. However, if your job title does not make that clear, consider including it. If you have a degree that is in a different field than your current job, it is less likely to be relevant to include it on your card. Company and cultural context play a role, too, so examine the cards of those in your field and consult with your co-workers.

As for how to use business cards, if you have met someone networking informally, hand them your business card at the end of an interaction *if* it has been positive and you want to stay in touch. A good way to get someone's business card is to offer yours first, as they will often respond in kind. If you have a negative interaction with someone, or they made you uncomfortable, don't give them your business card. If such a person asks you for a card, simply say that you have run out. If it is a more formal, prearranged meeting, it is customary to exchange cards at the beginning of the engagement. When you receive a card, make a point to look at it out of politeness.

Taking notes on business cards after you meet a person can be a useful way to remember details from the interaction, and some people will write additional notes or contact information on their own business cards for you. However, not everyone will be comfortable with you writing on their card. For example, in Japanese culture, it is impolite to do anything that marks or damages another person's card,[7] so avoid writing on someone else's card in front of them.

To keep track of the business cards you receive, you can use your smartphone to scan cards directly into your contacts. LinkedIn (after shutting down the CardMunch service) partnered with Evernote to offer card scanning and notetaking functionalities,[8] and the Google Lens feature can also be used for direct-to-contacts card scanning as well.[9] There are many options, and searching for "card scanning app" will produce review articles to help you discover the right one for you.

9.2.4 Food, coffee, and advance scouting

At a conference, you will regularly need to find a place to eat or a place to meet someone for a coffee. You can save time by looking in advance at maps of the venue and the surrounding area, including searching for restaurants that suit your tastes and budget, and noting them down or saving/labeling them. If you have time to arrive early and scout the area on foot, that's even better, though you may not have that luxury. Online research can also make it easier to arrange lunch or find a quiet place to sit down with someone. Bookmarking restaurants that are less obvious, and therefore less crowded with other conference attendees, can help you avoid long lines and keep you on schedule.

Packing snacks is also a good idea: if you end up overbooked, need to save time, or miss lunch for some reason, you can eat a granola or protein bar. Hunger can make you less agreeable,[10] and the effect is so common that the word "hangry," a portmanteau of "hungry" and "angry," has entered the English language. Staying fed will improve your attendance experience and performance. You can purchase shelf-stable, hearty, individually packaged snack foods before you depart for your trip or stop by a convenience or grocery store once you have arrived.

9.3 Presentations as Networking Opportunities

Attending and giving presentations is often the main goal of many conference attendees, with a focus on learning new research and techniques, or checking out the competition. These are also excellent networking opportunities, as sessions attract groups of people interested in a subject that may be relevant to you.

First, presenting at a conference is a form of public speaking (discussed in Section 7.7), and it is a wonderful networking activity. Preparing the presentation, practicing it, and giving it sharpens your communication skills. Sharing your research is important for your career, your research group or company, and the scientific community. It also brings you to the attention of your peers in a positive light and shares useful information with them. If possible and permissible, published recordings of your talk will continue to act in your favor as passive networking, as will the published proceedings. Staying until the end of your session gives people the opportunity to speak with you afterwards and make new connections.

There are also many networking opportunities for you as an attendee listening to talks. The question-and-answer (Q&A) period following a presentation is a big one. A relevant, thought-provoking question also lets the author know that you appreciate their work and were paying attention, which is nice for them. It also gives them an opportunity to add details they didn't share previously, and it gives you and the audience further insight on the topic through immediate access to the author. A good question is also an advertisement about you, and the sort of content that interests you, for the rest of the audience.

When you approach the microphone, first thank the speaker(s) for their presentation and for taking your question, and then state your name and where you work or what you do. It's a small moment of advertising for yourself and your company, and if you follow it with a good question, other attendees may seek you out to introduce themselves after the session. (In networking, it is desirable to have people come to you, when possible.) This introduction should be brief and, ideally, prepared in advance. Adapt it for the event. In addition to letting the rest of the audience know who you are, it provides useful contextual information for the speaker to answer your question.

At the Q&A, as well as other situations where you speak in front of a group, do not let the desire to be noticed motivate you to speak when you don't have something of substance to contribute. Don't be afraid to speak up, but strange, self-aggrandizing, or off-topic questions will only attract negative attention.

At the end of the session, conversations with speakers and other attendees are another networking opportunity. After watching a person's presentation, you will know something about their work and area of expertise, which gives you a great starting point to open a conversation. Speakers typically find it flattering and validating if someone stays to ask questions after their talk. If the presenter is a person you know you want to meet, attending their talk, asking them a question, and introducing yourself after the session is a great way to create a connection. Other attendees who have waited until the end of the session to ask questions are another self-selected group of people to network with, i.e., they care about the same subjects as you do. And if you have presented, it is a good idea to plan time after your session to give audience members a chance to speak with you or ask questions.

If a speaker you want to meet is giving a big presentation, say, a plenary talk, or is otherwise a conference-time celebrity, it can be useful to try and catch them before they go on stage. After their presentation, other people will try to get their attention, but before that the speaker will be relatively free (though not immediately before they go on stage).

9.4 Courses and Workshops

Courses and workshops, like presentation sessions, bring together a group of people who are interested in a given topic. If you care about that topic, there is a lot of networking utility to attending in addition to the content itself. A course or workshop will often have fewer people, which gives you a greater opportunity to get to know them and understand what they do.

Often, an instructor will ask participants to introduce themselves, answering questions such as where they work, the subject of their research, and why they are interested in attending the course. You don't have to wait until the professor asks the question; you can plan in advance how you are going to introduce yourself in a fashion that is relevant to the course material. This serves as an introduction to your instructor, so that they understand who is in the audience (which is important for being able to adapt their lecture), and it is your introduction to your classmates. Having a prepared introduction will also allow you to pay more attention when your classmates introduce themselves, and you can take notes about anyone you are especially interested in meeting.

Author Anecdote

I once encountered an introduction worst-case scenario during a course: I was running late and stumbled into the classroom just as the last person was giving their introduction. The instructor then asked me to introduce myself but didn't tell me what questions I should answer. I had not thought it over in advance, and without having heard anyone else's introduction to use as a guide, what I blurted out was only partly on-topic. A preplanned general introduction would have saved me. Also, when asked to introduce myself, I should have taken a breath and asked the instructor what questions he wanted me to address, so that I could give a more helpful and relevant introduction than I did by guessing.

If the course is long enough to have breaks, you can use that time to get to know your classmates, e.g., taking a coffee break or having lunch together. And if you scouted in advance for restaurants, you will have good suggestions about where to eat.

The questions you and your classmates ask during class also provide useful networking information. Not only do questions help to illuminate the course material and better your understanding, they give your classmates information about you, and vice versa. The type and content of a question reveals useful information about the asker. Off-topic or irrelevant questions, or interruptions, give a poor impression, so stay on-topic and be respectful.

9.5 Receptions

Receptions are quintessential networking events, and they come in a variety of formats. No matter the format, it is rarely a bad idea to show up on time, when few guests have arrived. This gives you a chance to familiarize yourself with the space and to meet or network with the organizers, so long as they aren't busy setting up.

In general, when you arrive at an event, collect and wear your nametag (if applicable), introduce yourself to the event staff, and look around the room, both in terms of the space (locations of food and drink) and the people. Don't be afraid to be alone for a few moments as you survey the room and the other attendees.

9.5.1 Cocktail-style events

A cocktail party is an event that lasts roughly two hours, where drinks and/or finger food are served, and guests are expected to circulate, i.e., have short conversations and move about the room, mingling with multiple people over the course of the event. These events involve a lot of social interaction, but just like an office holiday party (Section 8.2), they are business with social flair. Even with the festive atmosphere, they are professional events where you represent yourself and your school, institute, or company, so maintain business-appropriate behavior. That is not to say that you cannot enjoy yourself or the party, but do so in a way that shows good judgment in a professional environment.

Advanced preparation for a cocktail-style reception involves planning a relevant introduction, possibly an elevator pitch, a few good topics of conversation, and to restock business cards, if you have them. Check for a dress code if there is one, and make sure that your attire is appropriate. You can wear something interesting, such as a colorful tie or shoes, that can act as a conversation starter with others, but don't ignore the social norm entirely. Having a snack before going to these events is often a good idea as appetizers may not be served right away, and if you show up starved at an event with a buffet table, you may spend more time there than speaking with others. Going hungry is fine, but if you are so hungry that you would be irritable if someone stopped you to talk while you were trying to get something to eat, that's too hungry.

Standard behavior at a cocktail event is to circulate around a party, spending about eight to ten minutes with people and then moving to a new conversation. The short duration means that you will need to practice introducing others, self-introductions, maintaining conversation, and making graceful exits, as discussed in Chapter 5. Even if you feel comfortable with one person, they may have other people they want to speak with. Don't take it personally if they excuse themselves, as they may have enjoyed your conversation but have pressing obligations that compel them to move on.

You do not have to strictly rotate every ten minutes, but try to meet as many people as you can make meaningful connections with over the duration of the event. Whether or not you prefer to circulate at about ten minutes a person or have longer conversations with a few people is a personal preference. Whichever you choose, give your conversational partner your full attention. Do not let your eyes wander the room in search of another person to speak with, because this gives the present person the impression that you are not interested in them. You want to leave a positive impression, and acting like you are waiting for someone better to come along is unkind and counterproductive.

There are various strategies for how to approach a cocktail-style event. People who are not comfortable moving about the room would do well to station themselves in high-traffic areas such as the buffet or the bar, because people will naturally approach you. Another useful approach is to bring a buddy, who can introduce you to people you don't already know, and vice versa. You also have the advantage of getting to introduce each other to new people and say flattering things about each other that you could not say about yourself without sounding pretentious. If you brought a buddy, step away from them for a portion of the event; this diversifies your experience and means you can rescue each other from overly long conversations, as needed.

9.5.2 Meal-based events

Arrive promptly for meal-based receptions. Often, there is a cocktail hour or other period of networking before the meal starts, which is your opportunity to circulate. Once the cocktail portion is over (if there is one), you will *not* circulate during the meal, so your seating arrangement is important. Unless you are attending the event in order to see someone or several people that you already know, try to sit with new people. This may be your only opportunity to meet some of the new people at this event. You may occasionally need to meet up with someone at a broader networking event, but in that case, sit with them *and* some new faces.

Try to converse with everyone seated near you over the course of the meal. This can be in one larger conversation, individual conversations, or both.

During the meal, observe good table manners. Of course, what constitutes good table manners will vary by country, including what utensils you can expect to find in your place settings. If you have not dined in a particular culture before, do some advance research. Look up proper table manners, familiarize yourself with the kinds of food that may be offered, and how to use utensils such as chopsticks or snail tongs. Consider reviewing meal etiquette even if it is your native culture.

For a formal Western meal, the basics of table manners include putting your napkin in your lap at the start of the meal, waiting to start eating until everyone has been served, using you tableware (not your fingers) to eat, and chewing with your mouth closed with a minimum amount of noise (small bites can help).

9.5.3 After-parties and other informal gatherings

There are sometimes formally organized after-parties for dinner receptions, as well as privately organized, late-night party-type events. If you are invited, these types of events are often more casual and relaxed, and may involve food (typically appetizers) and/or alcohol. Such events can be a fun way to get to know colleagues and other researchers as people.

However, like a cocktail hour, these are not purely social events. Even though the setting is less formal, these are still people in your field who you know through work or professional channels. Although you may feel more relaxed, remember that your behavior can affect your work and career, and it is therefore important to maintain good decorum. Have fun, talk about personal subjects, and enjoy the party, but avoid cursing and taboo subjects.

9.5.4 Special notes on alcohol and juggling food

Alcohol is an interesting substance, both in its physiological effects and how it is treated across cultures. Make no mistake, it is a drug.[11] Like caffeine[12] or nicotine,[13] it is a commonplace and socially acceptable drug in many cultures.[14,15] Alcohol has a relaxing effect and acts as a social lubricant, which helps people feel at ease in a social situation.[16] But its inhibition-lowering effect can lead to bad behavior, and it can cause hangovers, spoiling the next day.[17] It also suppresses your immune system and can contribute to you catching a cold,[18] so especially at conferences, it is a good idea to moderate your alcohol consumption.

If you are conversing with someone who is clearly intoxicated, don't take their words too seriously and try to be understanding of their behavior. Some people's response to social anxiety and large events is to drink to relax, and it is easy to over-imbibe. Of course, remove yourself from the conversation if the person is being inappropriate or making you feel uncomfortable. If you worry about overindulging or don't care for alcohol, do not feel compelled to drink because others are. If you do drink, hydrate before, during, and after. Eating something before or during the event can help, too. Food slows the absorption of alcohol into the bloodstream, and water helps your body to process it, mitigating its negative effects.[19]

Some events serve both drinks and food. Ideally, you will want to have a free hand so that you can offer a handshake in greeting. If you are both eating and drinking, find a table where you can put your plate down or alternate between drinking and eating so that you can have a hand free.

Handling food and meeting people can be a challenge. Enjoy the food, but don't arrive so hungry that eating distracts you from meeting others. You can use your left hand to eat finger foods so that you can shake with a hand that has not been handling food or touching your mouth (handshakes are typically performed with the right hand; see Subsection 4.4.2) and avoid exposing your food to contaminants from other people's hands. Note that this strategy will *not* work everywhere. In some places, such as India and countries in Africa and the Middle East, it is taboo to eat with your left hand.[20,21] Another strategy is to avoid finger foods and only use utensils to eat.

9.6 The Exhibition

Whether you are exhibiting or attending, the exhibition is a great place to network, find equipment, parts, and products, and see the latest commercial developments. It also presents unique challenges as to opening and closing conversations, and how they should be navigated. The following subsections discuss strategies for approaching the exhibition.

9.6.1 Exhibiting, or working a booth

Exhibiting is not only about advertising for your company and looking for customers; it is an excellent way to grow your own personal network. You need to be ready to make conversation, answer questions about your company's products, and follow up with your new contacts.

If you see someone looking at your booth, allow them a moment to examine the booth before speaking to them. If they don't ask a question on their own, speak to them before they move away. Greet the person with a warm smile and a handshake before introducing yourself. Avoid the question, "May I help you?" It conveys no content specific to you and your company, and it is easy to simply say "no," leaving you little recourse. However, if you introduce yourself, there is a high probability that they will respond in kind, which gives you a chance to find out what they do and assess whether they are a potential customer. You can have a short, pleasant conversation with the person, even if they are not looking to buy your product or services.

Don't think of people who aren't potential customers as a waste of time. You don't want to get so absorbed in them that you turn other people away, but there are things you can learn from them, and if you make a positive impression, they may recommend their colleagues to you, or they may need your products and services at a later date. Speaking with anyone is good practice, especially if things are slow.

During slow times, avoid the temptation to play on your phone. This makes you unapproachable, and it reflects poorly on your company. If you need to answer a message or take calls, it is better to get someone to cover for you so you can step away. It is tiring and awkward work, but do your best to engage people in conversation, expand your network, and learn things from attendees, whether that is something technical about their research or a good restaurant nearby. You can also try to be a resource for them and answer any questions they may have, even if it's unrelated to your company. They will remember you fondly if you help, and it will reflect well on you and your company.

In terms of advance preparation, have an introduction for yourself ready, and a concise, informative elevator pitch about what your company offers. Have plenty of business cards. While they are a matter of preference for an individual attendee, business cards should be considered essential as an exhibitor. Offer your card to all potential customers, and give it to others who ask.

Because you are selling or advertising, the conversation will necessarily shift from an equal exchange to you speaking more about your products and services. Keep your explanations concise, and use your empathy to watch your audience for signs of interest, confusion, or boredom so that you can adapt your approach accordingly. If someone is bored or confused, you may have misunderstood the question or been talking for too long. You will spend more time speaking than you would in other sustainable networking conversations, but you still want to leave room for the other party to ask questions and make comments. It should not be a monologue.

If you are engaged in conversation with someone, and another person approaches your booth, acknowledge the presence of the new person. Excuse yourself momentarily from your current conversation and say something like, "Hello! I'm Clémence. I'll be with you in just a few minutes if you can wait," then return to your original conversation. If you have established that your original conversational partner is unlikely to be a customer, after greeting the new person, return to the original party to wrap up and excuse yourself, then return to the new person (if they have waited).

End conversations with a handshake, and say it was nice to meet them. Offer your contact information for follow-up questions, and ask for theirs. If you have a badge scanner at your disposal, ask if you may use it. If they have expressed a need for or interest in your products or services, give them some of your pamphlets and literature, as well.

9.6.2 Attending an exhibition

For those attending exhibitions, it's a good idea to have a plan; the bigger the exhibition is, the more important your plan will be. In your advance planning for the conference, look through the vendors and make a map of the booth numbers and where they are. Oftentimes, there maps of the exhibition distributed at registration, and if you like having a paper map, take one and circle the booths you want to attend. Product demo events are often held at the exhibition, as are career services and job fairs. It can be worthwhile to attend a job fair to see who is hiring, regardless if you are considering a change.

Even if you do not have any specific agenda items related to the exhibition, consider what you think might be interesting. Visit companies you already patronize to introduce yourself. Stop by companies that have employees who you already know to refresh your acquaintance. Create a prioritized list and a map so that you can make your visit as effective as possible. Random wandering has its own value, but a plan and a list will help ensure that you hit the important items on your agenda.

9.6.3 Visiting a booth

The easiest exhibition visits are at booths you have preselected. If you preselected them, you probably already know something about the company, whether you want to become a customer, are an existing customer, or have a connection with an employee. This context gives you a starting point for the conversation. Go to the booth, introduce yourself, and let them know your purpose. Get the name of the employee and learn about their role so that you can ask them pertinent questions (if they can't answer, get the contact info of the person who can). Share your card or contact information, get a card in return, and collect any relevant pamphlets or literature. When your conversation is finished, smile, offer a handshake (if culturally appropriate), and say goodbye. Then follow up (see Section 9.9).

If you arrive at a booth and the person you want to talk to is occupied, let them see that you are there so that they can greet you even if they cannot abandon their current conversation. If you don't have much time or would prefer not to wait, you can cut in as described in Section 5.5, give them your card, and say you want to talk but must stop by later. Even if you don't get a chance to talk in person, they know who you are and that you're interested, and the two of you can follow up later.

Networking becomes trickier if you are walking at random or if booth giveaways are your main reason for visiting. You may approach a booth out of curiosity, but feel free to move on unless you wish to stay and converse with the exhibitor. If you know that you are not a potential customer, you may fear irritating the exhibitor if you take their time with questions. This is a common awkward situation that you will encounter at exhibitions, and it can be difficult to navigate.

First, understand that a good exhibitor will not treat you poorly if you ask questions, even if you are not a potential customer. Be respectful of their time, and don't stay at the booth for a long time if you know you aren't going to buy anything; taking a few minutes to ask questions shouldn't be a problem. A chat with an exhibitor is a low-stakes opportunity to practice your networking and conversation skills. Additionally, there is an effect called "social proof," where people follow others under the assumption that those actions are correct.[22] According to this principle, at an exhibition, more people will visit a booth if there is already someone there engaged with the exhibitor.

9.6.4 Attendees meeting other attendees

While a lot of people at the exhibition may be on a mission and occupied with meetings or contacting certain vendors, not everyone is busy at all moments, which gives you opportunities to meet other attendees. Don't be afraid to introduce yourself to someone you don't know. If they are intent on something or in a conversation already, don't interrupt, but if you make eye contact with someone as you are walking the exhibition, it is perfectly reasonable to start a conversation.

9.7 Meeting Famous or Important People

You might meet someone at a conference who is famous or important, either in general or within your specialized community. When meeting such a person, it is good to acknowledge that you know who they are and that you are familiar with their work, but don't spend a lot of time expressing adoration of them. If you act like a fan, you will get treated like a fan and held at arm's length. If you act like a respectful peer, who is familiar with their work, you will have a better chance of making a memorable connection.

This person is like any other person, with interests, likes, and dislikes; make conversation accordingly. Just like people who are in executive positions and senior in their careers, they probably receive a lot more requests for assistance or their time than the average person, so be extra conscientious about the sustainability of your approach, and follow up promptly after the interaction to establish yourself in their memory.

9.8 Other Opportunities for Sustainable Conference Networking

9.8.1 Get to know the conference staff

Introducing yourself to conference staff, and getting to know them and their roles within the host organization, is a great sustainable networking opportunity. They are generally very friendly, helpful people who will appreciate you taking the time to introduce yourself, especially if you offer thanks, compliments, or feedback on the event. Staff will be everywhere within a conference, so there will be many of them to meet; be observant so that you can find the right moments to say hello, as they are often busy making things run smoothly. Note that there may be a difference between the staff of the organization that hosts the event and the staff of the facility where the event is held.

It can be worthwhile contacting organizing staff in advance of the conference to see if they need any volunteer assistance. If they are not familiar with you, it is unlikely that you will be given any tasks of great responsibility, but if you follow through and meet the staff at the conference, you will begin building rapport, and more volunteering opportunities will open up for you.

9.8.2 Volunteering

As discussed in Section 7.2, volunteering is far and away one of the best things you can do for your professional life, your network, and your community. Volunteering at conferences is a high-impact, short-term opportunity. By dedicating your time to help at a conference, you learn interesting new things and work alongside other volunteers with whom you will bond and develop lasting relationships. The organizing society benefits from the time and resources you dedicate to them, and the organizers get to know you, making them more inclined to help you when the need arises. Staff will be more likely to remember you if another volunteering opportunity comes up, without you even asking.

It can be difficult to find volunteering opportunities if you don't already know the right people, but once you make the necessary connections and get your first volunteering opportunity, more opportunities will arise. To start, search the organization's website and look for any information they have on volunteering. Also, check and follow any social media channels maintained by the organization. Your research might find contact information for the people responsible for organizing an event. If you can find any mutual connections to make an introduction, do so (there is a discussion on how to do this through LinkedIn in Chapter 11), but failing that, give them a cold call or email to introduce yourself and offer your assistance (see Chapter 12 for details on cold calls and emails).

Search for conference opportunities several months in advance, as conferences are complicated, and many things are planned early. Closer to the date, the organizers may be occupied with last-minute details and less likely to respond. But in general, they will be delighted to hear that you are interested in helping. Even if you don't find a volunteering opportunity, when you attend the conference make a point to get to know the staff.

Possibilities for volunteering at conferences include working at the registration desk, the help desk, the job center, as a room monitor, doing media coverage, moderating a panel, judging a competition, facilitating or leading workshops, and assuming leadership roles (once you become more established in the organization). Some volunteering opportunities may come with a waived registration or housing benefits, which can make travel easier if you are a student or find it difficult to afford attendance.

9.8.3 Coffee breaks

Coffee breaks, when everyone is out of the sessions and milling about, offer a great opportunity to strike up casual conversations with people. They are also great to attend with someone whom you may have met at the session you were in or presenting at, so that you can continue your conversation. Use your empathy and watch to see if a person makes eye contact and has open, receptive body language. If someone meets your eye and smiles back, that is a good indicator that they are open to making conversation. Coffee breaks can be used to practice opening and closing conversations, as they are typically brief, and to some extent you can behave the same way you would at a cocktail-type reception.

9.8.4 Personal meetings

An important part of networking at conferences is arranging your own meetings. These can be one-on-one meetings with friends or collaborators, for the purpose of catching up or accomplishing a specific goal. Or they can be gatherings with multiple people. You can invite a disparate group of friends to lunch or dinner for the purposes of cross-pollinating your network, or if you have a topic of interest and there is no event at the conference already centered around it, you can create a meetup for people with that shared interest.

Generally, you will want to do some advance prepreparation for meetings, including contacting people at least a week in advance, and finding good spaces for meetings, large and small. Scouting in and around the venue will enable you to suggest good locations. And if you want to host a larger event, you may want to make a reservation for a space or at a restaurant. Creating and hosting events will give you experience in organizing, is a service to your participants, and is a way for you to create great networking opportunities for yourself and others. See Chapter 7 for more on hosting and event organization for networking.

9.8.5 Poster sessions

Poster sessions are opportunities to meet authors and have one-on-one conversations with them on topics that you care about. Like the exhibition, it's not a bad idea to have a plan for what posters you want to see, but allow for some flexibility and wandering to discover things you might not otherwise. You can also use poster sessions to meet other attendees. As discussed in Subsection 9.6.3, being at a booth can attract others, and standing at a poster will have the same social proof effect. By engaging the author and starting a discussion, you may attract people who would otherwise be hesitant to ask questions but who want to listen. This is good for the author, because it allows them to share their research with a broader audience.

Author Anecdote

One of my more memorable poster session moments occurred as I examined a poster whose author was absent. I had been reading for a few minutes when another attendee began asking me questions about the poster. Confused, I did my best to answer based on what I had read, eventually realizing that they had mistaken me for the author. I confessed that I was not the author, and we had a laugh about it, followed by a nice conversation about our respective areas of research, and the poster, as well.

9.9 Generating Serendipity

While you want to dedicate most of your time to strategic efforts, it is important to leave some space for chance encounters and serendipity. You may not see immediately how someone could fit into your network, but serendipitous encounters can generate diverse connections. At a conference, you can almost be certain that the person will work in at least a tangentially related area, giving you a blend of diversity and relevance.

Receptions, the exhibition, coffee breaks, and poster sessions are spaces where casual conversation amongst strangers is a social norm and a great way to meet people you wouldn't otherwise. Being active on the conference app or social media while you are at a conference can also help you to generate serendipitous encounters. Your posts to let people know what events you will attend can enable meetups with people you might have missed otherwise. Being open to meeting people in spaces that aren't official networking venues, including around the venue or convention center, or walking to and from restaurants at lunch time, can generate fruitful and interesting connections.

9.10 Following Up

Following up is an essential aspect of networking, and you should learn to do it reflexively after a conference. You can begin sending follow-up emails during the conference, depending on your preferences and strategy, or schedule a follow-up meeting before the conference concludes. To prepare for sending follow-up messages, you can take notes over the course of the week detailing who you want to contact and why. Notes can be added to the back of a person's business card, in a notebook, or digitally on a phone or computer.

When you send follow-ups is a matter of strategy and preference. While next-day follow-ups are often considered ideal, because of the general chaos that conferences create for people's schedules, sending follow-ups within a week after the event is also acceptable. There is no one right answer about timing, and the circumstances of the meeting, your preferences, and the person you are contacting are all factors to be considered when following up. More details on follow-up format and the timing of messages is discussed in Chapter 10.

Exercises

(1)   Even if you are not attending a conference soon, make a list of items to do as part of your advance conference preparation and networking strategy. Think about how you want to organize your schedule, whether it will be written in a planner, on an electronic calendar, in the conference app, or some combination thereof. Whatever your approach is, codify it and your strategy, so that you have it ready. [Author's Note: I primarily use a Bullet Journal[23] and a secondary electronic calendar for my conference scheduling and planning.]

(2)   Think about the last time you attended a conference and see if you can find any business cards or contact information that you collected. Sort them to see if you remember any of the people; throw out any that you can't remember. Set the memorable cards aside to send belated follow-ups (it's almost never too late) when you get to Section 10.2.

(3)   When you have a conference you plan to attend, review this chapter and the strategy you created for Exercise 1. Think of your goal for the conference and begin preparing your schedule early, keeping volunteering opportunities in mind. Do this preparation incrementally, starting early, so that you are not burdened with the arduous task of building your whole schedule at the last minute, especially if you are presenting.

(4)   Do some self-analysis and think about how much time you feel that you need in terms of rest, self-care, and downtime during the conference, and factor those concerns into your schedule. If necessary, create some strategies or routines to help you relax or unwind after stressful situations that you may encounter at the conference. Try testing and practicing some of these activities at home when you feel stressed, so that you have something ready when you get to the conference. Select strategies that require space and equipment that will be accessible during the conference.

(5)   After attending a conference, note how things went and how you might change or improve your strategy and schedule next time. No plan or strategy is perfect; also, your goals will change each year, so regular reassessment of your conference experience will help you optimize how you use your time.

References

1. Wilson, M. E., "Travel and the emergence of infectious diseases," *Emerging Infectious Diseases* **1**(2) (1995).

2. Goscé, L. et al., "Analytical modelling of the spread of disease in confined and crowded spaces," *Scientific Reports* **4** (2014).

3. Rabie, T. and V. Curtis, "Handwashing and risk of respiratory infections: a quantitative systematic review," *Tropical Medicine and International Health* **11**(3) (2006).

4. "How to boost your immune system," *Harvard Health Publishing* (September 2014, revised July 16, 2018). Retrieved from health.harvard.edu/staying-healthy/how-to-boost-your-immune-system. Accessed on April 3, 2019.

5. "Why you should put your oxygen mask on first before helping others video," *Traveller* (August 1, 2016). Retrieved from traveller.com.au/why-you-should-put-your-oxyen-mask-on-first-before-helping-others-video-gqiikq. Accessed on April 3, 2019.

6. McCay, L., "Time to Stop Playing Business Card Scrabble With Our Qualifications?" *Huffpost* (October 4, 2012). Retrieved from huffpost.com/entry/business-card-tips_b_1938296. Accessed on April 3, 2019.

7. "Japanese Business Card Etiquette," *Japan Printing & Graphics, Inc.* Retrieved from japanprint.com/business-etiquette/japanese-business-cards-etiquette. Accessed on July 27, 2019.

8. "Evernote and LinkedIn perfect the business card," *Evernote*, evernote.com/cardmunch/Welcome.action.

9. "Google Lens," *Google*, lens.google.com.

10. MacCormack, J. K. and K. A. Lindquist, "Feeling hangry? When hunger is conceptualized as emotion," *Emotion* **19**(2) (2019).

11. "Alcohol," *Alcohol and Drug Foundation* (November 15, 2018). Retrieved from adf.org.au/drug-facts/alcohol. Accessed on April 3, 2019.

12. "Caffeine," *Alcohol and Drug Foundation* (December 10, 2018). Retrieved from adf.org.au/drug-facts/caffeine. Accessed on April 3, 2019.

13. "Tobacco," *Alcohol and Drug Foundation* (November 15, 2018). Retrieved from adf.org.au/drug-facts/tobacco. Accessed on October 3, 2018.

14. "Global Drug Survey 2015," *Global Drug Survey* (2015). Retrieved from globaldrugsurvey.com/the-global-drug-survey-2015-findings. Accessed on April 3, 2019.

15. Weinberg, B. A. and B. K. Bealer, *The World of Caffeine: The Science and Culture of the World's Most Popular Drug*, Routledge, Abingdon-on-Thames, UK (2004).

16. Fairbairn, C. E. and M. A. Sayette, "A social-attributional analysis of alcohol response," *Psychological Bulletin* **140**(5) (2014).

17. "Hangovers," *Mayo Clinic* (December 16, 2017). Retrieved from mayoclinic.org/diseases-conditions/hangovers/symptoms-causes/syc-20373012. Accessed on April 3, 2019.

18. Sarkar, D. et al., "Alcohol and the Immune System," *Alcohol Research: Current Reviews* **37**(2) (2015).

19. Konstantinovsky, M., "The doctor's guide to healthy drinking," *One Medical* (May 15, 2018). Retrieved from onemedical.com/blog/eat-well/healthy-drinking. Accessed on April 3, 2019.

20. Prakash, A., "The Rules For Eating With Your Hands In India, Africa And The Middle East," *Food Republic* (November 19, 2012). Retrieved from foodrepublic.com/2012/11/19/the-rules-for-eating-with-your-hands-in-india-africa-and-the-middle-east. Accessed on April 3, 2019.

21. "Culture and Etiquette," *Rough Guides* (2019). Retrieved from roughguides.com/destinations/asia/india/culture-etiquette. Accessed on April 3, 2019.

22. Kogan, R., "The Secret Power Behind Why We Pick Crowded Restaurants Over Empty Ones," *Fast Company* (August 29, 2013). Retrieved from fastcompany.com/3016506/the-secret-power-behind-why-we-pick-busy-restaurants-over-empty-ones. Accessed April 3, 2019.

23. "The Analog Method for the Digital Age," *Bullet Journal*, bulletjournal.com.

Chapter 10
How to Network Digitally and Online

"The problem isn't information overload, it's filter failure."
        ~Clay Shirky, author, from his keynote speech at the 2008 Web 2.0 Expo

10.1 The Power of Digital and Online Networking

A modern networking strategy is incomplete without an online or digital component. Whether you have watched the internet revolution as it started or you have grown up with internet access, digital and online activities for networking are now vital. In 2018, the global number of internet users increased by 7% to over 4 billion, and the number of social media users increased by 13% to 3.2 billion, indicating that it's not only new internet users who are adopting social media.[1] From 2005 to 2015, the percentage of the U.S. population that uses social media rose dramatically from 7% to 65%.[2] And the biggest increase in use over that time span wasn't the youth demographic, which hit 90% early—it was older users.

It is easy to feel overwhelmed by the plethora of options. The internet, apps, and social media have turned our lives into a continuous, high-volume news stream, and the flow of data is more than any one person can absorb. Although it is important to recognize the power of these tools and learn how to use them, your networking strategy must be selective to be effective. Without filtering and curation, social media and online networking can become a source of noise rather than useful signal.

Like all tools, digital ones can help or hurt us. The anonymity and distance (among other factors) provided by the internet can bring out the worst in some people,[3,4] and surely all of us have put something in writing at the keyboard that we never would have said in person. But used properly, social media can strengthen your relationships with people and help you to generate new and meaningful connections. Regular, easy contact with people, no matter where they are in the world, allows us to stay in touch and foster relationships in a way that would likely have been impossible before the digital revolution.

As powerful as social media and digital tools are, they work best in tandem with in-person interaction. This is the cyclical nature of online and in real life (IRL) networking; you want to do both. Meeting someone IRL can generate trust and rapport in a way that online interaction cannot.[5,6] Try to secure an IRL meeting with your new online contacts, if possible. Failing that, i.e., if distance makes it too great a challenge, then phone or video calls will do more than text. Reaching out to online contacts when you travel to arrange in person meetings is a great way to do this. The exact balance between your online and IRL networking efforts is going to depend on your personal preferences and circumstances, just make sure to maintain efforts in both arenas.

Think of social media and networking online as a large social event with many ongoing conversations. Just as you would not be rude or misbehave at an in-person social event, so too should you mind your manners online. There is the temptation to exercise less restraint online due to distance; we tend not to be as empathetic with words written on the screen as we would be if we could see the author in person. This is perhaps because we do not have the same cues from eye contact and body language that help us to relate. It is especially important to resist this temptation because online misbehavior can be saved, copied, and shared, as well as searched; it can come back to haunt you. Employers frequently conduct online searches about potential new hires, and negative or unflattering behaviors can affect your viability as a candidate for a job.[7] Again, being kind and gracious is not just the right thing to do, it is good for your career.

For the purposes of this book, networking activities are divided into two categories: active and passive (first introduced in Chapter 2). Active networking means taking action to meet people, e.g., attending an event or reaching out to someone. Passive networking refers to actions that increase your visibility so that other people to reach out to you, e.g., publications, a personal website, LinkedIn account, and social media presence. In effect, anywhere that your name appears online should be thought of as networking, whether you created it or someone else did. Good passive networking means having a positive and well-maintained online presence.

Digital networking allows you to follow trends, share your work and accomplishments, meet new people, connect others, maintain your existing contacts, generate useful content for others, find jobs and awards to apply for, learn, get new ideas, and promote yourself. It is an incredibly powerful, double-edged tool, and learning how to use it effectively, for the good of yourself and others, is an important part of sustainable networking.

10.2 Following Up with In-Person Contacts

Following up has been mentioned in other parts of this book, but because it is a thing that you will mostly do online, it is discussed further here. Following up is crucial, but most people don't do it well, even salespeople for whom it is part of their job.[8] Which means that having a good follow-up will give you a huge advantage over your peers. Confirm the person's preferred method of following up and then do it! A good follow-up will mention something specific that happened or what you talked about, making it personal and reminding the person of the time you spent together. You aren't required to have an agenda item; your message can simply say that you enjoyed meeting them and that you would like to keep in touch. If there is something you want to accomplish, you can introduce the idea and set up a meeting to talk about it, either on the phone or in person.

There is no official standard for when you should follow up. Some say within 24 hours after meeting,[9] others say within a week.[10] In his book *Never Eat Alone*, Keith Ferrazzi advocates following up immediately, if possible. Ultimately, you should assess the person, whether there is an urgent matter to discuss, and your personal preferences. You want to act while someone still remembers you, which depends on the person and the nature and circumstances of your meeting. When meeting a lot of people at conferences, it can be normal to wait until you are home to process your notes and the cards you received to make your follow-ups. This can be a good litmus test for whether you should follow up with someone: if you can't remember the person when you see their business card, then you probably shouldn't try to establish them as a connection. Under other circumstances, such as job interviews or after meeting someone famous or important, who may have trouble remembering you if you wait, you should follow up immediately. As a general rule, it's more important *that* you follow up than *when*.

Persistence can be important, because you may not get a response to your initial message. Suppose you met someone who said they would make an introduction for you, but you haven't heard back from them after your initial follow-up. Follow up again, and then possibly follow up once more after that. Always be polite—do *not* let frustration seep into your communications, because that would only decrease your chances of getting a response. Sometimes people go on vacation and miss your original message, or they are slow to respond due to an emergency or a tight deadline. Or they may not frequent the platform you used to contact them, in which case you might try another one. A general strategy is to send a follow-up three days after your first message (if you received no reply) and then a third message a week after the second if there is still no answer. Whether you should follow up beyond that will depend on your assessment of the situation.

Author Anecdote

My preferred method and platform for a follow-up is LinkedIn (see Chapter 11). I look over the person's card (if I got one), or I go through my notes, and search for the person on LinkedIn. Then I send them a connection request and a *personalized* message. If the person does not have a LinkedIn profile, then I send them an email. But if I pull out a business card and cannot remember who gave it to me, I don't follow up. I will still look them up on LinkedIn, as my memory of names is often not very good, so if I see their face it can spark the memory, in which case I send a message.

10.2.1 A special note on bad first impressions

You may occasionally end up in a meeting or interaction with someone that doesn't go well, which could happen for a number of reasons. The person might be having a bad day, be distracted by a work problem or an issue at home, or simply be a grouch. In short: it may have nothing to do with you. Unless the person's behavior was inappropriate or explicitly hostile, it's possible that they might respond differently on another day. In these instances, send a follow-up without any request for a reply. They may accept your gesture and respond, in which case you have salvaged the interaction, or they may not. Regardless, this good networking behavior will benefit you in the long run.

10.3 Maintaining Existing Contacts

While it is not necessary to be in constant correspondence with your network contacts, to network sustainably you need to be able to support your contacts based on their needs, interests, and circumstances. If you do not know those things, you cannot offer effective support. Check-ins don't have to be frequent; once a year can be enough for maintenance. If a contact tends to post a lot of updates to a social media platform that you share, such as LinkedIn, you may not even need to contact them directly if you also post regular updates that they can read. Because here too, the equitable and mutual flow of information is necessary.

Maintenance is especially important at the beginning of a networking relationship. After meeting someone, whether online or in person, it is vital to follow up, which can usually be done digitally. After that, check in occasionally, and share items such as useful articles, books, job opportunities, or relevant awards. You can ask about their work, offer congratulations, share your own news, or ask for advice. Reposting their content or giving them an endorsement on LinkedIn can also help you stay in touch and establish rapport.

Relationships which are well established, such as those that were forged over more lengthy periods, or in situations where you worked side by side, as in volunteering or graduate school, tend to be the tightest bonds, and may require less frequent contact afterwards in order maintain your connection, but they should not be neglected. Checking in with your friends or teachers from graduate school, the people you volunteered with etc. is important, because even if they will never forget you, their circumstances (and yours) will still be dynamic.

Using digital methods for contact maintenance such as texting, social media, and email, is convenient because these activities are asynchronous forms of communication. This means that both parties do not have to be actively participating at the same time to hold a conversation, whereas verbal conversation, in person or on the phone, requires both parties to be present at the same moment. Asynchronous communication is generally less intrusive, because it typically does not have to be answered immediately. When you do not need a rapid reply, this is a convenient way to connect that allows both parties to respond at their convenience.

10.4 Creating New Contacts Online

There are a variety of ways to generate new network connections online. Meeting new people online is similar to meeting people in person. It is easiest and smoothest if you are introduced by a mutual connection, but you should also reach out to people even when it requires a self-introduction. If you generate interesting content, whether it is a post, an article, or a comment on a thread, you create an opportunity for people to reach out to you.

10.4.1 Introducing yourself

When you identify someone that you would like to connect with who is not part of your company or immediate network, you will want to contact them online and introduce yourself. Do advance preparation and research the person before contacting them. Put their name into your search engine of choice, look them up on social media, see if they have a blog or a newsletter, and follow it. Look for ways that you can make an overture by offering them value, which can include following them on their preferred platforms, sharing their content, subscribing to their blog or newsletter, posting positive reviews of any books they have written, and using their hashtag, if they have one. Researching your potential contact is about respecting their time by being specific so that you can provide relevant context. If you want them to spend their time answering you, you first need to spend time researching them to find out what they do and what they care about.

When making new contacts online, you are less likely to be fruitful if you begin by asking favors, unless the favor is small and low effort, such as a simple question or a request for an informational interview (more on that below). It is better to establish trust and commonality with someone before you begin asking things of them. Better yet, do something for them first. It would be bad manners to immediately ask someone for a job in person (unless you are at a job fair), so apply the same rules and etiquette to your digital networking that you would in person.

Sometimes you will have to make a request in an opening message, but try to make that the exception and not the rule. In such cases, it is imperative that you research the person to find out as much as you can in order to personalize your message. Make your request clear, specific, and reasonable. "Reasonable" means that it is something that can accomplished easily, with little time or effort. If your request is vague, it puts the onus on the other party to figure out what you need, and if you don't know the person, they are unlikely to make that kind of effort for you.

Whether you are making a request or simply trying to start a new professional relationship, the message you send to introduce yourself should refer to *relevant* information that you have gathered about that person. Show that you prepared a message specially for them, rather than something generic. Avoid form messages, and let them know what about them prompted you to send the message.

Include information in your introductory message such as

(1) How you found the person (what brought them to your attention),

(2) Any mutual connections that you have,

(3) Who you are and what work you do,

(4) The things you have in common,

(5) What motivated you to send a message,

(6) Your request (if you have one) and how it could benefit them, or

(7) Something of value or interest to them.

These points provide context, which is very important when you are trying to make a new connection. It makes you real, relatable, and understandable, and you are more trustworthy when your motivations are transparent. Otherwise, you might be a scammer or a bot.

Because you want to be sustainable and not transactional, be careful with how your word items (6) and (7). If you make a request and immediately offer something in return, it may appear that your offer is contingent upon their compliance, which approaches that sleazy, transactional side of networking. You can tell them what the benefit will be for them if they answer your request, but avoid any "if you...then I" wordings or implication. If you make a request, wait until the request or task is concluded, then offer thanks and say, "please don't hesitate to ask if you need anything," or something similar. Be as specific if you can, which will make it more likely that your offer will be accepted.

Often, people will not respond to a self-introduction. Just like a follow up that goes unanswered, be persistent. You can send a few more messages, but keep the tenor light and cheerful. Don't let ego make you snippy and irritable. When (and if) you do finally receive a response, don't express annoyance that they didn't respond to you sooner (which would be self-defeating and awkward). Your goal is to keep your conversational partner comfortable, even if during a digital conversation; phrase your response as if they had responded to your first message.

You can generate new connections by contacting the authors of articles or other content that you enjoy. Look for any contact information listed with the article, find the author on LinkedIn, or search their name and some key words from the paper or article. Research them the way you would any other potential new connection, so that you can craft a personalized message. Include a congratulations on the publication, commenting on things you liked about it, and why it is relevant to you and your work. You can also ask them questions and offer assistance, which can spark discussion and generate both new friends and new professional contacts. Find these opportunities by reading journals, newsletters, news, etc. Such reading will also give you fodder for conversations.

10.4.2 Being introduced

While you can and should be making self-introductions, being introduced to someone by a mutual connection increases the chance that the new person will respond favorably. When people receive a recommendation from someone they already know and trust, they will be inclined to consider you as trustworthy. You may be introduced to someone because it occurs to them that the connection would be beneficial, or you can ask for an introduction. If there is someone you know you want to meet, look on LinkedIn to see if you have any mutual connections who could make an introduction. Researching the person you want to meet may also give you clues about other mutual connections that may not appear on LinkedIn, such as places they have worked, lived, and studied.

When you ask for an introduction, be specific. A vague question will get a vague answer, or none at all. For example, posting to your Facebook that you are looking for a job and asking, "Who can help me?" is unlikely to succeed. It asks your network to do the work for you, when it's your job to look through your contacts and ask a specific question to a certain person. As a general rule for networking, if you want a good answer, you need to invest the time to come up with a good question, which is a concrete, specific (reasonable) request addressed to a particular person or group. Research is important, because the more you know about a person (including who they know), the more targeted your question or request will be, and the more easily it will be fulfilled.

Accordingly, in your request for an introduction, provide relevant information about yourself and why you are interested in meeting the person of interest. Once your mutual connection has agreed to make an introduction, they should use the information you gave to explain to the third party why they are making the introduction. If your introducer fails to do this or conveys the information inaccurately, follow up as quickly as possible with the correct information and be diplomatic; don't embarrass your introducer, but do provide clarification as needed to prevent confusion.

Once you begin corresponding with the new person, always follow up with your introducer to let them know whether it went well or if the person did not respond. Whether someone has given you an introduction or advice, following up with thanks and describing the impact of their help will be appreciated, and that person will be more inclined to help you in the future.

10.4.3 Generating content as networking

Creating content that others can find is a valuable form of networking, referred to here as passive networking. Putting content out on your social media accounts, writing blog posts, papers or articles, and making thoughtful responses to other people's posts are all activities that raise your visibility and give others an opportunity to contact you. Part of your social media plan, as discussed below, should include generating content on select platforms, to create these passive networking opportunities.

If someone hasn't met you before, everything they know about you, i.e., the data upon which they will base their impression or assessment of you, is what they can find online. How you have crafted a profile, the quality and nature of your profile picture, and the content you choose to post is, for all intents and purposes, *you*, until they meet you in person. This makes it important to actively maintain your online presence.

Posting interesting things online can generate the same kind of fear of rejection that in person introductions can inspire, but remember that it is better to be memorable, if imperfect, than it is to be polished and forgettable. What you post should be kind, thoughtful, and checked for typographical errors, but it does not have to be perfect.

The content you generate informs your existing network about your areas of knowledge or current projects so that they can send the right opportunities your way. If you have posted a lot of useful information about, for example, cybersecurity, then when a connection of yours has a question about cybersecurity, your name will come to mind. And instead of writing individual people with your news (which you may still want to do in some cases), posting updates on blogs and social media provides similar information to many people at once. Consider this effort as a small, regular investment that can produce big results as time goes on.

The content that you post publicly online will network for you even when you are sleeping. If you ask good questions or post interesting and useful information in places where people can find it, you are advertising yourself and your interests, and people who like it can find you. However, if you lose your temper, are unkind or otherwise disrespectful, whether in a private or public forum, those comments can be saved and shared, so for your own sake and that of your networks and your communities, remain polite and professional, even if you disagree.

Author Anecdote

Even without making any efforts to look for jobs, simply having my LinkedIn profile filled out with my relevant experience regularly generates messages from people who are looking for someone with my skill set. While most of the messages come from recruiters, I have been contacted and found work I wasn't seeking by keeping my profile updated and attending to the messages I receive. This is my LinkedIn profile doing passive networking for me.

10.5 Informational Interviews

The informational interview is a process for learning about someone, their work, and their career. It is a great way to get to know someone better, to learn new career and technical information, and to expand your network. Informational interviews can be performed over the phone or in person and do not need to be referred to as an "informational interview" to be one. You can simply ask to have a conversation with someone about their work or research. These conversations can be anywhere from twenty minutes to an hour, depending on the person's availability.

A request for an informational interview is likely to be accepted because, as the name implies, it is only about information, requiring only a small amount of the person's time. A request for an informational interview lacks a specific agenda—you aren't trying to get job or something similar; the intent is to learn about the person and their work. If you want to make a different kind of request, such as for a job, you can do so, but be transparent about your intentions and do not call it an informational interview; doing so would be misleading.

When you find someone with whom you want to develop a relationship, and you have questions you would like to ask them, you can contact them and let them know you would like to set up an informational interview. This can be done in your initial email after you have been introduced by a third party or after making a self-introduction. The request involves a small commitment from the person, so be mindful of the time of year: around the holidays is generally not a good idea, and if the person resides in a different country than you, check if they observe holidays different than your own. Also be mindful of the relative time zones involved when scheduling an appointment.

Consider, too, the relative importance (i.e., workload) of the person you are contacting. People who are more prominent or senior will get more requests for their time than other people. The more important the person is, the more enticing your reason or offer of value will need to be, so again, researching the person in advance is very important. Do all of the things you would do for a formal interview: research the person, their company, see if they have a presence on LinkedIn or other social media, and read any papers they have published or watch recorded talks they have given.

If they agree to a phone call or meeting, pick a time, trade numbers in advance, and be punctual. During the interview, ask them about their job, what they like about it, the skills they use to perform their job, how they arrived at their current position, about their accomplishments, and if there is any way you can assist them. You can prepare these questions in advance and take notes during the interview. It is also okay to ask if they can suggest other people you could talk to on a particular subject (be specific), and if you have developed rapport, they will most likely refer you to more of their connections. Respect their time and don't run over the scheduled appointment, then follow up afterwards with thanks.

Note that while informational interviews can be procured and conducted in person, remote or digital methods provide you more options and freedom to perform them remotely.

Author Anecdote

I was only vaguely familiar with the concept of informational interviews, based on my academic and industry experience, when I became interested in working in science policy. I was introduced to someone with policy experience, and when we spoke, I was interested to hear that informational interviews are commonplace in her field and that a request for one would generally be accepted, not viewed as a surprise. Even if informational interviews are new to you, they are common in some professions, and requests will typically be well received. They are especially useful if you are considering career change, to hear more about the field you want to enter. Don't be afraid to give it a try!

10.6 Making Introductions for Others

Sometimes you will be the one to help others make new connections, which is a great way to give back to your network. There are two main scenarios where you will make digital introductions. First, you may have two contacts who have a common interest or goal, and you decide it would be worth introducing them. The other is when you are asked by one contact for an introduction to another.

Whether it was your idea or you were asked, before you initiate the introduction, consider the time and preferences of the people involved. It is generous and good sustainable networking to make introductions, but there a number of reasons why someone might not want to be introduced. They might not think the connection is a good fit; they might not be interested or able to help in the way requested; or they might be too busy at the moment. Thus, you should think of yourself as the gatekeeper of your own network. You want to understand why a person wants an introduction, assess the fit, and check with one or both parties before proceeding.

When someone asks for an introduction, ideally, they will explain why they want it and why they are interested in the other person. If they do not, ask for that information, so that you can decide whether you should proceed and be able to make a proper introduction with the necessary context.

If you proceed, contact the party (or parties) of interest. Let them know that a connection of yours is interested in meeting them, and why. Alternatively, if it was your idea, let each party know independently why you would like to introduce them. Ask if they are willing to be introduced; do not assume it. This is referred to as "the double opt-in," a term used by Adam Grant, author of the book *Give and Take*.[11,12] As mentioned above, there are a number of reasons why the answer might be no, and it spares them the unpleasant situation of having to decline *after* you have sent an introductory message, which could be awkward for everyone involved.

Should the person say no, or you decide not to proceed, decline and offer an explanation. You can say that the person is too busy or that you don't think they can answer the person's question. Be as polite and diplomatic as possible. While the best way to respond will be culturally dependent, responding with a prompt and polite "no" is preferable to answering with silence, which would leave the person wondering what went wrong. If compatibility was an issue, you can offer the person other possible introductions, if appropriate, or try to answer their question yourself.

If one or both parties agree to being introduced, you may then send a message to both of them. This message should include their full names and a few sentences about each of them, what they have in common, and why you think they should meet. Don't editorialize: "Susan is great!" is less useful than details such as, "Susan built a laser that got launched into space, and she's climbed Denali in Alaska." This necessarily involves some repetition, because you shared some or all of this information when confirming the introduction, but it lets each party know what information the other has.

Some people insist that you should never make a blind introduction, i.e., all introductions should be double opt-in. The decision will depend on how well you know the parties involved. If you're not familiar with everyone, it is best practice to err on the side of caution and seek permission before making the introduction. Asking avoids possibly inconveniencing one or more parties involved. However, if both people are close acquaintances, and you feel confident that they will not be bothered, you can proceed without the double opt-in. Whatever you do, use your best judgment and consider your contacts' preferences and time.

Following up with each party after the introduction is good practice to see how it went. Ideally, people would inform you without being reminded, but not everyone will realize that or remember to do so. Knowing how things worked out is valuable information about your contacts.

10.7 The Divide between Professional and Personal (or Not)

There is an increasing blurring of the lines between professional and personal when it comes to social media and online networking. To what extent you want to embrace, or resist, the bleeding of one into the other is a personal choice you will have to make for yourself. Certain platforms lend themselves more to personal subjects (such as Facebook) whereas others tend to be more professionally focused (such as LinkedIn), but almost any platform can be used for personal, or professional purposes, or both.

How personal you get in terms of what you share is just that, personal. The balance between sharing enough to let people know what is going on in your life and enable them to engage with you, and what is too much, is something that is different for everyone and every culture. Making yourself vulnerable by sharing your struggles and your failures makes you relatable and allows people to emotionally invest in you or share in your efforts. However, sharing too much (or the wrong things) can make you and others uncomfortable, and what that is will depend heavily on your network and your culture, as well as the platform you are using. What you share on Facebook is likely to be, and perhaps should be, different that what you share on LinkedIn or Twitter. It is something to think about and experiment with, to determine what works best for you.

Just as some subjects are taboos in conversation, some of these same subjects should be considered taboo in online conversation. As a general rule, if you are using an account in a professional capacity, avoid posting content that falls into the commonly taboo categories of sex, politics, religion, and money. And if it is not something that you would be comfortable talking about in person, don't post it online. In fact, considering that statements made online can be copied, pasted, shared, forwarded, have screenshots taken of them, be saved and effectively stored forever, even if you delete the original post, you should consider giving what you post even more scrutiny than what you say in person, in both personal and professional online spaces. The exception to the general prohibition on posting things like politics and religion in a professional space is if those are directly relevant to your work.

Depending on your job, you may need to use Facebook for professional purposes. In that case, if you want to keep a strict separation, you will have no remedy other than creating a secondary account and maintaining two, a strategy which many attempt and then discard as too much work. If you attempt to use one account for both professional and personal purposes, you should consider carefully the kind of content that you share, and pay close attention to the permissions and privacy controls available on that platform.

You may receive friend requests from professional connections on personal accounts, or connection requests from friends and family on professional accounts. Sharing certain personal information with your professional network may be inappropriate, but there is generally nothing wrong with sharing your professional life with friends and family. Add friends and family if you are comfortable doing so, as this increases the diversity of your network, but be more selective. But be more selective when connecting with otherwise professionally related people on personal sites.

Author Anecdote

I do not use my Facebook for professional purposes, which means that I miss participating in certain professional groups and the conversations in those groups, but it gives me privacy in a way that is important to me. I can post personal content without doubling-checking my permissions or worrying about sharing things with the wrong group. I also use a different name for my Facebook profile than the one I use professionally, as an extra precaution to prevent blurring my professional and personal life on this platform.

10.7.1 Privacy and permissions

It is a good idea to be familiar with and regularly review the privacy and permission settings of any social media platform that you use, especially if you want to keep a separation between your personal and professional lives. Decide how much you want strangers on the internet to be able to learn about you, and check that your settings reflect that. Your privacy settings can affect your reputation, networking opportunities, and your safety, so give them some careful attention.

10.8 Creating Your Online and Social Media Plan

As with all forms of networking, you should use digital and social media platforms strategically. There is a point of diminishing returns when it comes to the time and effort you invest in your online presence, and there is a risk of getting overwhelmed or diluting your efforts in an attempt to be part of everything. Part of your strategy should be to pick one or two platforms based on fit and goals, and become involved in greater depth, establishing yourself there rather than spreading yourself thin across multiple platforms. You can create accounts on many platforms, but regular activity on all of them would require an exorbitant amount of time. Link your lesser-used accounts to your more-active ones so that you can be found almost anywhere via a trail that leads to the places where you spend time.

It's important to be interactive on the platforms you select. Like in-person conversations, your goal is to dialogue, not monologue. Post your own content, but also look at and respond to the content of others. Only posting and never liking, replying to, or commenting on other people's posts is the equivalent of dominating a conversation with only things you have to say about yourself. Discussion and conversations in the comment section can lead to new network connections, so it behooves you to be active and comment on things that interest you professionally, and it creates value for the community.

With the constant deluge of information and the continuous proliferation of online networking, apps, and social media and messaging platforms, filtration and curation are important principles to observe. Filtering is about rejecting noise from the signal you are trying to observe, and curation is about selecting the pieces of information you want to see. Apply them to your platform feeds so that you get the kind of content you want. This process can be automated and outsourced to the platform itself, rather than performed manually by you, which would take a lot of time that you could spend on higher-impact activities. Your goal here is to efficiently increase the signal-to-noise ratio of the information in your feed. Chapter 11 will discuss how to manage your feed for various relevant platforms.

Diversity is important in your online networking strategy, with respect to the type of content and people you follow. This is easy to achieve on platforms such as Twitter, where users' posts are public by default and no permission is required to follow someone. A feed that displays information from a diverse set of people will boost your creativity and inspire new ideas.

A high-level plan for how to address your social media can make it more manageable. This plan should include things like how frequently you check and post on your chosen platforms, as well as the purpose of each account. Consistent usage is more important than volume, so create a schedule and regularly review and update your accounts, regardless of the frequency or volume.

Your plan should also address the sort of content you want to create. What do you want to be known for, considering the aggregate of your social media and digital footprint? This is what people will research if you send them a message and they haven't met you before. Employers consider this information, and you can use it to provide interesting and valuable material to your network. The content you create and release online is part of your introduction, so consider what you share in that light. You might want to take down some posts, in addition to curating what you share, in order to create an accurate and positive impression of yourself based on your output.

Use your circumstances and self-awareness to determine the type of content you want to create. Ask yourself what kinds of information, format, and platforms play to your strengths. Do you enjoy writing? A blog and guest posts or articles might be good for you. Are you better in conversation? Perhaps a podcast is the way to go. Are you a photographer? An Instagram account with an on-going photo project might be best. Maybe you are an excellent presenter in front of a live audience, in which case, look for speaking opportunities and try to get recordings posted online. You can generate content by promoting your friends' posts and successes, or sharing interesting articles. Again, imperfect action is acceptable, and whatever you are creating, you will improve. Don't let the idea that you need to know everything or be perfect at it stop you from getting started.

Only dedicate time to a digital platform if it is useful for your networking goals. If you build your networking goal first and your digital and online strategy second, then choosing the right platform will be easier. It will also make your efforts more productive. Join platforms and discussion forums relevant to your interests and make a reputation for yourself by answering questions, being helpful, or posting content you think will interest the group. Just as you want to give before you get in terms of networking sustainably, apply the same principle to your digital activities. Most of your posts should promote the work of others and generate useful content. Don't forget to self-promote, as well. If you give a presentation or publish a paper, share it with your online networks!

As part of your online and social media plan, regularly research your own name online. Use multiple search engines, such as Google, Bing, Duck Duck Go, and others, to see variations in the results. If there is negative information about you or someone with the same name on the internet, address it by removing it, pushing it to the second page of results (or beyond), or making your name more distinct (for more details, see Section 11.4).

10.8.1 Profile design

Most social media platforms offer not just a means of interacting but a profile that you can fill with details about yourself and your experience. For some platforms, the focus is the profile, while others have minimal profiles and focus more on content and user interaction. No matter how limited or detailed the profile, if you are going to use a platform, you should fill it out accurately (be authentic) and with an emphasis on information relevant to your networking goals (curation and signal-to-noise ratio). Your elevator pitch (see Subsection 5.2.4), distilled to no more than three sentences, is a useful statement to include. A professional and recognizable photograph is also important, discussed further in Chapter 11.

10.8.2 Digital networking and efficiency

Online networking and social media can become a huge time sink. The dopamine rush that we get from having our posts liked and discussed is a documented fact, and it is literally addictive.[13] This behavior makes good habits around the use of online networking methods important as a way to protect your time and productivity. Staying aware of how you spend your time is an important part of your digital networking strategy.

But how do you draw the line between necessary involvement and a waste of time? Ultimately, that will depend on you. Technology and networking should generally enhance our work lives, so if you notice that your social media and digital networking have begun to affect your productivity, you have gone too far. To avoid that, you want certain limits in place, such as a maximum permitted amount of time per day (or week), or only checking your accounts and answering messages once per day (or less frequently, depending on the platform).

Beware the trap of thinking that you can combine social media with a work task; multitasking is a myth.[14] What is referred to as *multitasking* is just the rapid shifting between several tasks, and because toggling between tasks takes effort and recovery time, these repeated interruptions hurt productivity.[15] In other words, you will accomplish more by spending thirty minutes on one task, followed by thirty minutes on a second task, than you would "multitasking" those two tasks for an hour. A useful limiter to prevent switching between work and social media is to delete apps from your smartphone, turn off non-essential notifications, and only check those accounts at a fixed time or for a limited amount of time.

A dedicated and consistent time of day, or day of the week, when you check specific platforms can help your efficiency and make it easier for others to correspond with you. If someone knows that you check your email first thing in the morning and then not again until the next day, then they will know when it's appropriate to send you a follow up if they haven't heard from you. By being consistent about when you respond, people will know when they can expect an answer from you. Predictability here makes communication easier.

Your strategy may be different for each platform, or you may need to check your work email throughout the day, but make sure you have a plan in place. The dopamine you get from checking social media, plus the momentary satisfaction of avoiding a difficult or boring task, can result in checking things mindlessly and more often than necessary. Make a conscious decision about how you want to use social media in a way that works for you, write it down, put it on your calendar or get an app that helps you track your usage, and execute your plan. You may find that your initial approach doesn't work the way you were hoping, but don't worry. Think of it as an experiment, take mental and/or physical notes, and try something else until you find a methodology that works for you. Technology and the internet should be treated as a way to enhance your networking and work efforts; it's a tool, not a goal.

Exercises

The following exercise will help you develop your online and digital networking strategy by generating an outline and ideas for the type of content you want to create. The next chapter will discuss various platforms, at which point you can add more details to your plan.

(1)   Search your name on Google, Bing, and any other relevant search engines. Are you on the first page of results? Are the results positive, or is there confusion, such as a famous axe murder who shares your name?

(2)   Based on your search results from Exercise 1, what kind of picture does it create of you? Is it good? Is it bad? Is it the kind of image you want? Or can you not be found? Take measures to improve what you find by removing anything unfavorable that you can or by changing the publicity settings on your relevant social media accounts. How to address negative information you cannot remove is discussed in Section 11.4.

(3)   Using your self-awareness, think about what kind of content you can generate that (a) interests you, (b) plays to your strengths, and (c) matches your career goals, both immediate and long-term. Whether it's writing articles, topics you would like to discuss, hosting a podcast, or types of information you would like to raise awareness of in your network, pick one or two things that you can focus on, and keep them in mind as you read the next chapter. This will help you identify what platforms would be best for you to use. Creating new, positive content can help you to address any negative information that you may not have been able to remove in Exercise 2; it can push negative items lower in the search results.

(4)   Continuing with your strategic plan, think about generating a schedule for yourself as to how you will dedicate time to networking. Consistency is more important than frequency. Schedule time at least once a month to search your name, update your status on your social media accounts, and like, share, or re-post your friends' and colleagues' content. Put your schedule on your calendar, plan to adhere to it for several months (until you generate some data), and then reassess.

References

1. Kemp, S., "Special Reports: Digital in 2018: World's internet users pass the 4 billion mark," *We Are Social* (2018). Retrieved from wearesocial.com/uk/blog/2018/01/global-digital-report-2018. Accessed April 5, 2019.

2. Perrin, A., "Social media usage: 2005-2015," Pew Research Center: Internet & Technology (October 8, 2015). Retrieved from pewinternet.org/2015/10/08/social-networking-usage-2005-2015. Accessed on April 5, 2019.

3. Santana, A. D., "Virtuous or vitriolic: The effect of anonymity on civility in online newspaper reader comment boards," *Journalism Practice*, **8**, 1 (2014).

4. "6 Reasons Why People Are Jerks On The Internet," *Likeable* (April 7, 2014). Retrieved from likeable.com/blog/2014/6-reasons-people-jerks-internet. Accessed on April 5, 2019.

5. Jiang, J. et al., "Neural synchronization during face-to-face communication," *J. Neuroscience* **32**(45) (2012).

6. Blenke, L. R., *The role of face-to-face interactions in the success of virtual project teams*, Dissertation, Missouri University of Science and Technology (2013).

7. Hoffman, A., "Job Applicant, Beware: You're Being Googled," *Monster* (2019). Retrieved from monster.com/career-advice/article/hr-googling-job-applicants. Accessed on April 5, 2019.

8. Brooks, M., "Following Up with Prospects: 90 Percent Never Do." *Sales Gravy*. Retrieved from salesgravy.com/sales-articles/closing-techniques/Following-Up-with-Prospects-90-Percent-Never-Do. Accessed on February 20, 2019.

9. Doyle, A., "How to Follow Up After a Networking Event," *The Balance Careers* (February 8, 2019). Retrieved from thebalancecareers.com/follow-up-letter-to-a-contact-met-at-a-networking-event-2063486. Accessed on April 5, 2019.

10. Salerno, C., "The Follow-up Email Template That'll Get You Responses (Almost) Every Time," *The Muse* (2019). Retrieved from themuse.com/advice/the-followup-email-template-thatll-get-you-responses-almost-every-time. Accessed on April 5, 2019.

11. Feloni, R., "The Terrible Networking Mistake That Almost Everyone Makes," *Business Insider* (January 8, 2015). Retrieved from businessinsider.com/most-common-networking-mistake-2015-1. Accessed on April 5, 2019.

12. Grant, A. M., *Give and Take: A Revolutionary Approach to Success*, Penguin, London (2013).

13. Haynes, T., "The Terrible Networking Mistake That Almost Everyone Makes," *Science in the News Boston* (May 1, 2018). Retrieved from sitn.hms.harvard.edu/flash/2018/dopamine-smartphones-battle-time. Accessed on April 5, 2019.

14. MacKay, J., "The Myth of Multitasking: The ultimate guide to getting more done by doing less," *RescueTime Blog* (January 17, 2019). Retrieved from sitn.hms.harvard.edu/flash/2018/dopamine-smartphones-battle-time. Accessed on April 5, 2019.

15. Jackson, T. et al., "Reducing the effect of email interruptions on employees," *International J. Information Management* **23**(1) (2003).

Chapter 11
Networking Platforms

"Social media is not a media. The key is to listen, engage, and build relationships."
~David Alston, technology and marketing startup entrepreneur

11.1 Know the Playing Field

The technology and software landscape changes quickly, but this chapter covers currently relevant platforms and their uses, various apps, and other forms of relevant remote networking, such as phone use and email. Certain players in the online domain have staying power and are likely to be relevant for a while to come, such as Facebook, Twitter, and LinkedIn. However, new competitors regularly enter the market, and there is no way to know for sure what will remain relevant, what will fade away, and what new platform may upset the status quo. For example, Google+ for consumers was shut down on April 2, 2019.[1] Regardless, this chapter covers currently relevant platforms and their uses.

The exercises at the end of Chapter 10 were designed to provide you with a general idea of how you would like to engage with your network via content, and to create a schedule for your digital and social media usage. As you read, look for platforms that will be useful towards these goals and plans, and make notes about which remote networking methods you would like to further research or pursue.

11.2 Suggestions for Basic Etiquette and Use

The same etiquette caveats that apply to in-person interactions (see Section 4.4) also apply in the digital realm. The applicability of the following suggestions will depend the scenarios and cultures involved. As you consider proper etiquette for remote, digital, and online networking, remember the core principles of sustainable networking: kindness and interacting in a mutually beneficial way that allows people to be comfortable.

Many of the methods of communication described here involve typed text, and the quality of that text is important. First, do your best to avoid misspellings and other typographical errors. Your text doesn't have to be perfect, but errors will add noise and distract from the message you are trying to communicate. When you send someone a message or make a post, re-read or proofread your messages. By cleaning up your messages, you make your reader or readers more comfortable, which reflects well on you and your communication abilities. On the other side, remember to be patient with the occasional typo: it happens to all of use.

Note that text written all in uppercase is, in many circumstances, considered to be the textual equivalent of yelling. And just as yelling is inappropriate during face-to-face professional interactions, so too should you consider it inappropriate in your professional digital networking. Text is also a difficult medium through with to communicate emotions,[2,3] so limit your use of sarcasm, which is easy to misunderstand in written form,[4] and consider possible ambiguities or erroneous interpretations of your wording.

Regarding the content of your text, always be professional and respectful, even if you believe you are speaking in a closed forum. It may be tempting to respond sharply to someone who is being rude or difficult, but remember that (a) it is possible that you have misconstrued their tone and meaning and they are perhaps not intending to create the impression that you are getting, and (b) if you lose your temper online, what you write in response can be reported, with or without the statements leading up to it as context. Your test to determine if something is appropriate to post is to imagine what would happen if it were shared with your whole network. If you wouldn't want that, don't post it.

It can be difficult to maintain your composure when you do not receive a response from people within your desired time frame. However, you do not know all of the details of the other person's life, and a circumstance that has nothing to do with you might keep them from responding in a timely fashion. Don't let impatience prompt you to send a grouchy email because you haven't received an answer. Following up is acceptable, but it should be positive, friendly, and professional. If you lose your temper and it turns out the other party was on vacation or away due to a death in the family, you will appear insensitive. Even if your worst fears are true and they are ignoring you, an irate response will bring negative attention, and it will not improve your chances of an answer.

At the other extreme, you might participate in a back-and-forth chat conversation via text message or email where you and the other party respond immediately. When an otherwise asynchronous form of communication is being used in synchronous fashion but you need to discontinue, it is generally good manners to excuse yourself, just as you would on the phone or in person. This lets the other party or parties know that you have to stop responding right away.

As for receiving and sending connection requests for social media accounts that you use professionally, avoid connecting with people you do not know. Only send or accept connection requests to and from people with whom you are familiar and would be willing to endorse on the strength of your reputation. You should be able to say something positive or supportive about the person's abilities. If they aren't someone you feel comfortable saying, "I know this person, and I recommend them," then don't send or accept a connection with them.

> **Author Anecdote**
> I was once contacted through LinkedIn regarding a job opportunity from a potential employer. This person opened with a personalized message and connection request. I answered their message and set up a call, but I waited to accept their connection request until after the call, which went well. They made a positive impression on me, and so I accepted the connection. A few weeks later, I received an email from a friend whom they had also contacted. He only accepted their request for a call because he had a mutual connection with them: me. He saw my connection with them as an indicator that they were trustworthy, because he trusted me. This is why I never accept requests from people I don't know; I don't want to mislead my existing connections.

The last chapter briefly discussed the value of being interactive. If online conversations are the equivalent of real-life conversations, then posting but never responding to others' posts is like monologuing instead of creating a dialogue. The principle of equitable exchange, which is important for sustainable networking, applies to online networking venues, too. Consistency is also helpful: it is hard to establish a reputation if you are never or seldom active. You do not need to be high frequency or dedicate large amounts of time to the enterprise, but try to be regularly and consistently involved on those platforms that you have chosen.

Finally, use good passwords for your accounts. A weak password, or the same password across multiple platforms, puts you at risk of getting hacked. If someone breaks into your account, then they will have access to a lot of your personal information, can imitate you or steal from you, and cause problems for your connections. If necessary, a password management system can help you remember your passwords. Strong, regularly updated passwords are important for both you and your network.

11.3 Platforms

There are many platforms, and it can be hard to decide which ones to use. When considering platforms, the key is to balance two factors: (a) where is your professional community most active, and (b) where are you most comfortable? You want to be where your colleagues are, and you want the best match for the type of content you wish to provide (play to your strengths). Pick one or two platforms where you will dedicate your time and attention. Don't try to frequently use many platforms, this will be an energy drain, and spreading yourself thin won't allow you to do each one well. Only use as many as you can do well, while conserving your time and energy for work productivity. The goal is to be efficient but also to have relevant content about yourself for others to find and to find ways to benefit your connections in a way that plays to your strengths.

11.3.1 Phone and video calls

Because phone and video calls are synchronous forms of communication, it is best to plan calls in advance, which ensures that the other person or persons are available when you want to speak. As a general rule, calls with more than two people should always be planned in advance due to possible schedule conflicts. You will sometimes achieve spontaneous calls between two people, but you can still run into scheduling conflicts. Using an asynchronous form of communication to schedule the call, such as email or text message, is the best practice. When scheduling a call, offer more than one possible day or time that works for you to give the person options, and let them know roughly how long you anticipate the call will be.

As with almost all networking, prepare in advance. Review your research on the person if they are new or if you speak with them infrequently. Have relevant materials or notes available for you to refer to during the call. Take the call in a quiet place in consideration of literal signal-to-noise. If you are making a video call, as opposed to an audio-only phone call, dress appropriately for the formality of the call. Also consider what will appear in the background of your image; position yourself and your webcam accordingly to eliminate visual noise. For example, don't take the call in your bedroom with a pile of clothes on an unmade bed in the background.

When you make the call, identify yourself immediately to the person who answers. Don't make them guess or assume someone will be able to identify you by the sound of your voice, even if you have scheduled the call for that time. Doing so only sets you up for an awkward situation if they get it wrong. There is also a possibility that an administrative assistant will answer the person's calls and that you will not reach the person directly. If you know this to be the case, you can state your name and that you have a call with Dr. Pak at 10:30 (fill in the relevant time and name).

If you are making an unscheduled call or a cold call (i.e., the person does not know you; see Section 12.6), don't ask to speak to the person at length. Instead, succinctly state your purpose, and ask if you could set up a time for a discussion or if now is an okay time. Even if your intended conversation is brief, ask if they have one or two minutes to spare before proceeding. This expresses consideration for the other person's time. If the answer is no, don't take it personally, and arrange to call back another time.

There are several considerations to keep in mind during a call. You may want to take notes, but do so with pen and paper, as typing on a keyboard can create unwanted noise. Your posture and body language during the call will affect your verbal delivery, even if it is an audio-only call. For example, people can differentiate smile types with only audio cues.[5] If you have an important call to make, either sit up straight at your desk or take the call while standing. If you are having a casual conversation, sitting in a relaxed fashion is fine. Always inform someone if you have them on speakerphone, and let them know who is present, lest they say something that they do not want overhead. Avoid eating and drinking while on the call: it can create unpleasant sounds or visuals for the other party and distract you when you should be giving them your full attention.

What you talk about during the call will depend on whether it is a meeting, a social call, or an informational interview. Phone conversations generally follow the same etiquette as in-person conversations. Resist the urge to fill silence, and allow for pauses in conversation so that everyone gets a chance to speak as needed. Refer to any notes you wrote in advance to ensure that you address all desired topics. If you accidentally interrupt the other person, which is hard to avoid with signal lag or the lack of visual cues, excuse yourself and say, "please go ahead." When you are finished with the call, thank the person for their time, say that it was nice to speak with them, say goodbye, give them time to respond, and hang up.

Send a follow up afterwards with another thank you. You can review any action items that were discussed (tasks to be completed after the call), or if there were none, you can simply say that you had a nice conversation. If there were people who couldn't attend a group call, include them in your follow up along with a summary of relevant information and the conclusions or actions going forward.

There are a variety of services that you can use for voice and video calls, including Skype,[6] Hangouts,[7] Zoom Meeting,[8] and WebEx,[9] to name a few. Many include audio-only, video, and group calling options but may require software installation, so set up the service before you plan to use it.

11.3.2 Email

Email is a great tool for traversing time zones that allows you to send messages at any time without intruding the way a phone call might. It is also good to use when you want to have a documented trail of progress, including agreed upon action items or a record of scheduling, which you cannot get on the phone. Storage and organization of correspondence is easy with email, and most people in STEM fields will use it, though some people don't use personal accounts with much frequency.

If you are using a personal email address for professional purposes, as opposed to an employer-provided one, make sure that the username and address are professional, ideally consisting of some combination of your name and initials. If your name is Mae McPerson, then usernames such as mmcperson, mae.mcperson, mcpersonm, and similar variations are good. Avoid usernames that are silly nicknames, off-color, or not clearly related to you and your work. The best email address is one that does not call attention to itself; it should be simple and make sense. If this means migrating to a new email address, do it.

Basic etiquette regarding text content and quality, as described in the general etiquette section, should be observed in email. Whether you are contacting someone new, following up, or touching base with a contact, use a succinct, descriptive subject line, and a brief, focused message. Re-read what you have written, pare it down, and check it for errors. It is slow and frustrating to decipher a garbled or rambling message, which will reduce your chances of receiving a response, particularly if you are contacting someone new. Having some kind of action item in mind is good, which can be as simple as suggesting a short phone call, if you are thinking of proceeding with some kind of business or collaboration with this person.

When you send an email but you don't get a response, don't be afraid to follow up. As mentioned previously, keep it polite, don't sound annoyed, and be persistent. Check your email regularly and answer in a timely fashion, ideally within 12 hours for business items, though sooner is better in most cases.[10,11] On the other hand, it is possible to check email too frequently; checking it less frequently can reduce stress.[12] Personal email can have longer response times, but the more formal a message is, the sooner you should respond. If the message is urgent, from a very important person, or states that it requires an immediate response, respond as soon as possible. If it is a longer message, requires some thought, or input from others, reply to say that the message has been received and when you expect to have an answer. If you discover a long-forgotten email in your inbox, respond to it and make a brief apology; it doesn't have to be elaborate, but be genuine, acknowledge the lapse, and do your best to respond to the message.

If you are included in an email that has been sent to multiple people, be judicious with your use of "reply all." No one likes to deal with irrelevant emails, so only reply to the necessary parties. Likewise, don't mass-forward chain emails. You only want to send thoughtful content, so forward content to one or two people if you think the information will be useful and relevant to them professionally.

When you are away from your email, write an automatic response with an appropriate message. It should include information such as when you expect to be back and how to reach you or who else to contact if the matter is urgent. Remember to disable the auto-responder upon your return.

11.3.3 SMS and texting

Texting, that is, the use of SMS and messaging apps, is another text-based, asynchronous form of communication. Compared to email, it is more immediate, because most people have notifications set up on their phones to let them know when a text message arrives, which is often not the case for email. This means that people tend to read and respond to their text messages sooner, making texting better than email for reaching someone quickly, making last-minute arrangements, or sending updates regarding in-person meetings. Even though it is an asynchronous communication method, the immediacy and notifications mean that you should text only during the normal hours when you would expect the recipient to be awake; if it is a formal relationship, restrict texting to business hours.

Texting is a remote but direct communication method, so it can be a temptation to communicate more informally via text message than you would in person.[13] Before you send a message, imagine making that statement in person. If the idea makes you uncomfortable, delete or reword your message until it passes the test. Like any kind of digital networking, your messages can be saved, shared, and publicized, and remember that some people have lost their jobs over private text messages.

Texting is generally not necessary for business purposes, even though it can be convenient. If you do not already have a texting feature or messaging app for personal use, it is probably not necessary to add it for professional use.

11.3.4 LinkedIn

LinkedIn is a social media website that focuses on business and professional connections, with 610 million users in 200 countries.[14] The United States is where it is the most popular, with 150 million users, but it is also popular in India (52 million users), China (44 million users), Brazil (34 million users), and the UK (25 million users), with a total of 562 million users in 200 countries.[15]

It is particularly valuable as a networking tool because of its ability to identify mutual connections you have with another LinkedIn user. The value of this tool cannot be understated. If you know there is a person you want to meet or get to know, and you can look them up on LinkedIn, the site will find your common connections, making it easy to know who to ask for an introduction. It also has many of the usual social media features, including a newsfeed, the ability to make posts that can be followed, groups related to workspaces, schools, and interests, as well as direct messaging. Video courses are also available.

The basic account for LinkedIn is free, and it is possible to participate fully in the LinkedIn community with a free account. A premium membership has more features, including the ability to contact people even if you're not connected (in the free version, you can only send messages to connections), see everyone who views your profile, get job listings curated for you, and more. For individuals, LinkedIn Premium Career currently costs $29.99 USD/month, with a one-month free trial available.

A LinkedIn account includes a profile page where you can list your education, work information, skills, volunteer experience, awards, publications, and more. Just as you should be networking for the job you want or the goals you have, you should write your LinkedIn profile accordingly. Complete it with as much relevant information as possible. Just as you can use your goals to curate what networking activities you pursue, use them to curate the content that you provide. If it does not support your goal or is unrelated to the job you do or want to do, it can serve as a distraction (reducing your signal-to-noise ratio), and it doesn't need to be included. At a minimum, fill out your "about" statement, your education and work history, and then carefully check it for typographical errors. The default URL for your account comes with a unique string of numbers at the end that can be difficult to remember, so take advantage of the URL customization feature. Replace the alphanumeric string with some variation of your name (you can make it more unique by adding your initials).

Endorsements of skills and recommendations are a part of the social media aspect of your LinkedIn profile. When you add skills to your profile, LinkedIn will automatically ask your connections for endorsements. This is done with just a few clicks. You can navigate to a connection's skill section of their profile and endorse their skills, which is a simple and easy way to do something helpful for that person. Recommendations are a similar feature, where you can write a statement saying how you know the person and what you think of them professionally. This takes more work than endorsements but carries more weight. If you had a bad experience with someone, it is generally not worth writing a bad public review; LinkedIn reviews are not the right venue for complaints and may reflect poorly upon you.

Another important part of your profile is your photo. It helps people to find you from among similar profiles and lets people know you are a real person (not a scammer or bot). Use a clear, professional-looking picture of yourself, including your shoulders and your face. You should be recognizable and dressed appropriately for your line of work. No photo, or a photo that is blurry, poorly cropped, or unprofessional, conveys a lack of attention to detail. If you want to go one step further and make your image more memorable, you can find a subtle and small way to push the norm of what is typical for your profession. Look at the photos of those who are in similar positions and lines of work, and find a way to make your photograph stand out while staying to theme, e.g., an interesting accessory, garment, or haircut.

When adding new connections, LinkedIn gives you a standard connection message when you send an invitation. It is essential to personalize the message, reminding the person of how you know each other, your real-life connection, etc., the same as you would in a follow-up email. Exceptions to this rule are people who you know, without any doubt, will remember you easily, such as people with whom you have a long-standing relationship. As a point of general etiquette, do not invite people you do not know to connect, and do not send impersonal connection requests to new acquaintances. Likewise, do not accept connections with people who you do not know. You do not want to publicly declare a connection, which is an implication of support, with someone you know nothing about.

In addition to a profile, you will have a newsfeed that shows posts and activity made by your connections; you can make posts, as well, which will be shared with them. Curate who you are following, populating your feed with useful information, rather than having to dig through irrelevant items to get to what you want. This process becomes more important the more connections that you have. There is a difference between following and connecting on this platform, and you can unfollow people without disconnecting from them. You can also order your feed by either most recent posts or top posts (though how LinkedIn determines a "top post" is opaque). It is also possible to follow companies and hashtags to see their content in your feed.

Whatever you post will show up in your followers' newsfeeds; currently, "following" is the default setting when you connect with someone. You can share articles that you find interesting, news stories, your successes (such as getting a promotion or getting an award), or your research or projects (so long as it is okay with your employer). Think about the kind of content you want to share: it should align with your goals, be valuable to your followers, and reflect the professional focus of the site.

There are also groups that you can join within the LinkedIn community that will give you content and discussions specific to their theme. Pick ones that accurately reflect your interests and goals, whether it relates to your current research, if you are trying to network into a new area or learning about a new subject. Group members can read posts, comment, and participate in discussions in a group, allowing everyone to get to know each other. Groups can be related to schools you have attended, research interests, employers, geographical location, and more. Join a few that interest you and fit your overall strategy. The groups you join will be displayed in your profile, giving others more information about you.

LinkedIn also offers job listings, some of which can be applied for directly through the site. Recruiters use the site, and your profile can be enabled to let them know you are looking for work. If your current employer is unaware that you are planning to change jobs, note that job-seeking activities, such as joining job-seeking groups, might be shared with your network, depending on your privacy settings. As your network likely includes current colleagues, review your settings with respect to job seeking, especially if you have not yet publicly shared that you are considering alternative employment.

11.3.5 ResearchGate

ResearchGate is another professional social media site, with a focus on publications and questions. A survey by *Nature* found that of scholars who regularly use social media, ResearchGate was the most popular site.[16] It allows users to share the texts of their publications with other users, as well as post and respond to research-related questions. Like LinkedIn, it offers a profile, newsfeed of items from the people you follow, job listings, and direct messaging, but there are no groups. Under your profile, there are site stats, showing how many times other users have read your publications, the number of publications you have listed, and how many questions you have posted or answered. These scores are compiled into an aggregate "RG Score," which speaks to the amount of research you have available and how many people interact with your content (includes Q&A), though there have been objections to the platform's opaque scoring methodology.[17]

Creating and maintaining an account is free, but you need an email address from a recognized institute or university; you can't sign up with a personal email address. When filling out your profile, include relevant details and a professional image of yourself, the same as for a LinkedIn profile. After signing up, you will be asked to identify your publications. You are automatically connected with your co-authors, and you can follow their activities and the publications of other researchers. You can share full-text versions of your papers, either publicly or upon request, and you can read and request the same from other researchers.

Be careful about publicly posting full texts of publications that are not open access. Copyright law varies from country to country, but generally, publishers of scientific research papers, not the authors, hold the copyrights for those papers. If the paper is open access and not behind a paywall, it is already freely shared, so posting it publicly is typically fine. However, if you go around a publisher's paywall by posting a copy publicly (even if you are the author), you may be in copyright violation. As a result of some lawsuits, ResearchGate has made substantial changes to its paper-sharing practices, and some authors receive take-down notices because of copyright violations.[18]

Whether or not you can legally share a non-open-access full-text paper with someone directly will depend on the circumstances and applicable copyright laws. The debate over open access, copyright, and modern publishing is a topic of rich debate, and is especially important to think about if you have an academic job with an emphasis on publications.

11.3.6 Facebook

As of this writing, Facebook is one of the most popular social networking websites in the world, with over 2.3 billion users,[19] and its primary focus for individual users is personal use. Users do not have to be individuals, and many businesses, public figures, and musical groups have accounts (pages) as well. While it is primarily personal for many people, some jobs will require you to have and use a Facebook account, blending the personal and professional. Decide how you want to use it and adjust your privacy settings appropriately. Some choose to maintain both a personal and a professional Facebook account, but the separation can be hard to manage.

Facebook accounts are free, and you can sign up with a personal email address. Features include a profile page, a newsfeed, direct messaging, groups, event listings, and a marketplace where you can purchase items for other users. Because of the personal nature of Facebook, connections are called "Friends." There is no way to recommend or endorse friends as you would on LinkedIn, but you can leave reviews for businesses and groups with pages. There is also no publications aspect, like that for ResearchGate.

Feed curation is important for Facebook. By default, when you add a friend you become a follower of their content. Like LinkedIn, you can unfollow people without unfriending them, and you have the option to follow pages created by business and organizations. Facebook gives you the power to categorize your friends into subgroups called "lists," such as "close friends," "acquaintances," and shared employers; you also can create your own list titles. This allows you to share posts with a specific group, and not with others, which is a key feature if you plan to keep the same account for both personal and professional uses. Further feed curation options include whether you see activities such as likes, comments, posts, tags, or posts in groups you joined.

All of these features come with many settings, and there is a lot to consider when it comes to privacy on Facebook. The company has been criticized due to its handling of user data,[20] and so it is worth the investment of time to explore the settings and think about what type of content you want to share and with whom.

11.3.7 Twitter

Twitter is a social media platform that covers almost any subject, both professional and personal. What makes Twitter unique is its character limit: text for a twitter post, called a "tweet," cannot exceed 280 characters. Images can also be posted, and the 280-character limit still applies. These features relate to the history of Twitter and its inception before smartphones and apps, when tweets were made via text message and limited to the 140 characters of standard SMS; it only recently doubled the character limit in 2017.[21] Tweets are publicly visible by default, which is part of Twitter's appeal as a public forum. Twitter has fewer features compared to LinkedIn and Facebook, including a limited profile, newsfeed (based on who and what you follow), making tweets, re-tweeting, commenting, and direct messaging.

Twitter is a continuous deluge of information, available to all, with approximately 500 million tweets sent *per day*, or over 5000 tweets per second.[22,23] Twitter does not have a groups function where you can seek themed information, so *hashtags* are used to navigate this massive flow of information. A hashtag begins with a #, called a hash or pound sign (though its little-known technical name is the octothorpe[24]), followed by keywords with no spaces, such as #womeninstem (for "women in STEM"). Many other social media platforms, including LinkedIn and Facebook, currently use hashtags, but the format originated on Twitter. It came into use during a wildfire in San Diego, CA, USA, when users began including the hashtag #sandiegofire in posts about the fire to make them more searchable. This is the purpose of hastags: to make it easier to search for specific information. By searching for #PhotonicsWest2020 instead of "Photonics West 2020," you only find tweets with the desired hashtag, as opposed to search results that include tweets about photonics, the West, and the year 2020. You can also follow hashtags as you would a person.

Because Twitter is public and searchable, it is highly interactive. If you are interested in contacting someone, possibly an author of a publication you liked, you might be able to contact them via Twitter by tagging them in a tweet, commenting on their tweet, or via a direct message. So long as the person isn't famous, in which case they will be continually deluged with tweets, there is a high probability they will see and respond to your message. Conversations started in the reply thread of a Tweet may also allow you to interact with people of interest. Reaching out to journalists on Twitter is a great way to make contacts if you are hoping to get press coverage, but make sure that what you want to share is relevant to the journalist you are contacting. Retweeting their stories and providing them with references, if they are looking for sources, is a great way to offer them assistance and make a good impression.

Twitter has a much more limited profile system, including your Twitter handle (@yourname), photo, URL, location, and a caption. The rest of your profile consists of your tweets, retweets, and comments, which puts more emphasis on a good profile picture and quality of the content that you generate. The URL that you use should link to a personal blog or a more extensive profile, such as LinkedIn. Because of Twitter's popularity, you may need to be creative in your use of initials to get your name. As with email, keep the username related to your name or career if you are going to be using it for professional purposes.

Your Twitter newsfeed is populated with tweets from the people or hashtags that you follow. Note that there is no distinction between following and connecting on Twitter, following is the only connection that exists. In addition to hashtags and people, you can follow lists, which are curated groups of profiles related by a theme. You can follow public lists made by others or create your own public or private lists. Lists help you organize the information you receive, allowing you to find what you want more efficiently.

In terms of the content you generate on Twitter, focus is good. If you are interested in a variety of subjects, create multiple accounts, each with a specific goal, so that they stay focused. Provide consistent, valuable information with your tweets, and you may establish yourself as an expert voice on the subject. Retweeting is how you can share the tweets of others with your followers, and you can re-tweet with or without an added comment. Sharing another person's content by retweeting them is helpful because it exposes them to a new audience (your network) and can potentially generate new connections.

11.3.8 Google Scholar Citations

You may already be familiar with Google Scholar, which is Google's search engine specialized for publications and patents. A Google Scholar Citations account allows you to keep track of your publications by listing all of them in one place, as well as listing your co-authors, and follow the publications of others. In addition, it calculates your h-index, a metric for an author's productivity and citation impact suggested by Jorge Hirsch in 2005.[24] An author's h-index is the highest value for which an author has published *h* number of papers that have been cited at least *h* times. Relative to LinkedIn and Facebook, a Citations account has few features, and like ResearchGate, its emphasis on publications gives it a more academic focus.

A Google Scholar Citations account is free, but you will need to sign up for a Gmail account to create one. Once you are logged in to your Google account, navigate to scholar.google.com and click on "My Profile," then follow the setup wizard. You will be asked to identify publications that are yours, but some of the suggestions may be erroneous, so select those that are accurate and that you want listed. There are fields you can fill out to include your affiliation, keywords related to your research, and a URL, which you can link to a personal website, blog, or your profile on another social networking site. There is also the option to include an image of yourself, which again, should be professional and clear. By default, your account will be private, so check your settings and make it public if you want to be findable.

11.3.9 Mendeley

Mendeley is a reference software that was purchased by the scientific publisher Elsevier in 2013. The web version includes social media services, as well. Much like LinkedIn, you can fill out your profile with work and research experience, education, publications, and research interest keywords. Features include a newsfeed populated by posts from other users that you follow (there is no distinction between connecting and following), groups based on research interests, a library where you can upload and store full texts of papers, a dataset search, and searchable job listings where you can upload your CV.

11.3.10 Forums

Forums are like public message boards, for which you typically need to register in order to post but can be read without any kind of account or registration. Forums can be useful for addressing highly specific subject areas and questions. Often, if you are researching a very specific question, you will find your answer online not in an article or paper, but in a forum thread. If you register, you can post your own questions, respond to the questions of others, and participate in discussions. Features typically include direct messaging and a minimalist profile that tracks the number of posts you have made. Answering questions in helpful and insightful ways supports others and performs active and passive networking; your answers will be publicly available for all to read long after you originally posted them.

To find a forum, search the topic area and include the word "forum." Check the forum content to see if it matches with what you are interested in, and if so, register to comment and post. You can read a forum for its content without posting, but you won't get the networking benefit if you don't interact with others.

11.3.11 Membership and alumni directories

If you are a member of a professional society or an alumni association, you most likely have access to a member or alumni directory. Log in to the society or association website to find it, and make your profile as complete as possible, including a photograph. Include an elevator pitch that is audience appropriate. If a field is available for it, provide the appropriate URL to link your preferred social media profile. A complete profile like this is a great form of passive networking that makes you more findable. See if any of the other organizations you associate with have directories where you can fill out a profile. These profiles do not require a lot of maintenance, but keep them updated every year or when you change location or employment.

These organizations and associations will often also have periodicals (for which you could write articles) and remote volunteering opportunities. Also look for member and alumni events at home and in other towns when you travel. Career and job services are sometimes available, and even if you aren't looking for new work, posting your CV (minus your phone number and home address, for your safety) can make you more visible.

11.3.12 Personal websites and blogs

A personal website or blog can raise your visibility, share your professional work and interests, and provide content for your community, consolidated in one place. And it gives you full control over the format and type of content. What you put on your website or blog should be relevant to your aspirational and career goals, and authentic to who you are and what you do.

Many websites offer free blogs and site builders, and if you want a personalized URL (which ideally contains your name or something to do with your work or research), it is generally inexpensive to purchase one. As with all your accounts, if you include an image of yourself, make sure it looks professional. Make sure that the aesthetics of the website are good, and if you're not sure, use a template and have a friend or colleague look it over. Include information (and links) to any relevant publications or research you have done, including your company website, journal papers, articles, and anything else that is relevant to your goals or personal brand. You can have an "about" page with fun facts if you want. Include appropriate contact information, such as an email address, so that people can contact you, as well as reasons to do so.

11.3.14 Other platforms

While some of the biggest and most professionally relevant digital networking platforms have been discussed, many more exist. The following list includes some other social media platforms and sites that might interest you:

(1)   **Instagram**: An app for sharing photos and videos with captions that includes a newsfeed populated by people or hashtags that you follow, a minimal profile, and direct messaging. It is like Twitter except for its emphasis on photos and no character limit on posts. Instagram is owned by Facebook.

(2)   **Periscope**: A video broadcasting/live streaming app that is owned by and can be used within Twitter. It broadcasts live video, tracks the number of viewers, and lets them comment during the feed so that you can respond live to questions.

(3)   **HootSuite**: A service that helps you manage your existing social media accounts. Free and premium accounts allow you to post updates simultaneously to multiple accounts, schedule posts in advance, and perform analytics across your synced accounts.

(4)   **Buffer**: A social media management service focused on content publishing that publishes and schedules content for social networks.

(5)   **TweetDeck**: A Twitter service for managing multiple Twitter accounts side-by-side simultaneously. For a single account, columns display the various tabs available in the Twitter app side-by-side.

(6)   **Nuzzel**: This service interfaces with your Twitter, Facebook, and LinkedIn accounts to highlight the most popular stories and topics in your network, among your friends of friends, or across a platform. You can use it to set up a personal, curated newsletter based on this content.

(7)   **WeChat**: This Chinese app shares many aspects with Twitter and Facebook, in addition to being a digital wallet and more. It is by far the most popular in China and a necessity for doing business there.

Most of the Chinese population uses it, and it is slated to become China's electronic ID system.[25] Note that users are required to use their full legal name to register for a WeChat account.

(8) **SlideShare**: This site, owned by LinkedIn, focuses on educating users on a variety of topics in the form of presentations, infographics, and videos. Users can share their knowledge by uploading their own content.

(9) **Zotero**: An open-source, independent reference management software and social media platform that offers groups and forums.

(10) **Pinterest**: A social media site that allows users to create and share "pins" of interesting images and information from the internet. Users collect pins on thematic boards, and features include following other users, as well as following boards and topics.

11.4 Search Engine Optimization

Search engine optimization (SEO) typically refers to the optimization of a website's structure and content to make it more visible in search engine results. Here it refers to making yourself more visible in the results when your name is searched. Rather than optimizing the content on a site, it means optimizing, creating, or removing the content associated with you that exists online.

What happens when you type your name into Google, Yahoo, or Bing? Are you the first search result? How common is your name? How many results are there? Is there another person with your name who appears more prominently? Do they have a bad reputation?

First, consider the accuracy of the results: are the things with your name on them about you? If your name is common, sharing results with other people may be an issue, so you can get creative with your initials or use a middle name instead of a first name, in order to make your name and search results more distinct. If your name is Sofia Maria Fernandez and a lot of other people show up in the results when you search for "Sofia Fernandez," you could instead use "Sofia M. Fernandez" or "S. Maria Fernandez." Many journal publications accept pseudonyms and do not require authors to use a legal name, so you have a lot of freedom as to what name you publish under, but whatever you use, strive for consistency.

Author Anecdote

My name, "Christina Willis," is common in the United States, where I reside, and so when I began writing technical publications in graduate school, I decided to exploit the fact that I have two middle names. To make myself distinct from all the other people in the world named Christina Willis, I use "Christina C. C. Willis." If you search that name on Google, I have the entire first page of results (as of this writing).

Second, consider the nature of the search results. You want the things that people find about you to be positive and consistent with your networking and career strategy. Negative information comes in two forms: accurate and inaccurate. Accurate negative information (whether it is true or not) is negative information about you that appears when your name is searched. If you posted this information yourself, take it down right away. If someone else posted the information, you can ask to have it taken down, but that may not be possible. The other possibility—negative information about another person with your same name—is referred to here as inaccurate negative information. This is where consistently having pictures of yourself on your accounts is helpful; if the negative information has someone else's face on it, even if it's the same name, people can determine that it is not about you. Whether it is accurate or inaccurate, the best solution to negative information that cannot be removed is to displace it to the second page of search results by creating positive content that appears higher in the results.

You can do this by creating your own website, making your profile on various social media accounts more prominent, writing articles, and so forth. If you fill out your profiles on the above listed social media sites and make them publicly visible with a relatively unique name, those accounts are likely to dominate the search results. A personal website, articles written by you, and your answers to forum posts (if you include your name) will also appear in searches. As part of your online networking strategy, keep these accounts up to date by logging in and creating some activity every month or so to keep the search results elevated. Again, consistency, not frequency, is key here, so don't let this habit become a time sink.

If your name is relatively common and you encounter issues with other researchers that possess the same name, an ORCID can help. This is a non-profit organization that assigns unique alphanumeric identifiers for researchers that can be used when submitting publications, applying for grants, or on social media accounts.[26] It addresses the issue of non-uniform name-order conventions across cultures and the fact that names are not unique identifiers.

Search your name regularly, including image and video searches.

Reputation management involves not just the things you say and share but also the things you *don't* say or post in public spaces. A kind and professional persona benefits the people you interact with and your career, and it will reduce the amount of time you need to spend improving your search results.

11.5 A Special Note on Physical Mail

While physical mail is neither online nor digital, it deserves mention here as a remote form of networking. There is a lot of advice on the topic of sending thank-you notes that is often not practiced within the American STEM community. However, expressing gratitude this way is recommended in the U.S., especially after job interviews.[27] Research shows that recipients appreciate thank-you notes far more than senders anticipate.[28] Post-job-interview notes as follow-ups appear to be a largely American phenomenon,[29] so it may not be necessary in other cultural contexts.

In the U.S., when someone has done you a favor, such as writing a recommendation letter, nominating you for an award, referring you for a job, or you want to make a special impression after a job interview, sending a physical note or letter is appropriate and gives special emphasis to your message. Sending hand-written, physical mail is becoming more uncommon, so it is a way to get yourself noticed, or to stand out from other job applicants. Include a business card in your note so that you are easily identifiable as the sender. Also make a record for yourself of when and to whom you have sent physical mail since it is not easily searchable the way email or other digital forms of contact are, and you may forget when you sent something.

Exercises

(1) Consider what platforms your peers and colleagues commonly use (or, if you are thinking of a career change, what platforms are popular in that field). Ask if you are not certain, and see if there are active groups on those sites that are pertinent to your research or work topics. Create a list of relevant platforms and prioritize them based on how active and relevant they are to you, and how they match the kind of content you want to generate.

(2) Select one or two platforms of the highest priority on the list you created. Create an account, or update your profile, if you already have one. Make sure your picture is recent and professional, and then fill out your profile as completely and relevantly as possible. Find and join one or more groups on subjects that interest you.

(3) Go back to the schedule you made in Exercise 4 of Chapter 10, and refine it as necessary with respect to these high-priority platforms. If you are using more than one platform, you can apply different schedules. Your activity doesn't have to be frequent or extensive, but at least once a month log in, post something of value, repost and like friends' content, or start or engage in conversations in a group that you joined. Commit a small amount of time consistently to this endeavor, and put reminders on your calendar or in your planner.

(4) For all other accounts on your list that are relevant but lower priority, create an account or update your profile, if you already have one. Fill it out as completely as possible, and link it to one or both of your high-priority accounts. Typically, you can enter a URL for a website, and that can be your profile on another platform. Doing this will make you more findable, with a path to the places where you are most active, without spreading your efforts thin over too many platforms. Update these lower-priority accounts occasionally, perhaps every 6 months or when you have a change in employment.

(5)   Keep using the account, or accounts, that will be your focus. Make regular use a habit but not a time-consuming one. Consistency is better than intensity. However, if you are struggling to do this regularly, you might be on the wrong platform or trying to produce the wrong content, so try something new. Experiment with your approach until you find what works for you as a consistent investment in your network.

References

1. Google, "Shutting down Google+ for consumer (personal) accounts on April 2, 2019," Google+ Help Center, published January 30, 2019. Retrieved from support.google.com/plus/answer/9195133. Accessed October 14, 2019.

2. Kruger, J. et al., "Egocentrism over e-mail: Can we communicate as well as we think?" *J. Personality and Social Psychology* **89**(6) (2005).

3. Byron, K., "Carrying too heavy a load? The communication and miscommunication of emotion by email," *Academy of Management Review* **33**(2) (2008).

4. Peters, S., "Why is sarcasm so difficult to detect in texts and emails?" *The Conversation* (March 8, 2018). Retrieved from theconversation.com/why-is-sarcasm-so-difficult-to-detect-in-texts-and-emails-91892. Accessed on April 4, 2019.

5. Drahota, A. et al., "The vocal communication of different kinds of smile," *Speech Communication* **50**(4) (2008).

6. Skype, skype.com.

7. Google Hangouts, play.google.com/store/apps/details?id=com.google.android.talk.

8. Zoom Meeting, zoom.us.

9. Webex, webex.com.

10. Morin, A., "Waiting For a Reply? Study Explains the Psychology Behind Email Response Time," *Forbes* (November 28, 2015). Retrieved from forbes.com/sites/amymorin/2015/11/28/waiting-for-a-reply-study-explains-the-psychology-behind-email-response-time/#317fb0069755. Accessed April 4, 2019.

11. Kooti, F. et al., "Evolution of conversations in the age of email overload," Proceedings of the Proceedings of the 24th International Conference on World Wide Web (May 2015). [doi:10.1145/2736277.2741130]

12. Kushlev, K. and E. W. Dunn, "Checking email less frequently reduces stress." *Computers in Human Behavior* **43** (2015).

13. Tagg, C., *A corpus linguistics study of SMS text messaging*, Dissertation, University of Birmingham, England (2009).

14. "About LinkedIn," *LinkedIn* (2019). Retrieved from about.linkedin.com. Accessed on April 4, 2019.

15. Feldman, S., "The Countries with the Most LinkedIn Members," Statista (November 29, 2018). Retrieved from www.statista.com/chart/16265/linkedin-country-members. Accessed April 4, 2019.

16. Van Noorden, R., "Online collaboration: Scientists and the social network," *Nature News Feature* (August 13, 2014). Retrieved from nature.com/news/online-collaboration-scientists-and-the-social-network-1.15711. Accessed on April 4, 2019.

17. Jordan, K., "Exploring the ResearchGate score as an academic metric: reflections and implications for practice," *Proc. Quantifying and Analysing Scholarly Communication on the Web* (30 Jun 2015).

18. Else, H., "Major publishers sue ResearchGate over copyright infringement," *Nature News* (October 5, 2018). Retrieved from nature.com/articles/d41586-018-06945-6. Accessed on April 4, 2019. [doi: 10.1038/d41586-018-06945-6]

19. Hu, J. C., "Social networks make the world's largest nations seem small," *Quartz* (September 12, 2018). Retrieved from qz.com/1386649/social-networks-make-the-worlds-largest-nations-seem-small. Accessed on April 4, 2019.

20. Perez, S., "Twitter officially expands its character count to 280 starting today," *TechCrunch* (November 7, 2017). Retrieved from techcrunch.com/2017/11/07/twitter-officially-expands-its-character-count-to-280-starting-today. Accessed on April 4, 2019.

21. Stricker, G., "The 2014 #YearOnTwitter" *Twitter Blog* (December 10, 2014). Retrieved from blog.twitter.com/official/en_us/a/2014/the-2014-yearontwitter.html. Accessed on April 4, 2019.

22. Twitter for Business, business.twitter.com. Accessed on April 4, 2019.

23. Trufelman, A., "Octothorpe," *99% Invisible* (December 16, 2014). Retrieved from 99percentinvisible.org/episode/octothorpe. Accessed on April 4, 2019.

24. Hirsch, J. E., "An index to quantify an individual's scientific research output," *Proc. National Academy of Sciences* **102**(46) (2005).

25. Liao, S., "How WeChat came to rule China," *The Verge* (February 1, 2018). Retrieved from theverge.com/2018/2/1/16721230/wechat-china-app-mini-programs-messaging-electronic-id-system. Accessed on April 4, 2019.

26. ORCID, orcid.org.

27. "Interview Follow-Up: Thank You Notes," *Harvard Law School*. Retrieved from hls.harvard.edu/dept/opia/job-search-toolkit/interviewing-and-following-up/follow-up. Accessed on April 4, 2019.

28. Kumar, A. and N. Epley, "Undervaluing Gratitude: Expressers Misunderstand the Consequences of Showing Appreciation," *Psychological Science* **29**(9) (2018).

29. Segal, N., "Should you send a thank you note for an interview abroad?" *Monster* (2019). Retrieved from monster.com/career-advice/article/send-thank-you-notes-abroad. Accessed on April 4, 2019.

Chapter 12
Networking the Job Hunt

"The job search is never about you… It is about what you, the job seeker, can provide."

~Alaina G. Levine,
Networking for Nerds (2015)

12.1 Don't Wait to Start

Networking can help you find job openings that are not formally advertised,[1] and it increases your chances of success with advertised positions. While it is possible to get a job without networking, using it as part of your job search will increase your options and the number of opportunities available to you, thereby increasing your probability of success. And whenever you change jobs, your network is an investment that goes with you.

Therefore, strategic and sustainable cultivation of your network should begin long before you need a new job. If you make sustainable networking a habit, you will have a broad and powerful network of people who trust you, know your interests, and will recommend you and send you opportunities. This chapter is located at the end of the book to emphasize the importance of putting your network first and cultivating it before you need anything from it. Most of your networking activities should not involve job hunting; it should mostly be the process of building sustainable, mutually beneficial relationships with others. Then when you need a new job, you will already have a helpful network of people in place.

A belief long held in networking is that typically it is *not* the people closest to you who are most likely to help you find new employment, but rather, the people in your network described as "weak ties." In 1973, Dr. Mark Granovetter showed that 56% of the people surveyed had found their employment through a personal connection, only 19% through so-called traditional means, and 10% by applying directly to an employer.[2] Of those who found their job through a personal contact, only 17% of them saw their personal contact regularly; most only rarely or never saw their contact, which is why they are referred to as "weak ties." The rationale is that weak ties have access to a different set of people and information than anyone close to you (whose information largely mirrors yours), and a weak tie therefore wields a lot of power in terms of opportunity availability.

More recent research has shown that the reason weak ties are typically more likely to help you find a job is that they are by far the most numerous type of tie in your network.[3,4] Considered at the individual level, stronger ties are more valuable than weak ties, but collectively, your weak ties are more likely to help you find new employment because they are much more numerous. Thus, regular, albeit infrequent, network maintenance is important, as is networking sustainably and trying to help others first. A weak tie is still a tie, and if you follow up or check in occasionally with someone, they will be more likely to respond positively to your requests and messages.

Under ideal circumstances, you will be the one deciding when to leave your job, not your employer. Life is often not ideal, however, and so it is possible you will one day be surprised by sudden unemployment. Whether the change is voluntary or not, you will rely on your network to help you get the job you want.

12.2 Planning the Change

If you are not where you want to be career-wise, strategically (and sustainably) creating new network connections can help you create the opportunity to find your dream job. To do this, you need to (a) know what you want to accomplish, (b) know who to ask for help, and (c) how to ask for help. Your networking strategy can include not just your goals but also ways that you can use your skills and knowledge to benefit your network and your current employer. If you know what you can offer to new connections, it is easier to network sustainably and effectively.

But where do you begin if you know that you want to a new job? If you are unhappy in your current job, consider what changes are needed to make it a better fit, what other jobs would be better, and why. If your ideal job is similar to your current job but in a different environment, then it may not be necessary to acquire new skills. But if the ideal job is significantly different than your current job, you will need to acquire skills, experience, and connections in this new field. The greater the difference between your current job and your ideal job, the longer you will need to prepare before you make the change.

Take actions to acquire what you need, e.g., sign up for courses and get relevant certifications, if such things are necessary for the job you want. If you are not sure what skills are necessary, do some research online and see if you have any contacts (or second-degree contacts) who work in the field of interest. Ask for an introduction or send a cold email (see Section 12.6). If you have a relevant connection already, ask for an informational interview (discussed in Chapter 10), letting them know that you are interested in their subject material and would like to learn more about how their job works. If the person is a secondary connection, ask your mutual connection for an introduction, or if you don't have one, send a cold email (see Section 12.6), and again, request an informational interview. By corresponding with someone who does the job (or one related to the one) you want, you can better understand the changes you will need to make and begin developing a new connection in that field. If you have an informational interview, follow up, be thankful, and offer relevant assistance.

Start looking at professional organizations, alumni groups, events, and societies relevant to the desired job. Join and attend so that you can meet people who are involved in the new area of interest. Participation will build both your experience and your network. Build rapport and help your new connections in whatever way you can; opportunities for further involvement and even employment may arise as you build Opportunity Momentum (refer back to Section 2.2 for more on Opportunity Momentum).

When you have acquired the necessary skills and experience, inform your relevant contacts that you are interested in making a move. Update your CV and your professional social media accounts. Look online where companies post the sorts of jobs that you want, and search the websites of companies and organizations that you are interested in working for. Check in with people that you know within the company, or with connections within the company, as you apply to see if they can give you any assistance or insight about the application process. You can also inquire directly to connections within a company about possible job opportunities that may not have been posted yet.

Sometimes, getting involved and getting to know people will bring opportunities for work or involvement without you needing to ask. To make that happen, you must communicate your skills and interests to your network, cultivate the right network for your goals, and network sustainably so that the people who you have helped trust you and feel comfortable recommending you.

12.3 When Change Is Thrust upon You

There are many factors that affect whether a company keeps you as an employee or lets you go. You can control the factors that relate to the quality of your work and your performance, but changes in the economy or your company's ownership are beyond your grasp and can put you out of a job. Even if your work is amazing, you may become unemployed. So what do you do?

You probably won't have the luxury or desire to spend a lot of resources acquiring new skills and network connections before you start a new job, so you will be relying on your existing network and skill set. Update your professional social media profiles if you haven't recently, post regular content, and use recent and professional-looking profile pictures. Update your CV and start posting it in relevant places, such as the career sections of your professional organization or relevant places within your alumni directories. Post an updated resume in places where you may have posted it previously. Do things like turning on the features in LinkedIn that let recruiters know that you are looking for work. Share your information in as many relevant places as possible. For your safety, remove your home address from any CV that you post publicly.

Develop a job-seeking elevator pitch (refer back to Subsection 5.2.4) that includes your most prominent qualifications (based on the type of work you want) and the type of work that you want. It should be brief and specific, but not narrow because that can over-constrain your search and make it hard to find work. With your elevator pitch prepared, send emails to relevant contacts, such as people who work in a company you would like to work for or in a geographical region of interest. Personalize all messages, include the pitch, and attach your CV or a one-page resume, so that the recipient can pass it along to others who could help. Just as you would for a planned change, look online and at company websites for job postings, apply, and then reach out to contacts at those companies, or ask your connections for introductions. Section 12.5 has more details on how to ask for help.

12.4 Recruiters

Recruiters are great people to know, even if you aren't looking for a job. Help them out when you can by asking what they are looking for and letting any relevant people in your network know about the opportunity. This generates a win-win situation for everyone involved, and if you have a good and established relationship with several recruiters before you start looking for work, it may make finding that next job much easier. When a recruiter calls you, talk to them even if you aren't looking to change positions, because you may have a friend who is a perfect fit.

It is also important to have your online self in order when you start talking to a recruiter about job opportunities. If the CV or resume you send them doesn't match your online information, it suggests either a lack of an attention to detail, or worse, that you may have fabricated details. Avoid this by making sure you have things up to date on all the platforms you use, as well as your CV. Recruiters will check the content you generate online, as will potential employers, so make sure it is consistent, current, and professional.

Recruiters network with each other, and while a recruiter you know may not have an opportunity for you, they may know another recruiter who does. If you've established a positive relationship with a recruiter, they will be more inclined to connect you with their own network. If you have developed relationships with any recruiters, once you have your digital persona updated and you are ready to start looking for a job, contact them with your elevator pitch, your availability, and a copy of your CV or resume.

12.5 How to Ask for Help from Existing Contacts

When reaching out to your contacts for assistance, you are more likely to get assistance (and better assistance) if you have a specific request. Being specific does two things: (1) it shows respect for the other person's time, and (2) it improves the likelihood of a helpful response. We are all busy, and by taking the time to craft a detailed request for someone, you are making it easier and quicker for them to respond, and the quality of information you receive in return will be better.

Consider a vague request versus a specific request: an example of the former would be a message saying, "I'm looking for a new job, do you have any suggestions?" This is an easy message to send quickly, but it puts the burden of problem solving on the other person. They have to guess at things such as what kind of job you want, whether you would be willing to relocate, and your availability. So the answer you would probably get is, "no," or if they are very patient, questions about the above, but not an answer. To generate a detailed request, for example, first look at job listings until you find one that seems to be good fit for you. Then look through your contacts to see if you know anyone or have any mutual connections at that company. If you have only a secondary connection, you could then send a very specific message to your existing connection, stating your interest in a certain position and asking for an introduction to the person your connection knows at the company. If you have a direct connection, you could send a message stating your interest in an advertised position and see if they have time to talk about the workplace. These specific approaches will generally produce better results.

But you don't have to start with a certain job posting to be specific. As discussed earlier, you can craft your job-seeking elevator pitch with specific information about you and the types of positions that interest you (work type, location(s), particular companies, etc.), and send that to your connections with a personal message and your availability.

Another important aspect of respecting the other person's time is only asking for things that you cannot do on your own. Being specific is part of this: you do the advance preparation to make your request a minimal amount of work for your requestee. You don't want waste the other person's time by asking them something that you can research. Not only does that waste time, it delays the arrival of your answer and has the potential to annoy the other person. In short: do as much of your own research and preparation as possible.

As discussed earlier, avoid making requests that are or look transactional. If you offer what you can do in exchange when you make a request, it can appear that your offer is contingent upon them doing what you are asking, i.e., it sounds like a transaction. So make offers to return any favor afterwards. Asking for help sometimes means being willing to be in someone's debt, so embrace it. This is not a bad thing. People like the people that they do favors for.[5,6] (This is sometimes referred to as the "Ben Franklin effect."[7]) Note that explaining to someone the value that you bring, or the potential positive consequences of meeting your request, is different than offering a favor in exchange. When asking for a favor, pointing out how the favor is mutually beneficial is a good thing.

As a rule, you want to be clear and polite when asking for help. Do not assume that a person will help you, or that you are entitled to their help. But neither should you act like you expect to be refused, apologize, or make excuses when you ask for help. These things are all noise that dilute your signal. Communication is best when the signal is clear and the listener doesn't have to decipher, extrapolate, or dig for meaning. Ask for what you need clearly and politely, without assumptions or apologies (so long as your request is timely and reasonable).

Two important aspects of clarity are concision and honesty. Everyone is busy, and email can be time consuming. Just like specificity, the more concise you are, the easier it is to absorb and digest the information you have sent. Few people have the time and patience to read a long email, so don't burden your requestee with too many words. Be clear and honest about your motivations, e.g., needing a job. Give that information upfront; don't make the other person dig for it, or they may not bother. People may feel suspicious is you don't explain your motives when you ask for something, and if you're asking for an introduction, your introducer will need that kind of relevant information.

Once you have prepared your request but before you send it, do a quick assessment to be certain if you are asking the right person. Some people may be willing to help but poorly positioned to do so. Based on what you know about the person's background, consider whether your message is clear and written for them. What contextual information should you include to make your request clear to that specific reader, and what have you added that is unnecessary? For example, if you are writing to someone with whom you worked in the past, you probably won't need to describe all of your qualifications (unless they have changed), but if you are writing to someone you don't know well, spending a little more time describing yourself will probably be necessary.

There is always a possibility that the person you *think* you want to get a hold of is not actually the person who can help you. If you provide (concise) contextual information about what you are looking for, then you may get redirected to the person you actually need. Don't automatically assume the most powerful person is going to be the right person. The most prominent and senior people also probably get the most requests, so that even if they could help you, they will have less available bandwidth to do so. It may be that the person you really need is two levels down in the hierarchy, and much more willing to accept your request.

Beyond the content of your request, and to whom it is addressed, there is also the logistical issue of timing and medium, and the intersection of the two. While it's fine to send an email late at night, it's not acceptable to make a phone call outside of certain hours. Also keep in mind holidays and school days, and do what you can to optimize the delivery of your request based on the information you have gleaned about the person you are contacting. Use the person's preferred medium of communication if you know what it is. The nature of your request may also determine the best medium. The bigger or more formal the request, the more investment your request should take, ranging up to an in-person meeting for something of great importance, or down to a simple text message for simple requests.

12.6 The Cold Email

In American English, "cold calling" means contacting someone with whom you have never spoken. There is an association in the English language between first meetings and coldness, including phrases such as "breaking the ice," and the term "cold call" appears to pre-date the invention of the telephone.[8] Networking can be a good way to get an introduction from a third party, in which case you avoid the "cold" scenario, but sometimes you will need or want to reach out to someone with whom you don't already have an existing or mutual connection.

When writing to someone for the first time, your goal is to optimize your signal-to-noise ratio (SNR). This is is good practice for all communications, but it is especially important when seeking a reply from a stranger. If there is a lot of noise in your message, such as typos, extraneous content, or a loss of signal due to missing context, your SNR will be poor. Apply the concept of SNR to your message, starting with the subject line, which should be brief, specific, and relevant.

Before you write your message, research the intended recipient, as you would for any new contact. Run their name through your favorite search engine, look for their employee profile, find them on LinkedIn, follow them on Instagram and Twitter, and read their blog, if they have one. Find any papers or articles they have published, and see if they have been mentioned in any news articles. You might find their CV or resume, and they could be listed in the directories of any organizations you have in common. If you know the person will be giving a talk or presentation that you can attend, do so. If you are inquiring about a job at this person's company, put some time into researching the company and its culture. This accumulation of information can help you to craft the details of your email or message, allowing you to include *only* the most salient information and improving your chances of getting a response.

Author Anecdote

My name is Christina, spelled with an "a" at the end, but I regularly get messages addressed to "Christine" with an "e." This mistake tells me that the sender was not paying attention to details when they wrote me—not the best impression. Don't be this sender. Double check the spelling of the name of the person you are contacting, and use the appropriate form of address. Getting someone's name right should be easy if you do your research and typo-check your message.

The rules that apply to asking for help apply here as well. Your message should be concise, clear, and honest. Be clear about your goal and your motivations; don't make the person guess, or you will seem suspicious. Explain the benefit to the person you are asking for help, if applicable. When seeking a job, state ways in which you feel you would benefit the company with your skills, experience, or work ethic. Support these claims (briefly) by mentioning previous employment or relevant publications, etc. Conclude with a specific actionable item, whether it's a phone call with the person or an introduction to someone else—whatever it is, keep it small and easy to fulfill. Asking for something difficult or time consuming in a cold email will increase the chance of your request being ignored. State that you appreciate the person's time, because you do. Consider including a signature that lists some of your accomplishments or social media links, but make them relevant to the request and succinct; otherwise, they are introducing noise.

Your message should include the following components, although the order will depend on the situation and your composition style:

(1) A brief, tailored introduction to yourself;
(2) Why you are writing;
(3) Why you are writing *that* person (and how you found them);
(4) What you are requesting;

(5) Ways in which responding will benefit the person, if applicable (Important: this differs from a transactional offer because the benefit is a *byproduct* of a response, not something given in addition after the fact);
(6) Attach a one-page resume or CV (if applicable);
(7) The action or outcome you are hoping to achieve; and
(8) A signature with your name and relevant links or accomplishments.

For example, imagine that you are an electrical engineer and you found a job opening at a company that designs consumer electronics. While researching the company, you found the name of another electrical engineer who works there. After researching that engineer, you might compose a message that looks like this:

Subject Line: Interested in working at ElectricWorld

Dear Dr. Dimitrov,

(1) My name is Jamir Feutmba, and I am an electrical engineer with experience designing compact, integrated electronics for commercial medical laser systems.

(2) I am interested in the open Senior Electrical Engineer position at ElectricWorld, (3) and I am writing to you because I see that you currently work in a similar position. I found you listed in the company directory, and I subsequently found the presentation on compact circuits from the Electro Thingamabobs 2019 conference; it was really good.

I think my skills would be a great match for the work that ElectricWorld does, and (4) I would love to speak with you about your experience there. It seems like a great place to work, and I would like to know more.

(7) Please let me know if you would be available to speak with me next Thursday or Friday, or another day if you are unavailable then.

Best Regards,
(8) Jamir Feutmba
www.jamirfeutmba.com

(6) P.S. I have attached my one-page resume if you would like more details on my background.

This message describes the motivation for the message and the desired outcome without being lengthy, and it concludes with a very specific, reasonable, actionable item. The statement about finding the recipient's conference presentation could be left out for brevity, but it lets the recipient know you did your research on them and allows you to pay a compliment. Note that employees often get referral bonuses if someone they refer gets hired, so during the call you could ask them to refer you for the position (if the call goes well), which may have a material benefit for them. Don't bring up referral bonuses as a topic of discussion, but be aware that they exist.

There is also the question of timing. In general, avoid sending messages on Monday or Friday, as these are the busiest days of the week, and people are either sifting through accumulated emails from the weekend or trying to finish tasks in preparation for the weekend. CoSchedule performed a review of multiple studies and concluded that Tuesday is the best day to send email, followed by Thursday, and then Wednesday in third place.[9] This same review found that 10 am / 10:00 is the best time of day to send, followed by 8 pm / 20:00; however, most important will be the time zone and local holidays of the recipient's location, which should be revealed by your research. Most studies on this subject are related to opening and click rates for marketing emails, so only use them as a general guideline in combination with your research and personal experience to choose the best time.

You may not get a response to your message right away, but if you follow up, do not express annoyance at the delay, which only decreases the likelihood of getting an answer. It is okay to follow up in a few days, three being a good number. Another follow up a week after that is reasonable as well, but if no response is forthcoming at that point, it is probably a dead end. Some people are more ambitious and will continue sending follow-up messages, but this is a personal choice that depends on your personality and what you know about the person you are attempting to contact. Sometimes this sort of persistence will pay off, and sometimes it may annoy the party you are trying to reach. Whatever you do, stay positive in tone, no matter how many follow up messages you choose to send.

If you can establish the person's preferred form of contact, use that, whether it's email, phone, post, LinkedIn, a tweet, or something else. Using the medium that the person is most comfortable with (and checks most frequently) makes it more likely you will get a response. You can try following up via a different medium if your first response goes unanswered, in case that person does not spend much time with that account or in case you have the wrong address or username.

12.7 Correspondence and Interviews

When you get a strong lead on a job, don't neglect your other networking efforts. Remember that until you have signed an offer, you do not have the job. If an opportunity falls through and you haven't stayed in touch about other opportunities, then you will have to start over. Pursuing multiple avenues at once can potentially generate more than one job offer at a time, which can give you amazing leverage during salary negotiation (and you should almost always negotiate). Your networking can also help you determine the right salary range.

The particulars of interviewing are outside the scope of this book, but some reading suggestions are given in Appendix B. However, consider that an interview is a networking opportunity, even if you don't get the job. During your interview, you will probably meet a variety of people with expertise relevant to your work or research. Ask for their contact information so that you can follow up and stay in touch; this can help you expand your network, whether or not you are offered or accept the job.

After an interview, always follow up with the hiring manager (and anyone else whose contact information you collected) to thank them for their time and let them know you are excited about the opportunity. While there is a fair amount of personal preference that plays into general follow-up timelines, for a job you should get back to the hiring manager *right away*. If you want to make a special impact, in addition to a timely email, a handwritten note can help you stand out and make you more memorable (mostly applicable in the U.S.; see Section 11.5). This is something most people don't do today in our hyperconnected online world, and it is more cumbersome, but it is a thoughtful gesture that can make a special impression.

If you got the lead for the job from your network, follow up with the relevant contact(s). Let them know if you got an interview, how it went if you did, and then follow up again later on to let them know if you did or did not get the job. This means possibly following up multiple times with updates for your referring contact. It lets them know that their effort was helpful and appreciated, and you should express your gratitude for their assistance, regardless of the outcome. Leaving someone in the dark doesn't let them invest in your outcomes. Keep your contact informed to give them the opportunity to commiserate or celebrate with you, building your bond with them.

12.8 Helping Others

At various points, you may be in a position to help a friend or colleague who is looking for work, or you may know of someone looking to fill a position. Helping others to find work is a great way to give back to your network, and having a diverse and powerful network will make you more able to do so. It generates goodwill and feels rewarding.

Ideally, you stay in touch with your contacts consistently, and names will occasionally spring to mind when you see a job opportunity. When that happens, send it along. When you are approached by others with requests, consider them, and accept if you can reasonably do so. Don't be afraid to turn down requests that are unreasonable, inapplicable to you, or poorly timed, but in those cases try to offer some kind of consolation assistance, such as referring a more relevant person, offering to help when you are less busy, or doing only one of several things asked.

If you find that a friend or colleague is looking for a new job, offer what assistance you can. Just as it is important to offer a specific request when asking for help, being specific when offering assistance makes it more likely to be accepted. Saying, "Is there anything I can do to help?" is a good start, but saying something like, "I would be happy to look over your resume," or, "Would you like an introduction to Bob Smith at McCompany?" is more likely to get a "yes." People often find it challenging to ask for help, but that doesn't mean that you can't be helpful; it just means that sometimes you will need to be more specific in order to have someone take you up on your offer.

Exercises

(1)   Assess your current position and responsibilities. Are you happy with your current circumstances? Is the work fulfilling for you? Is there anything you would like to change? Consider if there are different or additional responsibilities you would like to have in your current position. Can you get what you want in your current role? Your current company or institute?

(2)   Think back to the goals that you established in Exercise 1 of Chapter 2. If your current position doesn't match those goals, what position does? Where can you find it: advancement where you are, a different employer in your same field, or a different field entirely?

(3)   If you determine that you need a change, find job descriptions for the types of job that you want and compare the required skills and experience to your current abilities. Remember that people will often hire someone who doesn't fit all of the requirements, so consider applying even if you don't have all of the skills listed. If you see areas that need improvement, network to find ways to support that growth.

(4)   If you want to make a change, find people in your network, either first- or second-degree connections, who are already doing that job, and arrange informational interviews. Ask them questions about their job, and if you feel comfortable doing so, let them know that you are interested in a similar position. See what advice they have for you.

(5)   If you want to make a change and you have a mentor, discuss it with them. If you don't have a mentor, think about who might be a good mentor to guide you through the transition and work to establish such a relationship (refer back to Section 7.4 for more on mentoring relationships).

(6)   If you are happy with your current trajectory, share job opportunities with people in your network, and speak with recruiters when they contact you. Acknowledge the possibility that forces outside your control could disrupt your plans, and keep networking sustainably so that you have a healthy network to rely on if anything happens.

(7)   Even if you are happy with your current trajectory, periodically re-examine how things are going, perhaps every three to six months. If at some point you are ready for a change, proceed with the relevant advice and exercises in this chapter.

References

1. Rothberg, S., "80% of Job Openings Are Unadvertised." *College Recruiter* (March 28, 2013). Retrieved from collegerecruiter.com/blog/2013/03/28/80-of-job-openings-are-unadvertised. Accessed February 18, 2019.

2. Granovetter, M. S., "The Strength of Weak Ties." *American J. Sociology*, **78**(6), pp. 1360–1380 (1973).

3. Gee, L. K. et al., "Social Networks and labor markets: How strong ties relate to job finding on Facebook's social network," *J. Labor Economics* **35**(2) (2017).

4. Burke, M., "How strong and weak ties help you find a job," *Facebook Research* (March 31, 2016). Retrieved from research.fb.com/how-strong-and-weak-ties-help-you-find-a-job. Accessed on March 29, 2019.

5. Jecker, J. and D. Landy, "Liking a person as a function of doing him a favour," *Human Relations* **22**(4) (1969).

6. Gross, A. E. and J. G. Latane, "Receiving Help, Reciprocation, and Interpersonal Attraction," *J. Appl. Social Psychol.* **4**(3), 210–223 (1974).

7. Lebowitz, S., "Harness the power of the 'Ben Franklin Effect' to get someone to like you," *Business Insider* (Dec 2, 2016). Retrieved from businessinsider.com/ben-franklin-effect-2016-12. Accessed on March 29, 2019.

8. *The Oriental Herald, A Journal of General Literature*, Vol. XII, footnote on pg. 471 "cold call" (January to March, 1827). Retrieved from books.google.com/books?id=oRkYAAAAYAAJ&printsec=frontcover#v=onepage&q&f=false. Accessed on March 29, 2019.

9. Ellering, N., "What 14 Studies Say About The Best Time To Send Email," *CoSchedule Blog* (March 23, 2016, updated September 24, 2018). Retrieved from coschedule.com/blog/best-time-to-send-email. Accessed on July 28, 2019.

Conclusions

"Be excellent to each other."

~Ted (played by Keanu Reeves),
Bill and Ted's Excellent Adventure (1989)

No one is a perfect networker. Even people who are incredibly talented and effective, sustainable networkers regularly make mistakes or fail to execute best practices. But the point is not to be perfect. The point is to take action, experiment, and learn. There is no "after," as you continue to grow and improve. If doing all the right things in networking were easy, everyone would be great at it. Given the amount of mystery, confusion, and distrust that surrounds the concept of networking, that is clearly not the case. Being a sustainable networker means always being a work in progress and experimenting to find the methods that work best for you.

Those methods don't need to be grand, heroic, or time consuming. What networking looks like for you will be different than what it looks like for someone else, because we all have different strengths. But if you make kindness and generosity your baseline, and stay consistent in your efforts, you will build a network that will happily respond to your requests, just as you respond to theirs. Sharing what you have, what you know, and access to your connections creates a win–win situation that makes the world a better place to live, work, and do business.

If you are feeling overwhelmed or you think that you are too busy to network, start small. Do one relatively simple thing, such as making conversation with someone at work who you don't usually talk to or updating a social media profile. Next week, do another small thing. Keep going. These small actions will accumulate results over time if you do them consistently, but you need to do *something* to see a change. The more you do, the easier it gets.

Eventually, or even maybe right now, you might want to try something bigger, such as volunteering or taking an improv class. These bigger things can be amazing experiences that create learning and growth, but they may not all work out. Sometimes you might simply discover something you *don't* like. Don't let that discourage you: that is what experimentation is about. Collect the data point, reassess, tweak a parameter, and try something new. You'll get to know yourself better, and eventually you'll find activities that you love and that strengthen you as a sustainable networker.

Anywhere there are people, there are networking opportunities. Conferences and your workplace are rich opportunities, because of the professional commonality you share with the people involved. But other networking opportunities should not be overlooked, whether it's a festival, a meet-up, or making conversation on public transit. Meeting someone in the wild means they are less likely to have a professional common ground with you, but serendipitous encounters can result in interesting and fruitful connections. And even if a conversation with your seatmate on the plane doesn't become a useful networking connection, it is an opportunity to practice your conversational skills, work on dealing with rejection, or potentially make a new friend.

So practice, practice, practice. Experiment. Be kind. Interact. Follow up. And figure out what sustainable networking looks like for *you*.

Appendix
Suggested Reading

(* Works consulted in the writing of this book.)

* Alda, A., *If I Understood You, Would I Have This Look on My Face?: My Adventures in the Art and Science of Relating and Communicating*, Random House (2018).

* Cain, S., *Quiet: The Power of Introverts in a World that Can't Stop Talking*, Broadway Books (2013).

Campbell, E., *ESL Resource Book for Engineers and Scientists*, John Wiley & Sons, Inc. (1995).

Carnegie, D., *How to Win Friends and Influence People*, Musaicum Books (2017).

Duhigg, C., *The Power of Habit: Why We Do What We Do in Life and Business*, Random House (2012).

* Ferrazzi, K. and R. Tahl, *Never Eat Alone: And Other Secrets to Success, One Relationship at a Time*, Currency (2014).

* Gerber, S. and R. Paugh, *Superconnector: Stop Networking and Start Building Business Relationships that Matter,* Da Capo Lifelong Books, Boston (2018).

Goleman, D., *Emotional Intelligence*, Bantam (2006).

* Levine, A. G., *Networking for Nerds: Find, Access and Land Hidden Game-Changing Career Opportunities Everywhere*, John Wiley & Sons (2015).

* Liswood, L. A., *The Loudest Duck: Moving beyond Diversity while Embracing Differences to Achieve Success at Work*, John Wiley & Sons (2009).

* RoAne, S., *How to Work a Room: The Ultimate Guide to Making Lasting Connections, in Person and Online*, William Morrow (2014).

* Shepherd, M., *The Art of Civilized Conversation: A Guide to Expressing Yourself with Style and Grace*, Three Rivers Press (2007).

Taylor, J. and D. Hardy, *Monster Careers: Interviewing: Master the Moment that Gets You the Job*, Penguin (2005).

Index

Christina C. C. Willis is a laser scientist, writer, and public speaker, living and working in Washington, D.C. She specializes in novel, high-power laser development and has worked in metrology, laser tracking and imaging, and LIDAR applications. She was selected for the 2019–2020 Arthur H. Guenther Congressional Fellowship, which is co-sponsored by OSA and SPIE, through which she will serve a year in a Congressional office. In her free time, she enjoys yoga, running, and travel, and as of summer 2019, she has visited 39 countries.